# Monographs in Computer Science

*Editors*

David Gries
Fred B. Schneider

# Monographs in Computer Science

Abadi and Cardelli, **A Theory of Objects**

Benosman and Kang [editors], **Panoramic Vision: Sensors, Theory, and Applications**

Bhanu, Lin, Krawiec, **Evolutionary Synthesis of Pattern Recognition Systems**

Broy and Stølen, **Specification and Development of Interactive Systems: Focus on Streams, Interfaces, and Refinement**

Brzozowski and Seger, **Asynchronous Circuits**

Burgin, **Super-Recursive Algorithms**

Cantone, Omodeo, and Policriti, **Set Theory for Computing: From Decision Procedures to Declarative Programming with Sets**

Castillo, Gutiérrez, and Hadi, **Expert Systems and Probabilistic Network Models**

Downey and Fellows, **Parameterized Complexity**

Feijen and van Gasteren, **On a Method of Multiprogramming**

Herbert and Spärck Jones [editors], **Computer Systems: Theory, Technology, and Applications**

Heydon, Levin, Mann, and Yu, **Software Configuration Management Using Vesta**

Leiss, **Language Equations**

McIver and Morgan [editors], **Programming Methodology**

McIver and Morgan [editors], **Abstraction, Refinement and Proof for Probabilistic Systems**

Misra, **A Discipline of Multiprogramming: Programming Theory for Distributed Applications**

Nielson [editor], **ML with Concurrency**

Paton [editor], **Active Rules in Database Systems**

Poernomo, Crossley, Wirsing, **Adapting Proofs-as-Programs: The Curry-Howard Protocol**

Selig, **Geometrical Methods in Robotics**

Selig, **Geometric Fundamentals of Robotics, Second Edition**

Shasha and Zhu, **High Performance Discovery in Time Series: Techniques and Case Studies**

Tonella and Potrich, **Reverse Engineering of Object Oriented Code**

Allan Heydon
Roy Levin
Timothy Mann
Yuan Yu

# Software Configuration Management Using Vesta

Springer

Allan Heydon
Guidewire Software
2121 S. El Camino Real
San Mateo, CA 94403
U.S.A.

Roy Levin
Microsoft Research–Silicon Valley Center
1065 La Avenida
Mountain View, CA 94043
U.S.A.

Timothy Mann
VMware, Inc.
3145 Porter Dr.
Palo Alto, CA 94304
U.S.A.

Yuan Yu
Microsoft Research–Silicon Valley Center
1065 La Avenida
Mountain View, CA 94043
U.S.A.

*Series Editors:*
David Gries
Cornell University
Department of Computer Science
Ithaca, NY 14853
U.S.A.

Fred B. Schneider
Cornell University
Department of Computer Science
Ithaca, NY 14853
U.S.A.

ISBN-13: 978-1-4419-3472-7
e-ISBN: 0-387-30852-0
e-ISBN: 978-0-387-30852-4

Printed on acid-free paper.



9 8 7 6 5 4 3 2 1

springeronline.com

*To our former colleagues at the*
*DEC/Compaq Systems Research Center*

# Preface

The core technologies underlying software configuration management have changed little in more than two decades. Development organizations struggle to manage ever-larger software systems with tools that were never designed to handle them. Their development processes are warped by the inadequacies of their building and version management tools. Developers must take time from writing and debugging code to cope with the operational problems thrust upon them by their build system's inadequate support of large-scale concurrent development.

Vesta, a novel system for large-scale software configuration management, offers a better solution. Through a unique integration of building and version management facilities, Vesta constructs software of any size repeatably, incrementally, and consistently. Since modern software development occurs worldwide, Vesta supports concurrent, multi-site, distributed development. Vesta's core facilities are methodologically neutral, allowing development organizations a wide range of flexibility in the way they arrange their code repositories and structure the building of system components. In short, Vesta advances the state of the art in configuration management.

The idea behind Vesta is simple. Conceptually, every system build, no matter how extensive, occurs from scratch. That means that Vesta has a complete description of the source files from which the system is constructed, plus a complete and precise procedure for putting them together. By making these files and procedures immutable and immortal, Vesta ensures that a build can always be repeated. By extensively caching the results of builds, Vesta converts a conceptual scratch build into an incremental one, reusing previously built components when appropriate. By automatically detecting the dependencies between the system's parts, Vesta guarantees that incremental builds are consistent. What makes Vesta interesting and useful is its ability to do all this for software systems comprising millions of lines of code while being practical and even pleasant for developers and their management.

This book presents a comprehensive explanation of Vesta's architecture and individual components, showing how its novel and ambitious properties are achieved. Vesta's functionality is compared with that of standard development tools, highlighting how Vesta overcomes their specific deficiencies while matching or even exceeding their performance. Detailed examples demonstrate Vesta's facilities as they appear to a developer, and a particular methodology of proven utility for large system development shows how Vesta works on an organization-wide scale. For the reader who wants to see Vesta "with the covers off", the book includes a substantial treatment of the subtle and challenging aspects of the implementation, as well as references to the open-source code.

## Audience and Scope

The audience for this book includes anyone who has ever struggled with the problems of managing a substantial evolving software code base and wondered, "Isn't there a better way to do this?" While the book is not a "how-to" manual, it does demonstrate specific tools and techniques, founded on Vesta's core version management and building technologies, that are eminently practical. The Vesta system embodies and encourages principled development, and so will interest software engineering researchers, especially those inclined toward the creation of practical tools. Readers with a need to design and deploy configuration management solutions will find Vesta's flexible description language and build system a powerful, original approach to the persistent problem of coping with complex dependencies among software components.

The Vesta system builds on many computer science specialties, including programming language design and implementation, garbage collection, file systems, concurrent programming, and fault-tolerance techniques. Some familiarity with these topics is assumed.

## Acknowledgements

The Vesta system was many years in the making. The core idea behind Vesta first grabbed the attention of one of the authors of this book (RL) around 1979. The problems Vesta addresses — version management and system building — are as central to software development today as they were then, but in the past couple of decades the standard tools in this area haven't progressed much. Why not? We believe it is for the same reason that we still use the QWERTY keyboard: early *de facto* standardization on ultimately limiting technology. There are better system-building tools (and better keyboards), but they are non-standard. Standard system-building tools have brought software developers to a local hilltop. Vesta, we argue in this book, offers a view from a different, higher one.

The path to that hilltop hasn't been straight. The development of a practical system embodying our core idea — the notion of an exhaustive, machine-interpretable description of the construction of a software system from source code — proved surprisingly difficult. The first steps occurred in the context of the Cedar experimental programming environment [35, 36], A full-scale project to explore the subject didn't get underway for several years, as part of the Taos system at the DEC Systems Research Center (SRC). This project, called Vesta but later renamed Vesta-1, produced a usable but idiosyncratic system capable of repeatable, incremental, consistent builds of large-scale software. It saw significant use at SRC (but nowhere else) in the early 1990s [11,13,25,40]. Vesta-2, the subject of this book, came along several years later after considerable analysis of the use of Vesta-1, followed by a complete redesign and reimplementation.

Of course, no system just "comes along". The Vesta systems owe their existence to the hard work of many colleagues who generously gave their ideas, opinions, insights, code, encouragement, bug reports, and comradeship. With so many participants over so many years, it is impossible to thank them all, but we want to acknowledge a number of key contributors.

The initial inspiration for Vesta came from Butler Lampson and his work with Eric Schmidt and Ed Satterthwaite on Cedar and its predecessor systems at Xerox PARC. Butler guided our thinking on numerous occasions throughout the Vesta-1 and Vesta-2 projects, contributing to the designs for the system modeling languages and repositories. He also played a major role in designing the Vesta-2 function cache and weeder described in chapters 8 and 9.

The Vesta-1 system was developed by Bob Ayers, Mark R. Brown, Sheng-Yang Chiu, John Ellis, Chris Hanna, Roy Levin, and Paul McJones, several of whom also assisted in the analysis of Vesta-1's use that informed the design of Vesta-2.

Jim Horning and Martín Abadi, with Butler's participation, helped design the Vesta-2 evaluator's fine-grained dependency algorithm. Together with Chris Hanna, Jim also contributed to the design of the system description language and the initial implementation of the evaluator.

Bill McKeeman's incisive and insistent suggestions led us to make the description language syntax simpler and more readable. Our fingerprint package on which Vesta's repository and cache depend heavily descends directly from ideas and code of Andrei Broder. Jeff Mogul and Mike Burrows helped track down a serious performance problem in our RPC implementation. Chandu Thekkath helped with NFS performance problems and gave helpful comments on an early draft of this book. Emin Gün Sirer implemented the Modula-3 bridge and made several improvements to the performance of the entire system. Mark Lillibridge gave us many useful comments on an earlier draft of Appendix A. Cynthia Hibbard and Jim Horning provided numerous suggestions for improvement on various drafts of the manuscript. Neil Stratford coded an early version of the replication tools and some of the repository support for them.

Tim Leonard initiated our contact with the Araña (Alpha microprocessor) development group, which became Vesta's first real user community outside SRC, and Walker Anderson and Joford Lim led that group's initial evaluation of Vesta. Matt Reilly and Ken Schalk championed the use of Vesta in the Araña group, seeing it through to eventual adoption and production use. Both were involved in the port of Vesta to Linux, and Ken has become the driving force in evolving the present open-source Vesta system. It is through his tireless efforts that developers unconnected with the original work at DEC have an opportunity to evaluate Vesta as a practical alternative to conventional configuration management tools. Scott Venier created Vestaweb, a very useful web interface for exploring a Vesta repository.

Finally, we owe a debt of gratitude to Bob Taylor, whose regular encouragement kept us from abandoning Vesta when it seemed unlikely it would ever see use outside the research lab. Without Bob's unflagging support over many years and two companies, Vesta would probably never have happened.

This book, like the Vesta system itself, has been many years in the making. It began as a Compaq technical report [27], and we thank Hewlett-Packard for permission to use portions of that report. We also are indebted to John DeTreville for the Vesta logo that appears on the cover. But the book would not exist without the support of two key individuals. Fred Schneider, as series co-editor for Springer's *Monographs in Computer Science*, persuaded us to undertake the production of this book when the complexities of our day jobs made it seem impossible. Our editor at Springer, Wayne Wheeler, showed remarkable patience in the face of repeated underestimates of the work involved. We are grateful to Fred and Wayne and the staff at Springer (notably Frank Ganz, Ann Kostant, and Elizabeth Loew) for their continuous support during the preparation of the book, and we hope that the result justifies their faith.

Palo Alto, California
December 2005

*Allan Heydon*
*Roy Levin*
*Tim Mann*
*Yuan Yu*

# Contents

## Part II The User's View of Vesta

## Part III Inside Vesta

## Part IV Assessing Vesta

*Software Configuration Management Using Vesta*

# Part I

# Introducing Vesta

The first part of this book sets the stage for an in-depth presentation of the Vesta system. Chapter 1 presents the key problems that Vesta addresses and lays out the essential properties of Vesta's solution. Chapter 2 provides some technical background on Unix, the operating system on which Vesta is implemented, chiefly targeted at the non-specialist. Chapter 3 then surveys the architecture of the Vesta system, presenting its major components and their interactions, and laying the foundation for a more detailed survey of Vesta's functionality in Part II.

# 1

# Introduction

This book describes Vesta [26,28,43], a system for software versioning and building that *scales to accommodate large projects*, is *easy to use*, and guarantees *repeatable, incremental, and consistent builds*. Vesta embodies the belief that reliable, incremental, consistent building is overwhelmingly important for software construction and that its absence from conventional development environments has significantly interfered with the production of large systems. Consequently, Vesta focuses on the two central challenges of large-scale software development — versioning and building — and offers a novel, integrated solution.

Versioning is an inevitable problem for large-scale software systems because software evolves and changes substantially over time. Major differences often exist between the source code in various shipped versions of a software product, as well as between the latest shipped version and the current sources under development, yet bugs have to be fixed in all these versions. Also, although many developers may work on the current sources at the same time, each needs the ability to test individual changes in isolation from changes made by others. Thus a powerful versioning system is essential so that developers can create, name, track, and control many versions of the sources.

Building is also a major problem. Without some form of automated support, the task of compiling or otherwise processing source files and combining them into a finished system is time-consuming, error-prone, and likely to produce inconsistent results. As a software system grows, this task becomes increasingly difficult to manage, and comprehensive automation becomes essential. Every organization with a multi-million line code base wants an automated build system that is reliable, efficient, easy-to-use, and general enough for their application. These organizations are very often dissatisfied with the build systems available to them and are forced to distort their development processes to cope with the limitations of their software-building machinery.

Versioning and building are two parts of a larger problem area that is often called *software configuration management* (SCM). The broadest definition of SCM encompasses such topics as software life-cycle management (spanning everything from requirements gathering to bug tracking), development process methodology, and the specific tools used to develop and evolve software components. Vesta takes the view that these aspects of SCM, although important to the overall software development process, can be sensibly addressed only after the central issues of versioning and building. Further, in contrast to most conventional SCM systems, Vesta takes the view that these two problems interact, and that a proper solution integrates them so that the versioning and building facilities leverage each other's properties. That integrated solution then serves as a solid base upon which to construct facilities that address other SCM problems.

## 1.1 Some Scenarios

To motivate Vesta's focus on versioning, building, and their integration, here are some scenarios that conventional software development environments do not always handle well.

**Scenario 1.** A developer must check out a library to make a change necessary for his currently assigned task, but he can't because someone else has it checked out.

*The problem:* the source control system doesn't allow parallel development.

**Scenario 2.** Dave is having difficulty debugging a change because a library used by his code is behaving in an unexpected way. The library is a large and complex one but was built without including information required by the debugger. Dave knows nothing about the procedure for rebuilding the library to include the debugging information he needs.

*The problem:* the build system does not support the parameterization necessary for the developer to be able to say easily "rebuild this library including debugging information" and as a result, he must delve into the library's build instructions to determine how to set the necessary switch and build it manually.

**Scenario 3.** Alice is ready to begin debugging a substantial new feature, but to do so she requires several other components to be rebuilt with a new definition for a data structure that they share. She is unable to do this herself without setting up an environment comparable to that used by her organization's nightly build.

*The problem:* the build system and process do not enable developers to build substantial subportions of the complete system in order to test and debug their changes with other affected components.

**Scenario 4.** Susan, a developer in California, learns that her colleague Anoop needs to build Susan's software component at the Indian development lab. She would like to help, but is uncertain about the ways in which her component depends on local conditions that may be different in his development environment. She also has no way to determine what additional files she needs to send to Anoop in order to ensure that her component will build properly in India.

*The problem:* the build system does not ensure that building instructions are complete and capture all dependencies.

**Scenario 5.** Fred types "make", and his program compiles and links without errors, but it exhibits mysterious bugs. After a long fruitless debugging session, Fred tries "make clean; make" to build the program from scratch. The program then works.

*The problem:* the build system trusts the developers to supply dependency information rather than computing that information itself, and Fred — or some developer who had previously worked on this program — left some out.

**Scenario 6.** A developer comes into work and performs a "sync" operation, which copies recently checked-in files to her workstation. This keeps her local file tree from falling too far behind the work her colleagues are doing. However, after building her code with the new files, she finds that it no longer works as it did yesterday. There's no easy way for her to find the problematic change or to roll back to where she was before the "sync".

*The problem:* the version management system provides only coarse-grained updating and supports versioning only in the central code pool, not on behalf of individual developers.

**Scenario 7.** A developer is implementing a new feature. In the course of the implementation, he decides that the approach is flawed, so he deletes what he has been doing and goes home. Overnight, he has an idea about how to salvage a significant portion of his previous work, but since he didn't check the code in before deleting it from his workstation, it's gone.

*The problem:* the version management system provides no support for versioning except in the shared source pool, so it can't help the developer in this situation.

**Scenario 8.** John needs to make a small change to a library, so he checks it out. He makes the change, but when he tries to compile, the compiler gets a mysterious fatal error. He reports the problem to his colleague Mary, who checked in the library the previous day. Mary tries the same build on her workstation and it works. After some head-scratching and discussion, they discover that John and Mary have different versions of the compiler. Investigating further, they find that John was supposed to download a new compiler several weeks before, but the email telling him to do so came when he was absorbed making a delicate change to his code, so he put the message aside and ultimately forgot about it.

*The problem:* the build system and build instructions do not reflect or capture dependencies on the versions of tools used during the build process.

**Scenario 9.** A customer reports an error in an old but still supported release of a product. The developers attempt to reproduce the problem, but they are unable to rebuild the old system from source. Investigation reveals that a third-party library used in the old release was not included in the build tree and that when an updated version of that library was installed for use in a later release of the product, it overwrote the old one.

*The problem:* the version management and build facilities are not integrated and do not require that build instructions constitute a complete description of the system, causing an essential component to be inadvertently discarded.

## 1.2 The Configuration Management Challenge

The common theme highlighted by the preceding scenarios is the failure of conventional software configuration management systems to address the realities of building and evolving large systems. Effective SCM becomes more difficult as the size of the software system grows, as the number of developers using the SCM system increases, as the number of geographically distributed development sites grows, and as more releases are produced. To handle large-scale, multi-developer, multi-site, multi-release software development, an SCM system must guarantee that builds are *repeatable*, *incremental*, and *consistent*. Existing SCM systems generally fail to provide at least one of these properties (see Chapter 10 for specifics).

**Repeatability.** When multiple versions are being developed in parallel, the ability to repeat a previous build exactly is invaluable. For example, if a customer reports a bug in an older version of a product, developers must be able to recreate the faulty program, debug it, and develop a modified version that fixes the bug (scenario 9).

Repeatability is an easy goal to state and to appreciate, but a difficult one to attain. Most build systems in use today do not guarantee repeatability because their build results are dependent on some aspect of the building environment that the system does not control. This produces the all-too-common situation in which one developer says to another, as in scenario 8: "It works on my machine, what's different about yours?"

**Incrementality.** For the practical development of large systems, the builder must be incremental, reusing the results of previous builds wherever possible. Without reliable incremental building, a development organization is forced to perform some (if not all) of its builds from scratch. The slow turnaround time for such scratch builds increases the time required for development and testing. Incremental building, on the other hand, allows many developers to efficiently edit, build, debug, and test different parts of the source base in parallel. (Contrast with scenario 3.) Even large integration builds that combine work from many developers can be accelerated by incremental building — any components that have already been built, whether in the last integration build or in isolation by individual developers, are candidates for reuse.

Good performance in the incremental builder itself is also important. As software systems grow, even incremental building can be too slow if the running time of the builder (exclusive of the compilers and other tools it invokes) depends on the total size of the system to be built rather than the size of the changes. This problem can easily arise. For example, a simple incremental builder might work by checking each individual compiler invocation in the build to see whether it must be redone. If these checks have significant cost, such a builder will scale poorly. Indeed, this is the norm in most SCM systems.

**Consistency.** The build process performs a sequence of actions on source files (files created by developers, also called *sources*) and derived files (files previously created by the build system, also called *deriveds*). A build is *consistent* if every derived file it incorporates is up to date relative to the files from which it was produced. The obvious way to achieve consistency is to perform every build from scratch (that is, starting from sources), which of course sacrifices incrementality. Correspondingly, a partial system build introduces the potential for inconsistency because some derived file may be out of date with respect to a source file, to another derived file, or to some aspect of the build environment on which it depends. When this happens, the semantics of the source and derived files no longer correspond. Such a system generally exhibits unwanted behavior that is difficult to debug, as in scenario 5.

Achieving these three essential properties is thus the central challenge for an effective SCM system.

## 1.3 The Vesta Response

This book shows how the Vesta system successfully addresses the SCM challenge. Specifically, it explains and justifies the claim at the beginning of this chapter:

> Vesta is an SCM system that *scales to accommodate large software*, is *easy to use*, and guarantees *repeatable, incremental, and consistent builds*.

Vesta subdivides the general problem of versioning into *version management* and *source control*. Building breaks down into *system modeling* and *model evaluation*.

**Version Management.** Version management is the process of assigning names to evolving sequences of related source files and supporting retrieval of those files by name. Some SCM systems apply version management to derived files as well, in the sense that derived files receive versioned, human-sensible names just as sources do. By contrast, Vesta's version management assigns human-sensible names to sources only, while derived files receive machine-oriented names and are managed automatically.

**Source Control.** Source control is the process of controlling or regulating the production of new versions of source files. Operations commonly associated with source control include *check-out* and *check-in*, which respectively reserve a new version name (typically incorporating a number) and supply the file or files to be associated with a previously reserved version name. Source control may be coupled with concurrency control as well, so that checking out a particular version may limit the ability of other users to check out related ones. Vesta adopts a unique perspective on source control, quite different from that of conventional SCM systems, that enables it to avoid the kinds of problems evident in the scenarios of the preceding section.

**System Modeling.** A *system model* describes how to build all or part of a software system. It names the software components that are combined to produce larger components or entire systems, names the tools used to combine them, and specifies how the tools are applied to the components. *Configuration description*, *system description*, and *building instructions* are equivalent terms for system model.

Conventional build systems typically do not require and therefore rarely have comprehensive building instructions. Instead, they depend on the environment, which might comprise files on the developer's workstation and/or well-known server directories, to supply the unspecified pieces. This partial specification prevents repeatable builds. The first vital step toward achieving repeatability is to store source files and build tools immutably and immortally, as Vesta does, so that they are available when needed. The second step is to ensure that building instructions are *complete*, recording precisely which versions of which source files went into a build, which versions of tools (such as the compiler) were used, which command-line switches were supplied to those tools, and all other relevant aspects of the building environment. Vesta's system models do precisely that.

**Model Evaluation.** A system model can be viewed either as a static description of a system's configuration, or as an executable program that describes how to build the system. *Model evaluation* means taking the second view: running a *builder* or *evaluator* (the terms are used synonymously) to construct a complete system by processing and combining a collection of software components according to a system model's instructions.

By following those instructions to the letter, the builder performs in effect a scratch build of the system. Completeness of the instructions makes the build repeatable, but for practicality it must also be incremental. Incrementality means skipping some build actions and using previously computed results instead, an optimization that risks inconsistency. To ensure that an incremental build is consistent, the Vesta builder records every dependency of every derived file on the environment in which it was built. This includes dependencies on source files, other derived files, the tools used in the build, environmental details, and the building instructions themselves. Then, if anything on which a derived file depends has changed, the builder detects it and performs the necessary rebuilding. If not, the builder can be incremental and skip an unnecessary rebuilding step. Recording dependencies for use in this way is obviously impractical unless automated, and worthless unless exhaustive. Vesta's coupling of automated dependency analysis and incremental building distinguishes it from conventional SCM systems.

As these brief descriptions indicate, the four central topic areas are not independent. For that reason, the remainder of the book does not address them in order, taking instead a top-down approach. Part I presents an overview of Vesta's architecture. Part II describes the Vesta system as a software developer sees it, emphasizing the user-level concepts rather than the implementation. This part examines Vesta's facilities for storing files and manipulating them in the course of the development cycle. It also introduces the language in which system models are written and shows how it is used to describe large systems effectively. By the end of Part II, the reader will understand why Vesta is easy to use and how it can scale to handle large software systems while guaranteeing repeatable, incremental, and consistent builds.

Part III examines the implementation of the functionality described in Part II. Achieving each of the key properties — repeatability, incrementality, consistency — requires the solution of significant technical problems. This part focuses on those problems and their solutions, providing sufficient description of the relevant parts of the implementation to evaluate Vesta's design and engineering choices.

Finally, Part IV compares Vesta against other leading SCM systems, both in function and performance. It shows that development organizations need not sacrifice the former for the latter; the key SCM properties are achieved with similar or even superior performance as compared to "industry-standard" builders.

# 2

# Essential Background

The essential problems of software versioning and building transcend particular platforms and development environments. Nevertheless, concrete solutions to those problems are created for specific platforms and environments, and Vesta is no exception. The Vesta designers sought to address the central issues in a way that was minimally dependent on the environment, but inevitably there are dependencies of style, terminology, and implementation detail. This book presents Vesta in sufficient detail that these dependencies are visible, which therefore requires that the reader understand something of that dependent context.

To this end, this chapter presents a brief overview of the environment in and for which Vesta was originally built: Digital Equipment Corporation's Tru64® operating system.[1] Tru64 is a multi-generation descendent of the Berkeley (BSD) version of Unix. Vesta uses few notions that are peculiar to Unix, so the key Vesta concepts and most of the technical specifics transfer easily from Unix to other popular operating systems. Those specifics of Vesta are nevertheless shaped by the Unix context, so this chapter outlines that context as background for the material in the remainder of the book.

Readers who are conversant with Unix can quickly skim this chapter or skip it entirely. Those who are unfamiliar with Unix will likely find that the essentials described below have natural analogs in the environments with which they are familiar. This brief chapter is certainly not a reference on Unix concepts.[2] It occasionally sacrifices a bit of technical precision in the interest of remaining concise and conveying the key ideas necessary to understand Vesta, a fact that Unix and Tru64 aficionados will undoubtedly recognize.

[1] Vesta has been ported to a number of other Unix platforms, including Linux.

[2] The classic reference is Kernighan and Pike [33].

## 2.1 The Unix File System

### 2.1.1 Naming Files and Directories

File names are subdivided into a *name* and an *extension*, separated by a period ("`.`"). This is only a convention; Unix has no machinery for associating semantics with file extensions, as is the case for some other operating systems (e.g., Microsoft Windows®). File extensions are very frequently used to identify the "type", that is, the internal format, of files. Because extensions are only conventional, they may be of any length, although between one and four characters is typical. For some kinds of files, the absence of an extension is the norm, but in such cases the usage of the file is such that a single fixed name (like `readme` or `Makefile`) is commonly used.

A *directory* is a collection of names, each of which may identify a file or another directory. These names do not distinguish the things they name; thus, the name `foo.bar` might be a directory or a file, although conventionally a name with an embedded dot is used for a file, not a directory.

The files and directories on a disk partition are arranged in a tree-structured name space. (This is a simplification, to be corrected shortly.) Within this tree, a *path* (sometimes called a *filename path*) is a sequence of names separated by the character "`/`". The root of the tree is named "`/`", so a path from the root might be `/x/y/z`. In such a path, every name, with the possible exception of the last, must be a directory, so in the path `/x/y/z`, `x` is a directory containing a directory named `y` containing `z` (`z` may name either a file or a directory). A path like `/x/y/z` is called *absolute* because it explicitly originates at the root. A path like `x/y/z` is called *relative*, meaning that it is to be interpreted relative to some directory that depends on the context in which the path is used.

Every directory contains the special name "`.`", which refers to the directory itself. Every directory except the root also contains the special name "`..`", which refers to the directory's parent in the naming tree.

### 2.1.2 Mount Points

The file name space that Unix programs and users see is created by connecting the directory trees on individual disk partitions via a mechanism called *mount points*. A directory tree $T_1$ is attached to a particular node $N$ in tree $T_2$ by *mounting* it there, that is, by effectively splicing $T_2$ so that $N$ becomes the name of the root of $T_1$. So, for example, if `a/b/c` names a file in $T_1$ and `x/y/z` is a path in $T_2$, mounting $T_1$ at `x/y` makes the file accessible as `x/y/a/b/c`. Note that, as a result of the mount, `x/y/z` is no longer in the name space.

The mount point mechanism enables the construction of large file name spaces out of the smaller ones that correspond to individual disk partitions. The individual disk partitions may be on separate computers; that is, a mount point may span file servers connected by a local area network. File servers may implement their file systems differently as long as they adhere to recognized protocols, of which NFS [49, 54] is a particularly common one. Vesta's storage machinery (Chapters 4 and 7) exploits this property.

### 2.1.3 Links

It is customary to think of a Unix file system as a tree of directories with files at the leaves. Even ignoring the loops created by "`.`" and "`..`", this is not entirely accurate, because of *links*. There are two distinct kinds of links, *hard* and *soft*, with rather different properties.

A hard link connects a Unix directory entry to a file. A file is a container for a sequence of bytes and is identified by an integer called the *inode* number, which is unique within the disk partition on which the file resides. The directory entry for a file associates a file name with an inode number, making that association a hard link. There may be more than one hard link to the same file, and all hard links have equal status, in the sense that the file remains extant until the last of them is deleted. Unix users rarely see inode numbers and many are unaware of the concept of hard links because they never create more than one link to a file. However, in a system that manages versions of groups of files, hard links are a useful concept.

A soft link (more commonly called a *symbolic* link) provides a more general method of referencing files outside of the directory tree structure. While a hard link pairs a file name with an inode number, a symbolic link pairs a file name with a path. That path may name a file or, less commonly, a directory. When a name in a file path corresponds to a symbolic link, the link is effectively interpolated (or expanded, like a macro) at the point at which it occurs. For example, if `y` is a symbolic link with value `a/b/c`, the path `x/y/z` is equivalent to the path `x/a/b/c/z`. Unlike a hard link, a symbolic link may "dangle"; that is, it may name a non-existent file (although this is rarely desirable). Also, a symbolic link may point anywhere within the file name space, while a hard link can reference a file only within the same disk partition as the directory since inode numbers are relative to a partition.

### 2.1.4 Properties of Files

The set of properties, or metadata, associated with a Unix file is fairly spartan, unlike some other file systems. We have already noted that the type of data held in the file is not explicitly stored; instead, naming conventions (the file extension) are used to encode this information. Sometimes file version information is encoded in the file name as well; for example, text editors that create backup versions of the file they edit often use a naming convention to represent these versions. There are other naming conventions that are occasionally used to simulate file properties, such as beginning a file name with a "`.`". This indicates a "hidden" file; that is, one that the standard directory listing program, `ls`, should by default omit. These conventions, while undoubtedly useful in various contexts, are purely conventions. The Unix file system doesn't understand the properties they encode.

Unix maintains with each file a trio of times called the file's `mtime`, `atime`, and `ctime`. Respectively, these record when the file was last modified (written), accessed (read), and had its other Unix-maintained properties change. These properties include its *permissions*, which control access to the file. While access control is not emphasized in Vesta, it does figure in the machinery for propagating files between sites, so the Unix access control mechanism is briefly covered here.

In a Unix system, the principals for access control purposes are *users* and *groups*. Strictly speaking, both users and groups are identified by integers, although tables maintained by the system administrator (stored in the file system as `/etc/passwd` and `/etc/group`, respectively) map these integers to human-sensible names. It is therefore customary to say, for example, that the owner of a file is `smith`, while in reality `smith` is a user name that translates to, say, user ID 342. A group ID maps, via a system table, to a set of user IDs that it is deemed to contain.[3] Access control principals are local to an individual Unix system; that is, Unix has no notion of principals whose identity spans multiple systems.

Every file has an associated *owner* (a single user ID), and an associated *group* (a single group ID). Every file has a set of nine mode (or permission) bits, three each for the owner, the group, and the *world*, and these three bits control access for reading, writing, and execution. For example, a commonly used system utility program would likely grant execution permission to everyone, while a program under active development might grant no access to the world, but all permissions to its associated group, which would likely be the group of users involved in its development.

Given this structure, the access checking algorithm is straightforward. The accessor is first assigned to a class of access. If the accessor's ID equals the owner's ID, the accessor gets owner access. Otherwise, if the accessor's ID is a member of the file's group, the accessor gets group access. If neither of these cases applies, the accessor gets world access. Then, for the operation being performed, the appropriate access control bit (read, write, execute) within the class is examined, and the operation is permitted or prohibited accordingly.

The access control scheme applies to Unix directories as well, except that, since it is meaningless to execute a directory, the third mode bit of each class is used to control searching of the directory instead.

For administrative purposes, Unix has a distinguished user ID, often named "`root`", for which the access control check always succeeds regardless of the actual permission bits.

## 2.2 Unix Processes

When a Unix program is loaded and started, it consists of a single *process*. For many programs, a single process is sufficient, while others find it necessary to create additional processes by *forking*. Processes are arranged in a tree, and the action of forking creates a new child of the process that performs the fork operation. Processes do not share memory[4] but a parent can pass parameter information when it forks a child

[3] The integers that identify users and groups lie in distinct name spaces; that is, a particular Unix system might have a user 342 and a group 342, and these have no relationship to each other.

[4] This is a simplification, since some Unix variants do permit interprocess memory sharing.

and can establish byte-stream communication channels, called *pipes*, between its children. Also, processes can communicate indirectly through the file system.

Because processes are fairly heavyweight (that is, they have a large amount of state information) and because the methods for communicating between them are limited, some programs use *multithreading* within a process. In a multithreaded process, the threads of control share the memory and most of the other state information associated with the process (e.g., parameters passed by the parent and pipes to other processes). There is very little per-thread state, making it efficient to switch execution contexts between threads of the same process.

A process receives parameters from its parent as a vector of text strings. The format and meaning of these strings is program-specific, although there are a number of standard conventions. Typically, parameters include input and/or output file names and options that alter the program's behavior. Collectively, the vector is sometimes called the *command line*, because when a program is launched from the shell (see below), the command line typed by the user is parsed to create this vector.

Every process has a view of the file system name space that is defined by two directories, called the *current* or *working* directory and the *root*. The working directory is the context used to interpret relative paths used by code within the process. For example, `x/foo.c` is interpreted by looking in the working directory for a directory named `x`, then looking in it for a file named `foo.c`. The root directory is used as the starting point for absolute file names, that is, paths beginning with "`/`". Both of these directories are established by the process's parent at the time the process is forked. This is an important subtlety, for most Unix users think of "`/`" as having a fixed meaning for all processes. While this is frequently the case in Unix installations, it is not inherent, and Vesta exploits the ability to control the meaning of the root directory for selected processes, as discussed in Section 5.2.3.

An executing process communicates with its surrounding environment through input/output channels called *file descriptors*. A file descriptor is simply a small integer that identifies an open file, a pipe, or a device such as a user's keyboard or display screen. Three file descriptors have particular conventional uses and are generally passed to a process by its parent: `stdin` is an input stream frequently used to supply the input data to a program, `stdout` is an output stream frequently used to deliver the results of a program, and `stderr` is an output stream used to report errors. While these streams often satisfy the I/O needs of a simple program, a more complicated one that needs to read and write multiple files may not use them at all and instead perform its I/O through file descriptors that it explicitly opens.

## 2.3 The Unix Shell

The shell is a program with which a Unix user interacts after logging in. Its job is to accept commands from the user and execute them. There are a number of popular Unix shells that differ in their details, but all provide a way for the user to type in the names of programs to be executed and to supply parameters to them. The shell also provides ways to direct where the streams `stdin`, `stdout`, and `stderr` go.

With this key feature the user can create *pipelines* that connect the inputs and outputs of multiple programs to manipulate a stream of data in complex ways. Much of the power of Unix derives from this mechanism, coupled with a rich set of programs, called *filters*, that are designed to be combined in pipelines. By providing some simple control flow machinery for conditional execution and looping, the shell enables the construction of *shell scripts*, which are, in essence, simple applications formed by aggregating and sequencing the execution of individual Unix programs.

In the simplest case, however, the shell simply parses the typed command line and forks a process to run the specified program. For example, when the user types

```
/bin/cc -O2 -g foo.c
```

the shell interprets it to mean "fork the program `/bin/cc` as a process and provide as its parameter vector the three strings `-O2`, `-g`, and `foo.c`". The other state information required by the process, such as the root and working directories and the three standard file descriptors, is set by default (and of course the shell gives its user ways to alter the defaults).

The shell also provides a way to define *environment variables* which are passed implicitly to programs invoked from the shell. An environment variable is simply a name and associated text string. Its meaning is established by code executing as part of the process. As the name suggests, these variables generally encode some information about the environment of the process. Environment variables are generally passed unchanged to a child process by its parent.

A common use for environment variables is to define a *search path*, a sequence of directories whose members are sequentially interrogated when a certain kind of file is being sought. The shell itself defines such a variable, called `PATH`, that is the sequence of places to look to locate a program to be executed. For example, if the `PATH` variable is defined as

```
PATH=/usr/local/bin:/usr/bin:/bin
```

and if the user typed

```
cc -O2 -g foo.c
```

the shell would sequentially search the three paths `/usr/local/bin`, `/usr/bin`, and `/bin` to find the first directory in which the program `cc` exists, then execute it. If that directory happened to be `/bin`, then this command line would have the identical effect as the one two paragraphs above. (`/bin` is the directory conventionally used for standard program binaries and is therefore generally a component of this search path.)

## 2.4 The Unix Programming Environment

The conventions of the Unix programming environment were developed initially based on the semantics and needs of the C programming language [34], and most other programming languages that have since been added to the environment have followed those conventions as much as possible.

C programs are typically created from source files stored in a number of related directories, plus one or more binary libraries. The source files are identified by names ending in `.c`, libraries are identified by the file extension `.a`. Each source file is compiled by the C compiler, producing object code in a file with extension `.o`. An executable C program is then linked together by the program `ld`, which reads a set of object files and libraries and writes a single executable file, which conventionally lacks a file extension.

The source files that make up a program generally need to share definitions, including the names of functions defined in other source files or libraries. These definitions are typically grouped in *header files*, conventionally with extension `.h`. To incorporate the definitions in a header file, a C source program uses the `#include` statement. For example:

```
#include <stdio.h>
```

This statement instructs the C compiler to locate the file `stdio.h` and insert its contents as though they appeared at this point in the source program. Although the programming language imposes no structural requirements on a header file, it is a common methodology to use a header file to define the interface to the functions provided by a library. So in this example, `stdio.h` might define the interface for the standard I/O library `stdio.a`, which would be included on the command line that links the program.

A *library* is a collection of object files (also called an *archive*) processed by a program named `ar` so that they may be selectively included during the linking of a program by `ld`. A program that includes `stdio.h` may use only a few of the functions it defines, and therefore only the code that implements those functions rather than the entire contents of `stdio.a` need be linked in.

As a program grows in size, it becomes unwieldy to use explicit paths to name all the files involved in its construction. Instead, the C programming environment tools (chiefly the compiler, `cc`, and the linker, `ld`), use search paths to locate header files and libraries, respectively. Moreover, the standard system libraries and the header files needed to use them are stored in well-known directories, which, by default, appear at the end of these search paths. The specifics vary in different versions of Unix, but the idea is the same. For example, the compiler might use a search path named `INCLUDEPATH` to find header files, whose default value might be:

```
INCLUDEPATH=.:/usr/include
```

This search path instructs the compiler to look for header files first in the current working directory (‘`.`’), then in `/usr/include`.[5]

[5] As any experienced Unix developer knows, search paths are fragile. Vesta's system description language (Section 5.2.2) provides a more robust way to bind names to specific file paths.

## 2.5 Make

While it is possible to compile and link Unix programs directly by typing shell commands or running shell scripts, this is too cumbersome for anything but the simplest applications. As a result, virtually every Unix programming environment includes Make [18] or one of its many variants. Make is a program that automates the build process. It takes as input a *Makefile* that encodes a set of dependencies among files and a set of actions to be taken to build a piece of software from those files. The underlying idea is simple: Make repeatedly considers, by examining the dependency rules, whether any file is out-of-date with respect to those it depends on, and if so, it executes a designated action that brings the file up-to-date. A typical rule states that an object code file, `foo.o`, depends on its associated source file, `foo.c`. If Make discovers that `foo.o` is older than `foo.c` (or missing entirely), it executes an action associated with the dependency rule, which typically compiles `foo.c` to produce an up-to-date `foo.o`. These actions are essentially short shell scripts. Thus, a Makefile provides a simple way to group together a collection of related actions for building the components of a program and specifying declaratively the circumstances under which those actions are to be taken. Moreover, if the dependencies are completely specified, Make can rebuild a software system incrementally following a change to one or more files.

From this very brief description, we can highlight three significant properties of Make:

- dependencies are specified manually by the programmer;
- only dependencies involving files can be expressed; and
- build decisions depend entirely on relative file modification times.

All of these have been recognized as shortcomings in various contexts, and many of the variants of Make exist precisely to try to correct these deficiencies. Later chapters examine Make in much more detail, contrasting it with Vesta's approach to building software systems.

# 3

# The Architecture of Vesta

Chapter 1 briefly introduced the central SCM problems of building and versioning. This chapter and those in Part II describe how Vesta is designed to solve these problems and show how the Vesta system creates a development environment in which software builds are repeatable, consistent, incremental, and scalable.

## 3.1 System Components

We begin with an architectural overview of Vesta and the major functional behaviors of its components. Figure 3.1 shows these components, with those that are most visible to the ordinary developer toward the left and those that are mostly hidden within the implementation or visible only to administrators toward the right. The components in the bottom row are shared servers; at each Vesta installation, or *site*, there is exactly one instance of each. In contrast, the components in the top row can execute on any developer's machine, and most of them typically run on every such machine.

The *repository server* handles long-term data storage. It provides an abstraction similar to, but with significant differences from, the Unix file system abstraction. Vesta users manipulate files and directories in the repository using two sets of tools shown at the upper left of the figure: *standard file browsing and editing tools* and *repository tools*. Developers use the former set of tools for browsing, listing directories, editing, comparing files, and so on. These are precisely the tools of a standard Unix environment (that is, **ls**, **emacs**, etc.), and they work with files in the repository as they would with an ordinary file system. Developers use the repository tools to manipulate files and directories in ways that are unique to Vesta and do not fit the standard file system paradigm, to be discussed in more detail in Chapter 4.

The *evaluator* is Vesta's builder; it evaluates (that is, it executes) system models written in Vesta's system description language to construct complete software systems from their constituent parts. The evaluator makes use of one or more *run-tool servers* to execute standard build tools like compilers and linkers. It invokes the

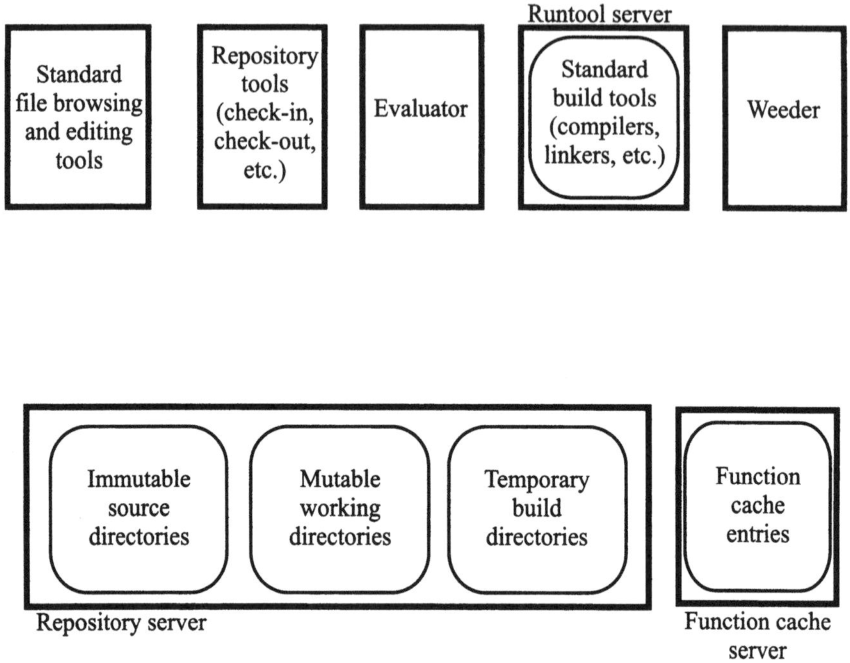


**Fig. 3.1.** The major components of the Vesta implementation.

*function cache server* to store intermediate and final results of each build for later reuse.

The *weeder* is a utility invoked by a Vesta administrator, not a developer. It serves as a garbage collector for Vesta's long-term storage, removing unwanted files and other persistent data structures.

These components of the Vesta system interact in different ways to implement source file management, system building, and storage management, as discussed in the following sections.

### 3.1.1 Source Management Components

Figure 3.2 highlights Vesta's source management components — those that implement source control and version management — and shows how they interact. Chapters 4 and 7 describe these components in detail.

Source management occurs in two classes of directories implemented by the Vesta repository: *immutable* and *mutable*. Developers use immutable source directories to hold versioned, immutable source files (or *sources*, for short).[1] Of course,

[1] When we speak of *source* files, we mean any file stored in the Vesta repository that is not created through the execution of the Vesta evaluator (builder). From Vesta's perspective, such files are "handmade", since Vesta has no rules (system models) for constructing them. Obviously, files whose contents are typed by a Vesta user are sources. But, by this defi-

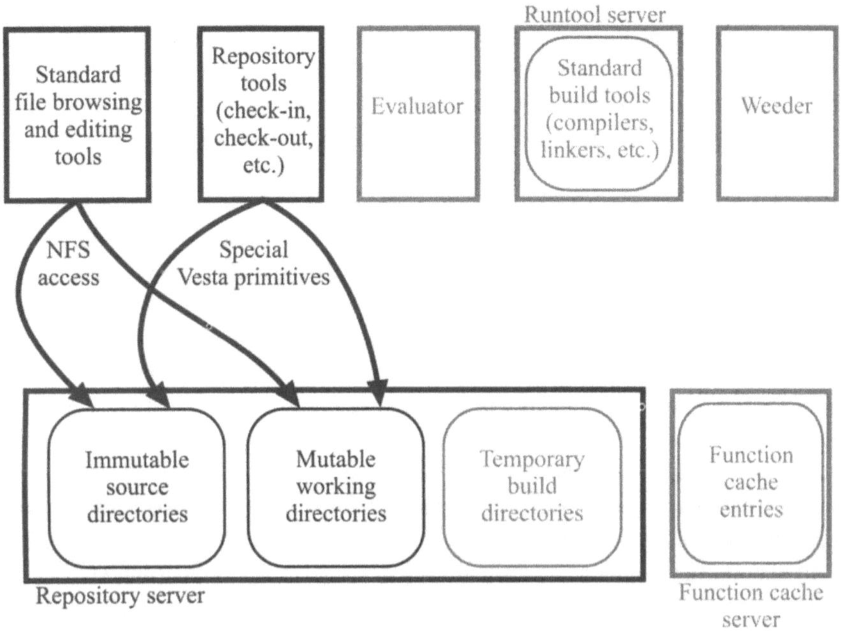


**Fig. 3.2.** Source management components and their interactions.

these immutable files must be created somehow; mutable directories provide the place for this to happen.

The Vesta repository stores immutable sources in a hierarchical name space, similar to a Unix or Windows directory tree. Every version of every source is included in the tree. Different versions of the same source are distinguished by having a version name or number as a component of their pathnames. The repository makes this tree available as a network-accessible file system, using the standard NFS protocol [49, 54]. Thus, ordinary file browsing and editing tools running on any user workstation capable of being an NFS client can access all versions of all immutable sources directly. The repository also makes mutable directories available in the same way. These two file systems are typically mounted (see Section 2.1.2) and appear in the developer's file name space as `/vesta` and `/vesta-work`, respectively.

In the repository, sources are conventionally grouped in *packages*. A package is a collection of related files, such as the sources to build a single program or library. By convention, Vesta sources are versioned at the package level, not at the level of individual files. This means that a version of a package consists of a directory tree of related files, and all the versions of a package are subdirectories of a single package directory. Contrast this with the more conventional method of versioning

---

nition, binary files such as build tools and libraries copied into the Vesta repository from elsewhere are also sources.

every source file (e.g., RCS [60]), which provides no natural means of identifying which versions go together.

Like many source control systems, Vesta uses a check-out/check-in paradigm, but the process works in a slightly unusual way. Because source files are immutable, a check-in operation never deletes existing files or renders them inaccessible. Instead, check-out/check-in operations add to the name space of package versions.[2] Checking out a package reserves a version name and makes a working copy, in a mutable directory, of the existing files and subdirectories from the package's previous version (if any). Standard tools can then be used to modify, create, delete, or rename files and directories in the working copy. The builder operates only on immutable snapshots of the working copy, not on the working copy itself. These snapshots, which are immutable source directories, are taken by the repository tools at the user's direction as part of the build process. Checking in the package binds the previously reserved version name to the last snapshot of the working copy. Check-in, snapshotting, check-out, and other repository operations that do not fit the NFS file access paradigm are handled by the repository tools. As Figure 3.2 shows, the tools work by invoking special Vesta repository primitives through a remote procedure call (RPC) interface.

To support development of software across geographically distributed sites, the repository server at one site can replicate some or all of its sources to repository servers at other sites, communicating through an RPC interface (not shown in the figure). Vesta's support for this *partial replication* is described in Section 4.3.

### 3.1.2 Build Components

Figure 3.3 highlights the Vesta components that participate in a build. Building is quite a complex process, involving many components that interact in subtle ways to ensure that builds are repeatable, incremental, and consistent.

The Vesta evaluator is the center of the build process. The evaluator reads a system model and acts on it, building what the model describes. It begins (arrow 1 in the figure) by reading the model from an immutable directory in the repository. A model describes how to build a software system from source, and the sources it references are also stored in immutable directories. Models are written in the Vesta system description language (SDL), a small functional programming language whose data types and primitives are specialized for software construction. In this language, a typical primitive function call causes a single source file to be compiled, while a more complex function might compile and build an entire library. Chapters 5 and 6 discuss Vesta's SDL and system models in some detail.

Whenever the evaluator encounters a function call in a model, it consults the function cache (arrow 2 in Figure 3.3) to determine if a sufficiently similar call has already been evaluated and remembered from a previous build. If so, the evaluator reads the result from the cache instead of evaluating the function again. This is the

[2] These additions to the name space actually use *appendable* directories, a variant of the repository's immutable directories not shown in Figure 3.2. As the name suggests, an appendable directory has limited mutability; names can be added but not deleted.

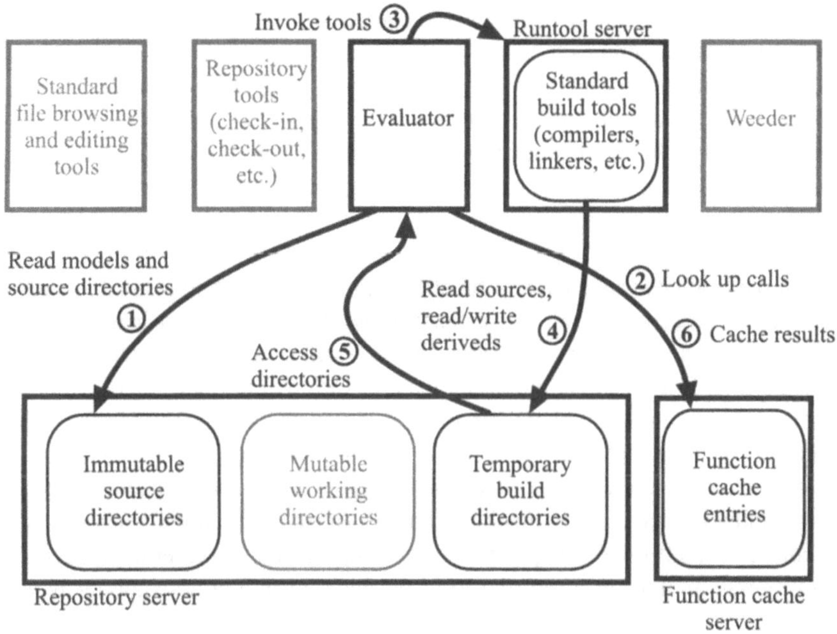


**Fig. 3.3.** Component interactions during a build.

basis for incremental system-building: using cached results to avoid redundant reconstruction. A function cache "hit" can occur at any level in the call graph of a Vesta model, from the leaves (usually individual calls to a standard build tool such as a compiler or linker) up to the root (the entire build). Most other build systems lack this ability; that is, they implement the equivalent of function caching only at the leaves. As a result, they don't scale well to large builds. Chapter 8 explains in detail how the evaluator and the function cache work together to implement incremental building, and Chapter 11 documents the performance benefits.

What does it mean for a previous function call to be "sufficiently similar" to the current one? That is, what is the set of conditions under which the evaluator will get a cache hit? The complete answer is quite complicated and will occupy our attention for much of Chapter 8, but we can catch a glimpse of it here. In order for use of a cached function result to be sound, Vesta must ensure that all the names and values on which that result depended are the same in the current evaluation environment as they were when the cache entry was created including, for example, the names and contents of all the header files used in a C compilation. Hence, when Vesta evaluates a function, it records the dependencies that the function's result has on names and values in its execution environment. These dependencies are *dynamic*, meaning that the evaluator records only what is referenced during this particular evaluation, rather than estimating the dependencies by static analysis of the system models and other source files involved.[3] The dependencies recorded are also *fine-grained*, meaning that when a part of a composite value is referenced, the evaluator records a dependency on just that part, not on the whole value. (For now, think of a composite value as a directory, so that a fine-grained dependency identifies the members of the directory on which a function evaluation depends.) On cache lookups, a hit occurs whenever the evaluator can find a cache entry for the current function whose dependencies were bound to the same values in the entry's original environment and the current environment.

When the evaluator encounters a function call and cannot find a suitable cache entry, it must evaluate the call. For a function written in the Vesta language, the evaluator does this itself. For a primitive function call that invokes a tool, it must execute the tool. It does so via the *runtool server* (arrow 3 in Figure 3.3), which is responsible for running the tool and reporting its outcome back to the evaluator. The evaluator invokes the runtool server using a remote procedure call, and the runtool server can therefore reside on a remote machine. This arrangement enables Vesta to support parallel compilation by invoking runtool servers on multiple machines and to support cross-platform development by invoking the runtool server on a machine with a different architecture from the local machine when a cross-compiler is not available.

Build tools execute in an *encapsulated environment*. That is, Vesta controls not only the tool's command line and environment variables, but also the entire file system content that the tool sees. While a tool is executing, Vesta monitors and records each file system reference that it makes, since these represent dependencies that must be recorded in the eventual cache entry for the tool invocation. Figure 3.3 shows the interactions among components that accomplish the recording. When a tool begins execution, it has a unique file name space separate from any other tool execution and which the repository server and evaluator collaborate to provide. File accesses made by the tool actually go to special *temporary build directories* (arrow 4) provided by the repository. (These directories are invisible to users and their special properties are transparent to the tool.) The repository notes the first reference to each file or directory made by the tool and calls back to the evaluator (arrow 5 in Figure 3.3). Using the unique name space for this tool execution, the evaluator resolves the binding for the name and records that binding as a dependency of the current tool invocation. The evaluator returns the result of the binding to the repository, which then adds it to a tree of temporary build directories for this tool invocation. The repository can then satisfy subsequent accesses to the same name from these directories. At the conclusion of a tool execution, the repository reports to the evaluator the new files and directories that the tool created (and any other file system changes the tool made) as its output.

After the evaluator finishes executing a function call, it writes a new cache entry (arrow 6 in Figure 3.3) to record the function result and its dependencies. The function cache server maintains these cache entries persistently for an entire site so that

[3] For example, in building a C program, if a particular .h file in the environment is not used, no dependency on it is recorded.

each new build can benefit from work done previously, and a build requested by one user can benefit from work previously done on behalf of another user.

As a final step, not shown in Figure 3.3, the evaluator can *ship* the results of the build. That is, it can copy some or all of the results of the evaluation's top-level function call to ordinary files and directories, making them available outside the Vesta cache.

### 3.1.3 Storage Components

Figure 3.4 shows the three pools of long-term disk storage used by Vesta components and illustrates the operation of the *weeder*, an administrative tool for reclaiming disk storage space that is no longer needed.

As shown at the bottom of the figure, the repository has a private storage area for directory entries and the function cache has a private area for cache entries, but they share a common pool of storage for source and derived files. This file pool is managed using garbage collection; that is, when neither a source directory nor a function cache entry references a file, it can be deleted. At different times in its

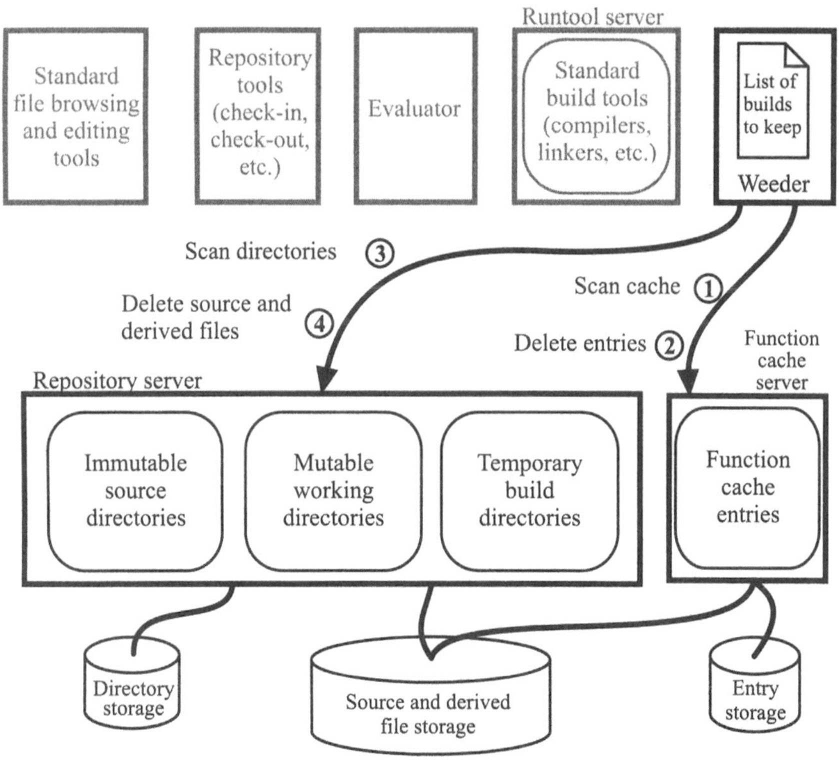


**Fig. 3.4.** Disk storage and the weeder.

history, the same file can be referenced by a directory, a cache entry, or both. The operation of the file pool is discussed in detail in Section 7.1.1.

As builds are performed, cache entries and derived files accumulate in the function cache and the file pool, which can eventually grow to consume the available disk space. However, because the function cache is just a cache, its entries can be freely deleted without affecting the repeatability or consistency of builds (just future performance, due to fewer cache hits). When disk space gets low some cache entries must be deleted to reclaim space in both the entry storage and the file pool. However, deciding which entries to remove and which to retain is a task that cannot be entirely automated; Vesta users and administrators must together decide which ones are worth keeping, based on their knowledge of what builds are likely to be requested in the future.

Unwanted cache entries and derived files are deleted by the Vesta weeder, which an administrator runs periodically. Given a specification of which build results to keep, the Vesta weeder deletes all cache entries that did not participate in those builds (arrows 1 and 2 in Figure 3.4). (In the terminology of the garbage collection literature, the input specification to the weeder is the set of *roots*.) The weeder then contacts the repository (arrows 3 and 4 in Figure 3.4) and deletes all files in the shared pool that are no longer referenced either by remaining cache entries or by the repository directory structure.

Since weeding can take considerable time (minutes to hours), the function cache, repository, and weeder are designed so that the weeder can be run concurrently with users' activities without adversely affecting normal build performance. Thus, the weeder is essentially invisible to Vesta users. Chapter 9 shows how concurrency and invisibility are achieved.

### 3.1.4 Models and Modularity

There is one other component of Vesta that is implicit in the preceding figures: system models. Chapters 5 and 6 cover the writing and use of system models in considerable detail, but in the present context what matters is that they are *modular*, meaning that each model can import other models and use the functions they define. Thus a model that describes how to assemble a collection of sources into a subsystem can be used by higher-level models that assemble subsystems into a complete system.

Modularity is essential in managing the description of large systems, but it is important for building small programs too. In a modern programming environment, even a small "hello world" program is compiled and linked against a large runtime library of input/output and operating system interface routines. Moreover, the commands needed to invoke compilers, linkers, RPC stub generators, and the like can be complex. Vesta provides a *standard environment* model that encapsulates these libraries and common building actions and makes them available to user-written models in a simple form. The standard environment can be quite complicated internally without exposing any of these complexities to the ordinary user. For example, it can build some or all of the standard libraries and tools from source. At the same time, because it is written as a model rather than being hard-wired into Vesta's implementation, more advanced users can modify or extend the standard environment to suit their unique needs, or even replace it entirely.

Modularity is important even when writing system models for individual applications. One might not immediately think to organize an application's system model so that it can be imported, but by doing so, one can then write a *release model* that imports one version of the standard environment and builds a whole collection of applications using it. Thus a development organization that maintains a suite of applications can easily create a consistent release in which all the applications are known to have been built with the same tools against the same libraries.

## 3.2 Vesta's Core Properties

The Vesta components and architecture outlined in the preceding section deliver four essential properties needed for effective software version management and construction: repeatability, consistency, incrementality, and scalability.

**Repeatability.** A Vesta build description represented by a collection of system models gives a complete recipe for building a software system from versioned sources. That is, a build description brings every relevant aspect of the construction environment under Vesta's control, including environment variables, library archives, build tools, and immutable sources. Because the build description contains complete information and because system models and the source files they reference are immutable and immortal, executing the build description produces a repeatable result.

**Consistency.** A build system that aspires to perform consistent builds must know the dependencies of every derived file. Vesta detects and records all such dependencies automatically in the course of building by encapsulation of tools and by fine-grained dependency analysis. By using automatic detection rather than relying on human-supplied (and thus error-prone) dependency specifications, Vesta can collect all the information needed to determine what building actions are necessary, and can thereby ensure that the results of its builds are consistent.

**Incrementality.** Incremental construction means exploiting past work to perform as little new work as possible. To this end, Vesta caches the results of individual tool invocations as well as larger units of work, such as the construction of entire libraries. Moreover, it automatically associates with each cached result complete, fine-grained dependency information that specifies precisely when that result may be safely reused. Since the results reside in a shared, site-wide cache, each developer can benefit from the builds of all others, maximizing the opportunity for incremental construction.

**Scalability.** In a sense, scalability is the central challenge that Vesta faces, since for small systems repeatable, consistent builds are easily carried out by brute force and incrementality is unimportant. Thus, scalability considerations pervade the Vesta architecture and implementation.

Two examples of design for scalability have already surfaced in the overview above. First, the repository's directory structure allows for a flexible hierarchy of packages, and the system description language allows build instructions to be written in a modular fashion and to import other build instructions in a hierarchical structure. Hierarchy provides one of the few ways known to "divide and conquer" the complexity of large-scale software configurations, enabling manageable scaling. Second, Vesta does not limit cooperative development to a single site. As a software system grows larger, its development becomes more likely to involve programming teams at multiple, geographically distributed sites. Groups at different sites may need to share only some of their sources. Vesta's ability to partially replicate a repository's contents supports scaling of development operations beyond a single site.

Scalability is fundamentally different from repeatability or consistency, which are essentially binary: either a system exhibits them or it doesn't. Scalability is really a design parameter. At the time work began on the version of Vesta described here (Vesta-2), an earlier prototype (Vesta-1) was being actively used to build and evolve a code base of 1.4 million source lines. A natural objective for Vesta-2 was to accommodate a system at least an order of magnitude larger.[4] Coincidentally, anecdotal data suggested that, at the time, the largest software systems in industrial settings that were built as a single consistent unit comprised 10-20 million lines of source code. From these two observations came a design target of 20 million source lines for a system that Vesta-2 should be able to build, and the implications of that target shaped the specifics of the system described in the remainder of this book.

## In Summary

This chapter surveyed Vesta's architecture and sketched how its components work together to provide repeatable, incremental, consistent, and scalable system construction. With this background, Part II presents a detailed view of Vesta's functionality as it appears to a developer, and Part III provides an "under the hood" look at the implementation techniques that deliver that functionality.

[4] It is a truism that a quantitative change of an order of magnitude in a fundamental assumption for a system induces a qualitative difference in that system's design and/or implementation.

# Part II

# The User's View of Vesta

The next three chapters survey Vesta facilities that an individual developer sees. Chapter 4 describes the development cycle, Vesta's unconventional mechanisms for naming, organizing, and manipulating files, and Vesta's support for geographically distributed development. Chapter 5 presents the primary features of the system description language that is used to define how software systems are built. Chapter 6 shows the language in action by examining how a typical system is described with Vesta system models and how that description affords both the developer and the development organization great flexibility without sacrificing repeatable, consistent, incremental builds.

# 4

# Managing Sources and Versions

The Vesta repository provides long-term storage of source and derived files. The repository has two kinds of clients — users and the evaluator — who require distinct sets of services. Users are mainly concerned with sources. They read existing source files and create new ones. The evaluator is concerned with both sources and deriveds. It reads system models, and it invokes tools that both read sources and deriveds and write out new deriveds. This chapter examines the repository services as they appear to software developers who use Vesta. The evaluator-specific facilities are covered later in Section 7.1.

A Vesta user interacts with the repository chiefly through a set of *repository tools*, which provide a particular interface to the functions implemented in the *repository server* (recall Figure 3.2). The repository tools present to the user a particular style of source naming, storage organization, and development process using the general-purpose storage facilities of the server. These specifics are the subject of Sections 4.1 and 4.2.

It is worth noting that while the approach taken in these tools is of proven utility, it is by no means "hard-wired" into Vesta. On the contrary, the tools are quite malleable. They are short programs invoked from the Unix command line, each fewer than 1,000 lines of code and readily changed. Most of the complexity is located in the repository server. Thus, a development organization can, with a small investment of programming, adapt the repository tools to support their preferred naming conventions and development process. The reader can therefore think of these tools as a fully worked-out example of a development process, one that has proven to be both convenient and practical.

This chapter first examines the central notions of file naming and organization, then shows how a user actually steps through the development cycle using the repository tools. It next describes how teams at multiple sites coordinate their development activities using repository replication, and closes by discussing the metadata facilities the repository provides.

## 4.1 Names and Versions

### 4.1.1 The Source Name Space

The Vesta repository provides a hierarchically structured source name space, similar to a Unix or Windows directory tree, but with a few additional features and restrictions to support configuration management. Users see the source name space as a subtree of the file name space visible on their workstations. As a result, users can use all their existing, familiar tools for browsing ordinary files and directories equally well on repository files and directories.[1]

To support Vesta's guarantee of repeatable builds, source files have two key properties not generally found in ordinary file systems: *immutability* and *immortality*. Immutability means that once a file is created and placed in the source name space, the file's contents cannot be modified. Immortality means that a file, once created, cannot be deleted. Together these properties support repeatable builds by ensuring that source files remain available and unchanged indefinitely.

Of course, it would be impractical to enforce these properties without exception for every source file. Deletion is sometimes unavoidable (for example, to address a lack of disk space or to comply with a licensing agreement) and mutability must be possible in order to populate directories. To address these realities without sacrificing the goal of repeatable builds, the Vesta repository carefully limits how file mutation and/or deletion occur. It ensures that all source files *accessible by the evaluator* are immutable, which is necessary in order for caching to work. The repository allows source files to be deleted, but it does not allow a deleted source's full pathname to be reused later for a different source. Thus, repeating a build will either access the identical files that were accessed previously or will fail because some source file has been explicitly deleted.

The Vesta repository supports two kinds of directory with limited mutability: *immutable* and *appendable*. *Immutable directories* provide larger immutable units than single files. Once an immutable directory is populated with files and placed in the source name space, it cannot be changed. Every file and subdirectory in such a directory must be immutable too, allowing the entire tree rooted at it to be treated as an immutable unit. *Appendable directories* support and enforce Vesta's rule that names cannot be reused. New names can be created in the directory, but existing names cannot be unbound or freely rebound to different files.

However, the repository does allow certain carefully limited forms of rebinding, involving special entities called *ghosts* and *stubs* (to be explained shortly). If the Vesta evaluator encounters a ghost or stub during a build, it halts with an error message, does not produce a result, and does not record the error in the Vesta function cache. Therefore these cases of rebinding cannot cause the same build to produce

[1] The repository server achieves this seamless integration by exporting the source tree as an NFS volume that is then imported and mounted (see Section 2.1.2) by client machines. However, the server also exports two remote procedure call (RPC) interfaces for access to features that do not map well onto NFS (see Figure 3.2 and Section 7.2.6).

different results on different occasions. As with deletion, they can at worst cause a build that succeeded on one occasion to fail on another.

Ghosts support Vesta's deletion semantics. When a user deletes a file, stub, or subdirectory from an appendable directory, Vesta replaces the deleted item with a ghost. The ghost prevents the old name from being reused; Vesta does not allow a name bound to a ghost to be rebound to anything else, and attempting to delete a ghost has no effect.

Stubs support more specialized features of Vesta: name reservation (Section 4.2) and partial replication (Section 4.3). A stub is a placeholder for a file or directory that may be supplied in the future. In some situations, a stub replaces an existing file or directory. If this happens, the stub can itself be replaced only by the original file or directory, or by a ghost.

Obviously, ghosts and stubs are unconventional file system notions. They appear distinctively in the file system name space created by the Vesta repository as zero-length files that cannot be read or written.

The entities that can appear in source directories — files, directories, ghosts, and stubs — are collectively called *objects*.

### 4.1.2 Versioning

Software systems that are under active development constantly grow and change through modification of the files they contain. How can an append-only name space of immutable files and directories support software development? The answer, of course, is to adopt a naming convention in which each pathname includes a version number. Instead of modifying a file or directory in place, one creates a new version.

Most file systems and software development tools that support versioning place the version number at the end of a pathname, associating it with the individual file. By contrast, the repository server imposes no requirement regarding the location of the version number within a pathname, and the repository tools implement versioning at the level of directory trees, not individual files. Since this placement is unusual, it merits closer examination.

Most programs consist of several files that make up a logical unit, which Vesta calls a *package*. A package always includes one file of building instructions (a system model) and typically consists of several closely related files of code, interfaces, and documentation, perhaps organized in a tree of subdirectories. Large programs are generally decomposed into several packages, each relatively independent of the others. It is natural to store each package as a separate directory or directory tree.

When a package is modified, often several files in it must change together for consistency. In most version control systems (of which CVS, discussed in Section 10.1.2, is representative), every file is versioned separately, and hence a separate data structure and tools are required to keep track of which versions of the files in a package go together to make a coherent version of the whole package. In Vesta, each coherent package version simply corresponds to one immutable directory with one hierarchical file name, with the version number as a component of the name. For example, the directories `thread/5` and `thread/10` would be versions 5 and 10 of the thread package, and the files `thread/5/foo.c` and `thread/5/foo.h` would be corresponding versions of its components `foo.c` and `foo.h`. If `foo.c` is unchanged between two versions of a package, the repository transparently links the same immutable file into both version directories; only one copy exists on disk.[2]

The repository makes all package versions directly available for browsing and building at all times. A user can easily see what is in a particular version simply by looking in its directory, and can easily compare two versions with standard tools like Unix's **diff**. This is in contrast to version control systems like CVS that implement file versioning without integrating it into the general file naming hierarchy, thus making versioned files invisible unless a user views them through a special tool or performs a special operation in order to copy the file into the regular file name space.

A secondary reason for versioning at the level of directories is that standard Unix and Windows tools do not understand version numbers appended to file names. Vesta effectively "hides" the numbers from the tools by placing them earlier than the last component in the pathname. For example, a Unix C compiler more naturally deals with file names of the form `2/foo.c` than `foo.c/2` or `foo.c;2`. The repository server can support all three of these versioning schemes, since it allows immutable files to be placed directly in appendable directories, but the standard repository tools supplied with Vesta support only the first form of versioning, as a design choice.

While package-level versioning naturally groups related file versions, it does not help in the assembly of a large software system from multiple packages. Some mechanism is still required to identify which versions of the packages go together to make a coherent system. Vesta provides that mechanism in the system description language, not the repository. One might argue that if a mechanism for naming package versions is included in the description language, then one might just as well use that mechanism to name individual file versions and dispense with package-level versioning in the repository. Although this approach is technically feasible, it would be far less convenient for users than Vesta's chosen one, for models would then be cluttered with large numbers of versioned file names instead of containing only a few versioned package names.[3] In addition, a package version represents a development "step" taken by an individual developer, while the combination of multiple packages typically involves multiple developers. (More on this later in this chapter.) The dynamics of these activities are different and are best addressed with different mechanisms.

### 4.1.3 Naming Files and Packages

A hierarchical name space gives great freedom in assigning names to files. To avoid chaos, one needs to organize the name space, that is, one must establish conventions on how files are named so that people can find them. Vesta's repository server does not enforce any particular naming convention, but the repository tools do. Figure 4.1 shows part of a typical repository directory structure.

[2] This link is analogous to a Unix hard link; see Section 2.1.3.

[3] Indeed, an early precursor of Vesta adopted this file versioning approach, with the result that its system models were nearly unreadable.

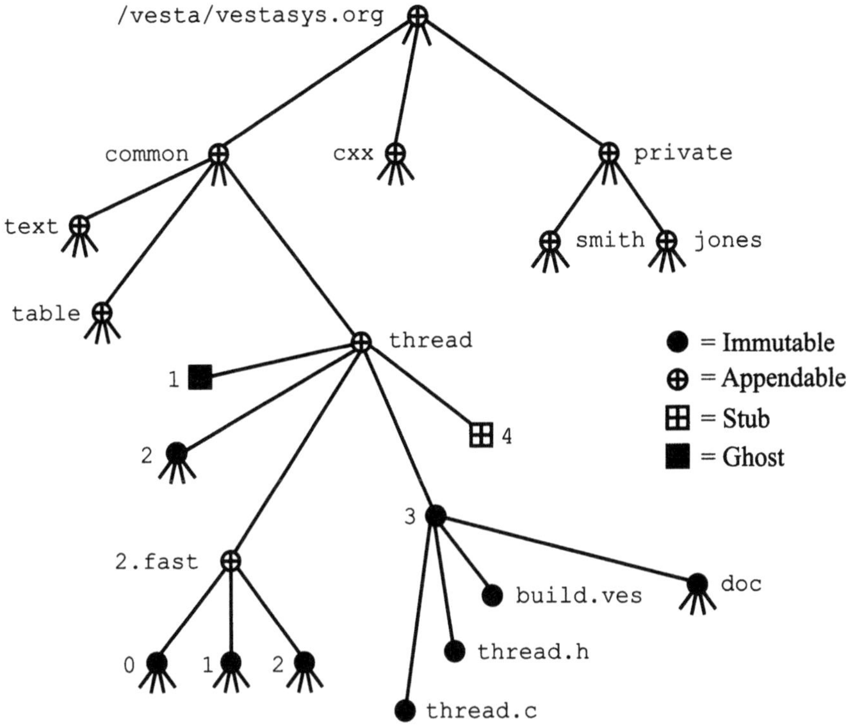


**Fig. 4.1.** Naming convention example.

The root of the subtree in the figure is `/vesta/vestasys.org`. This name is chosen to be unique across all Vesta sites, for reasons discussed in Section 4.3.

Below the root is a tree of appendable directories used for categorizing packages. In this example, packages that are generally useful are placed in the `common` directory, packages that are part of the C++ compilation system are in `cxx`, and private packages owned by users Smith and Jones are in `private/smith` and `private/jones`. This portion of the directory tree is purely conventional and arbitrary, and the repository tools place no restrictions on it.

At the next level down in the tree are individual packages such as `text`, `table`, and `thread`. The thread package is shown in detail in the figure. The immutable subdirectories `thread/2` and `thread/3` are versions of the package. `thread/3` is shown containing three immutable files and an immutable subdirectory. Version `thread/1` has been deleted, leaving a ghost in its place to keep the name from being reused. The name `thread/4` is bound to a stub, reserving it for a new version that a user is working on and has not yet checked in.

The appendable directory `thread/2.fast` is a *branch* of the thread package. While versions 1, 2, 3, ... represent the main line of development, the versions under `2.fast` are another line of development branching off from version 2. Essentially, `thread/2.fast` is a new package, whose version 0 is identical to version 2 of the thread package. Branches can give rise to further branches; for example, a branch from `thread/2.fast/1` might be named `thread/2.fast/1.bugfix`.

## 4.2 The Development Cycle

The sequence of steps that users typically go through when evolving software is the *development cycle*. The outline below shows the cycle and identifies the Vesta command used in each step. The command **vesta** is the Vesta evaluator, and the other commands shown are repository tools.

1. Check out a package: **vcheckout**
2. Modify the package
   a) Edit: any text editor
   b) Advance: **vadvance**
   c) Build: **vesta**
   d) Test
   e) Go back to step 2a until done.
3. Check in the results: **vcheckin**.
4. Optionally go back to step 1.

### 4.2.1 The Outer Loop

In the outer loop of the development cycle, a user checks out a package (step 1), modifies it (step 2), and checks in the result as the next version (step 3). One trip around this cycle constitutes a *session*. The check-out step creates a mutable working copy of the package. Modification of this working copy occurs during the inner loop of development, discussed below. After modifications are completed, the check-in step writes an immutable snapshot of the working copy into the repository.[4]

The repository tools implement a simple concurrency control scheme as part of check-out. Checking out a package reserves a name (which of course includes a version number) for the version that is to be checked in later. No other user can reserve the same name, and normally only the user who reserved a name is given permission to check the package back in under that name. By default, **vcheckout** tries to reserve a version number that is one greater than the highest checked-in version. Thus, if two users use **vcheckout** in the default way on the same package name, one will get an error.

For example, in Figure 4.1, a user (say, Jones) has checked out the thread package with the command **vcheckout common/thread**, thereby reserving the name `/vesta/vestasys.org/common/thread/4` for the next version. The reservation appears in the repository name space as a stub, owned and writable only by Jones. If user Smith asks to check out the thread package too, he will be told that

[4] Both check-out and check-in use copy-on-write to improve time and space efficiency, as described in Section 7.2.4.

version 4 is already reserved by Jones. Thus alerted, Smith can speak to Jones and make sure their intended changes will not be redundant or conflicting. He can also plan for the eventual merging of source code that is likely to be necessary.

If Smith wants to proceed in parallel with Jones, he can ask **vcheckout** to reserve a different version number, in one of several ways. If Smith is making a single variant version, he can choose a name outside the main sequence of versions, say `thread/3-smith`. If Smith is starting a new line of development that may proceed for several versions before merging back into the main line, or may never merge back in, he can create a branch using the **vbranch** tool. In our example, Smith could type **vbranch common/thread/3.smith**, which would create a new branch with the specified name. Version `common/thread/3.smith/0` would be identical to `common/thread/3`. Smith could then check out the branch and work on it as in a normal package. Finally, in the unusual case in which Smith's changes are meant to subsume Jones's completely, Smith can leapfrog Jones by explicitly asking **vcheckout** to reserve version `thread/5`.[5]

In none of these cases does Smith need to "break a lock," as would be necessary in the concurrency control schemes implemented by some other version management systems (see RCS [60], for example, discussed in Section 10.1.1). Vesta does not lock the old version from which Jones started; instead, Vesta reserves the new version name by creating a stub for it. There is nothing to interfere with Smith starting a different line of development that branches off from a common old version.

Once Jones has successfully checked out the package, she goes through the inner loop of the development cycle (discussed next). When Jones has finished modifying the package, she invokes the **vcheckin** tool, which replaces the reservation stub that was created by **vcheckout** with an immutable snapshot of Jones's mutable working copy. It also deletes that working copy, so that Jones cannot inadvertently continue to edit it after her session has ended.

### 4.2.2 The Inner Loop

The inner loop of the development cycle is the familiar edit-build-test sequence, with the addition of one step that is unique to Vesta: the *advance* operation. Editing occurs in the mutable working directory created by **vcheckout**. However, the Vesta evaluator will not read files in this directory because it guarantees build repeatability by building only from immutable sources. So, after editing and before building, a Vesta developer invokes the **vadvance** command, which makes an immutable snapshot (copy) of the developer's mutable working directory and writes it into the repository name space under a new version number within the session. It is this set of files that the **vesta** command supplies to the evaluator for building.[6]

[5] It's worth emphasizing that these uses of the name space are conventions implemented entirely by the repository tools. Their semantics are not understood by the repository server.

[6] The reader may find it surprising that **vadvance** is used on every iteration of the inner loop of the development cycle. To be sure, this simplifies the evaluator implementation, but these intermediate snapshots have value in their own right. Recall scenario 7 in Section 1.1.

To keep the many snapshots created during a session from cluttering the shared name space, the repository tools put them in a directory that is separate from the main-line versions of the package, called the *session directory*. A session directory is essentially a branch with a special name, created by **vcheckout**. The versions created in a session directory are generally of interest only until the package is checked in.

### 4.2.3 Detailed Operation of the Repository Tools

The preceding overview of the outer and inner loops of the development cycle provides the background for a detailed look at the way the Vesta repository tools manage the name space at specific points in the cycle. Figure 4.2 illustrates the complete operation of **vcheckout**. Initially, `thread/3` is the latest version of the thread package. When user Jones types **vcheckout common/thread**, the system creates the reservation stub `thread/4` and the session directory `thread/checkout/4` in the repository's appendable source tree `/vesta`. It creates the mutable working copy `jones/thread` in a separate mutable directory tree named `/vesta-work`. The session is given an initial version `thread/checkout/4/0` whose contents are immutable and identical to the last checked-in version in the main line of development, `thread/checkout/3`. The working copy initially has the same contents as well, but it is fully mutable.

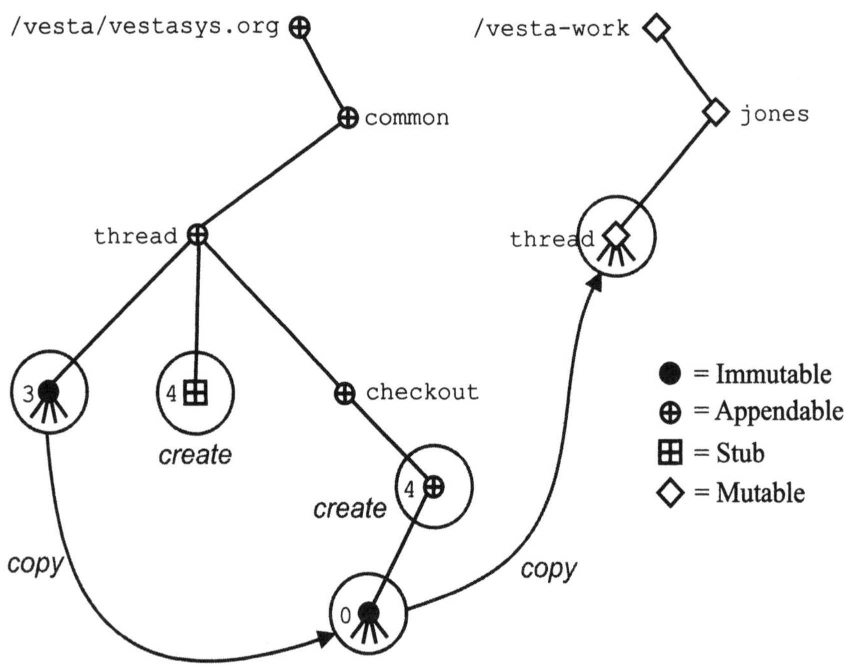


**Fig. 4.2.** Action of the command **vcheckout common/thread**.

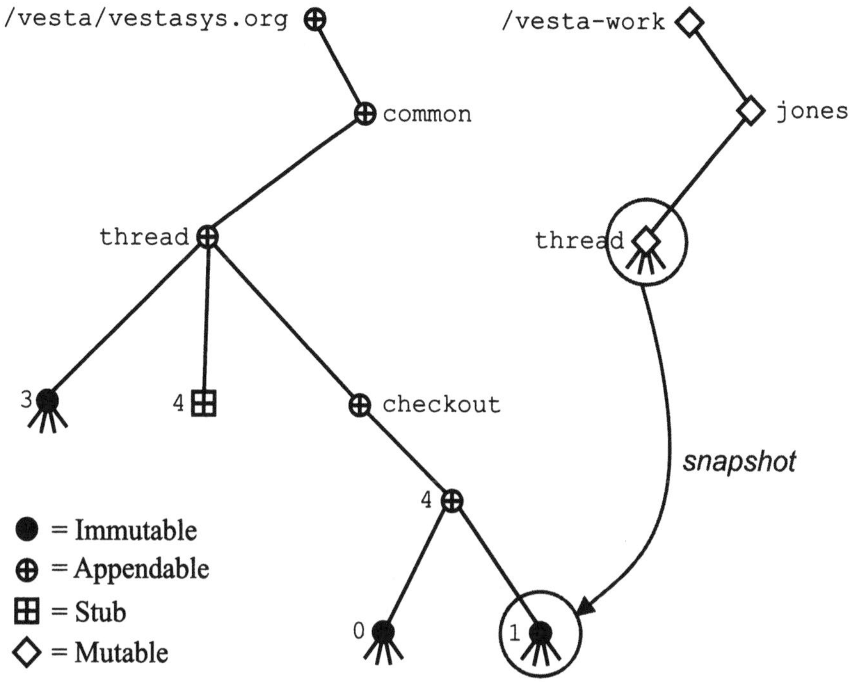


**Fig. 4.3.** Action of **vadvance** in the directory `/vesta-work/jones/thread`.

Jones can now edit the files in her working copy with any text editor or other file manipulation tool. She can freely create new files or subdirectories and delete or rename existing ones, using ordinary commands and tools.[7]

Whenever Jones wants to try compiling her modified files, she types **vadvance** to save an immutable snapshot as the next higher version in the current session directory. Figure 4.3 illustrates the operation of **vadvance**. The tool simply makes an immutable copy of the working directory in the package's session directory. The name of this copy is the next available version number in the session. Jones can of course use **vadvance** even when she is not about to do a build. For example, she could use it to checkpoint her current work in preparation for making experimental changes.

Jones uses the **vesta** command to invoke the Vesta evaluator to build the latest version in the session. (For convenience, Vesta provides a simple shell script that combines **vadvance** and **vesta** in a single command.)

Next, if her program has built without errors, Jones tests it. If changes are needed, she returns to the editing step and goes around the inner loop again. Any time Jones needs to reexamine an old version or undo a change, she can simply look back at the old snapshot — whether it is in the current session, an old session, the main line of

---

[7] For example, the Unix commands **cp**, **mv**, **rm**, **mkdir**, and **rmdir** work without modification on files and directories in Vesta working directories.

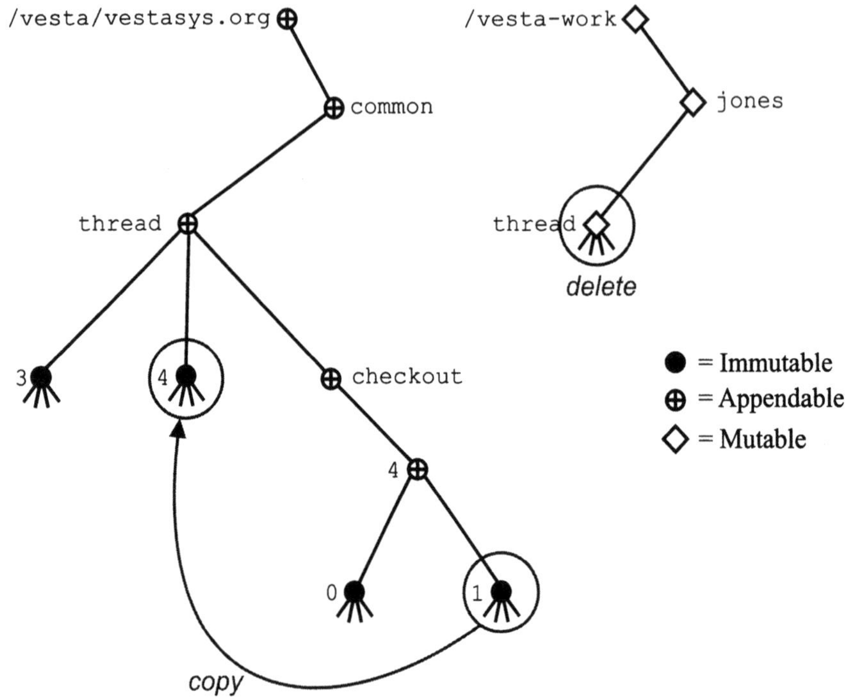


**Fig. 4.4.** Action of **vcheckin** in the directory `/vesta-work/jones/thread`.

checked-in versions, or elsewhere — and compare or copy the files to her working directory.

Finally, when Jones is satisfied, she ends the outer loop of the development cycle by running **vcheckin**, as mentioned earlier. Figure 4.4 illustrates this operation. Note that check-in does not itself snapshot Jones's working copy of the package; instead it uses the snapshot made by the most recent advance after verifying that the working copy has not been modified since then.

### 4.2.4 Version Control Alternatives

The preceding sections emphasized that the specifics of version management and concurrency control are implemented by the repository tools, not by the repository server. Other version control styles can be readily implemented in the repository tools without changing the server. For example, only small changes to the repository tools would be required to support concurrent versioning in the style of CVS [23]. In concurrent versioning, there is no locking or reservation of version numbers at all. New version numbers are chosen at check-in time rather than check-out time. To support this, **vcheckout** would be changed to omit stub creation. **vcheckin** would be altered to use the version number recorded by **vcheckout** to test whether any newer version has been checked in since the one the session started from. If so, **vcheckin** would prompt the user to merge changes. With this version control regime, it would also be appropriate to alter the naming convention for session directories slightly, because the present convention makes the session name a function of the reserved new version name.

Vesta does not provide any special tools for merging changes made along different branches, largely because the repository semantics make it easy to merge branches using commonly available tools. Vesta keeps track of the versions created along all the branches, all the way back to the common base versions from which they diverged, and manifests each one as an ordinary file system directory. Thus, a developer can easily use standard directory-oriented tools, such as **diff**, **diff3**, and **patch**, perhaps augmented with some simple shell scripts for convenience. In contrast, RCS and CVS require special variants of these tools that are integrated with their versioning systems. Of course, a development organization may choose a particular set of conventions for naming versions in the Vesta repository and might find it useful to build a version comparison/merging tool that understands those conventions. Because the repository makes the version structure manifest within the ordinary file system name space, such a tool is easy to write and requires no knowledge of or access to Vesta repository internals.

### 4.2.5 Additional Repository Tools

A few other repository tools round out the development cycle suite.

The **vcreate** tool creates a new package containing no versions. A user can then check out the new package and add files to it. When a package has no versions, applying **vcheckout** to it creates an empty directory as the working copy.

The **vsessions** tool provides a simple graphical interface for managing checked-out packages. The tool displays the latest version number in each session belonging to its user. It provides an Advance button for each session, which simply invokes **vadvance** on it.

The **vlatest** tool displays the latest checked-in version number of a given package or of all the packages and branches in a given directory tree.

The **vwhohas** tool lists the user (if any) who has checked out either a given package or all the packages and branches in a given directory tree.

The **vhistory** tool shows a change log for a package, listing all past versions and the comments supplied by users at check-in time.

The **vupdate** tool creates a new version of a system model in which the version numbers of imported models have been revised according to the state of their packages in the repository and instructions from the user who invokes the tool. For example, a user can specify to **vupdate** that the new model should reference the latest checked-in version of all imported models, a fairly common operation.

The **vimports** tool lists the transitive closure of a model's imports.

### 4.2.6 Mutable Files and Directories

Section 4.2.2 showed how mutable files and directories are used in the inner loop of the development cycle. In principle, these could be ordinary files and directories provided by the host file system, but Vesta realizes significant performance advantages by implementing them in the repository server. The semantics of the repository's mutable files and directories closely resemble those of the host file system. That is, objects in a mutable directory can be created, deleted (without leaving ghosts), or renamed as desired, and mutable files can be modified freely. As seen by the user, the repository's mutable directories are essentially identical to ordinary file system directories,[8] but the repository implements special additional operations for use by the repository tools to optimize the development cycle. These operations efficiently copy data between mutable and immutable directories, making **vcheckout**, **vadvance**, and **vcheckin** nearly instantaneous regardless of the number of files in the package. These special operations are accessed through a repository server RPC interface, since they do not fit within the NFS protocol used for standard file system manipulation.

## 4.3 Replication

The preceding section described the development cycle, focusing on a user's manipulation of files in a repository. Increasingly, large software systems are developed in parallel at geographically distributed sites. The Vesta repository was therefore designed to make it easy to replicate sources at many sites. To enable developers to work independently, the replication design allows each repository to operate mostly autonomously. Only a few operations depend on the ability to access more than one repository at the same time.

### 4.3.1 Global Name Space

Conceptually, Vesta sources are named in a single name space that is global across all Vesta repositories. The name space is organized as a tree, illustrated in Figure 4.1. Its root is `/vesta`. Each repository stores a subtree of the global name space, typically making it available as `/vesta` in a standard Unix file name space via a mount point (see Section 2.1.2).

Replication exists when two or more repositories store subtrees that overlap, meaning that the same path from the root exists in more than one repository. Two repositories that hold the same subtree are said to be *replicas* for it. When this occurs, Vesta ensures that the replicas *agree*, that is, the repository's replication machinery maintains an *agreement invariant* on the portions of the global name space replicated at the various repositories. This invariant is discussed in detail in Section 7.3.2, but intuitively it means that no name is bound to different values in different repositories.

[8] An esoteric note for Unix experts. Vesta does not implement symbolic links in mutable directories, and does not allow multiple hard links to a mutable file. Symbolic links are forbidden because it would not be meaningful to copy a symbolic link into the immutable part of the repository; it is unclear what a symbolic link there should mean if the Vesta evaluator were to encounter one. Multiple hard links are forbidden to simplify the bookkeeping and to guarantee that a mutable file never has to be copied when making an immutable snapshot. In practice, these limitations are inconsequential.

Vesta uses *partial replication*; that is, each repository can replicate all, part, or none of the data stored in any other repository. Partial replication extends the fundamental Vesta property of build repeatability to hold not just within a single repository, but globally across all Vesta repositories that agree. The agreement invariant does not ensure that a particular build can be carried out at any repository. Since replication is partial, a build that succeeds at one repository may fail at another because some of the necessary sources are missing. However, the agreement invariant does ensure that if all sources required for a build are present at two repositories, then the build will produce identical results at both.

Vesta uses a global naming convention to make it easy for new sites to adopt Vesta without inadvertently creating source names that clash with those at other sites. As a result, two sites that initially know nothing of each other and share no sources can later decide to cooperate and take replicas of each other's files. Under this naming convention, when a new Vesta site wants to create sources that are initially not shared with any other site, the site administrator puts them under a new directory immediately below `/vesta`, named with an Internet domain name that the site owns. Because domain names are unique, the new sources acquire globally unique names without the need for any special coordination across repositories.[9]

Sources that are to be distributed widely should be named carefully, so that the names make sense to the people who will be using them. For example, the Vesta system's own sources are publicly available under a directory named `/vesta/vestasys.org`, an intuitive name not associated with a particular machine. The use of domain names in the global name space supports unique name creation without cross-repository coordination, but those names imply nothing about the locations at which files are stored. There is no guarantee that files with a particular domain in their pathname reside on a machine in that domain, or even that any such machine exists. Naming and file location are separate notions.

Domain names provide a simple way to add names to the root directory `/vesta` without conflicts, but sites also need a way to add names to directories deeper in the tree without causing disagreements between replicas. Vesta uses a simple concept of *mastership* to achieve this. For each appendable directory, other than `/vesta` itself, one repository's replica is designated the *master*. The master is the only replica that is required to hold a complete set of the names in the directory, so new names can be added to the master freely with no need for communication with other repositories. In contrast, a non-master appendable directory can add names only by copying them from another replica.

Mastership also applies to stubs. The stubs described in Section 4.1.1, which serve as a placeholders for data that has yet to be created, are actually master stubs. A non-master stub, on the other hand, is a placeholder for data that may already exist in another repository. Non-master stubs are used chiefly in master appendable directories, where they allow the directory to hold a complete set of names without requiring all the named objects to be present in the same repository. Mastership

[9] This mechanism is not perfect, because Internet domain names can be deregistered and later reregistered to some other owner, but has been adequate for practical use.

has some additional significant properties and subtleties — in particular, it can be transferred from one replica to another — which are discussed in Section 7.3.

### 4.3.2 A Replication Example

Figure 4.5 shows an example of two repositories that partially replicate each other and are in agreement. They are the Eastern and Western repository of the imaginary Vesta Systems Organization. The figure illustrates several common patterns that occur in real Vesta usage.

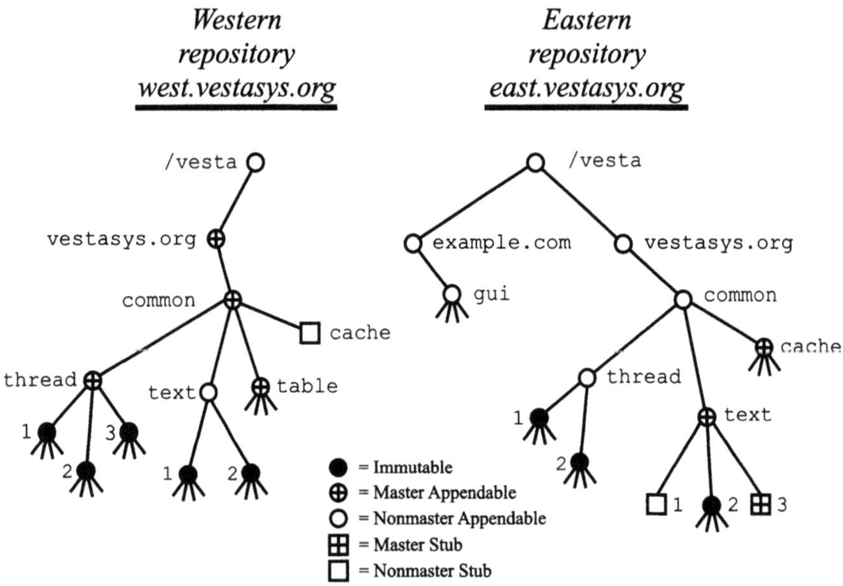


**Fig. 4.5.** Two repositories that agree.

As noted above, the root directory `/vesta` is not mastered at either repository, and the names directly under it look like Internet domain names. In the western repository, `/vesta` contains a subdirectory named `vestasys.org`, which holds the master copy of the organization's files. The eastern repository has a similar but non-master `vestasys.org` subdirectory, as well as one named `example.com`.

Partial replication occurs at several levels of the tree. At the top level, part of `vestasys.org/common` is replicated in the eastern repository. The western copy has a complete list of names — `thread`, `text`, `table`, and `cache` — while the eastern copy is lacking `table`. The western copy does not have the contents of the `cache` directory, but does have a stub with that name as a placeholder. This ensures that no other repository will create a different `cache` directory that would clash with the copy in the eastern repository and violate the agreement invariant. The eastern repository also contains a partial replica of `/vesta/example.com`, a subdirectory that does not appear in the western repository at all.

One level down, in the `thread` package, the western copy is master and has all three versions that currently exist, while the eastern copy currently lacks version 3. The `text` package demonstrates that a directory need not have the same master as its parent; it is mastered at the eastern repository and its parent is not. Perhaps when first created it was mastered at the western repository and later moved to the eastern repository, since version 1 is present in the west but not in the east. Since the eastern copy is master, it must have a complete list of names, so it has a stub for version 1, perhaps inserted at the time it received mastership. In addition, the eastern copy has a master stub for version 3. This master stub is a placeholder for an object whose content has not yet been supplied (typically a reservation created by **vcheckout** as described in Section 4.2). The master repository is free to replace it later with a different type of object, but thereafter it cannot be changed back to a master stub.

### 4.3.3 The Replicator

Vesta provides a replication facility, the *replicator*, that copies data between repositories while preserving the agreement invariant. The facility is available both as a standalone tool **vrepl** and as a library that can be called by other tools.

The replicator can "push" sources from the local repository to a remote one, "pull" sources from a remote repository to the local one, or copy sources between two different remote repositories. It takes as input the network addresses of two repositories — a source and a destination — and a set of pathname patterns specifying the data to be replicated. The replicator walks the directory tree of the source repository to find all paths that match the patterns and copies to the destination repository those that are not already present there. Continuing the example in Figure 4.5, assume that a developer using the western repository issues the command

```
vrepl -d east.vestasys.org
      -e+ /vesta/vestasys.org/common/table/LAST
```

The command replicates (pushes) the highest-numbered version of the `table` package from the western to the eastern repository. (The `-d` indicates the destination of the transfer. The source is omitted and defaults to the local repository.) More complicated patterns are possible and common. The full pattern language extends the one provided by the Unix shell. For example, it adds the pattern `LAST`, which matches the highest version number that is not a stub. Prefixing a pattern with + adds the objects that match it to the set to be copied; prefixing it with - removes them.

The replicator also has a feature that replicates all the files needed to do a particular Vesta build. Chapter 6 explains the organization of system models in detail, but for the moment it is sufficient to know that every package contains a system model that specifies how the package is to be built and that system models import other system models to create a complete description of the components needed for a particular build. By convention, the root model for the build of a package is named `.main.ves`. Referring again to Figure 4.5, assume that a developer using the western repository issues the command

```
vrepl -s east.vestasys.org
      -e@ /vesta/example.com/gui/4/.main.ves
```

The command replicates (pulls) into the western repository from the eastern repository all the source code needed to build version 4 of the `gui` package, including the entire programming environment (libraries, compilers, etc.) required by the build. Note the pattern specifying the `gui` package is prefixed by the `@` character. This directs the replicator to start from the specified system model, to form the transitive closure of the imported models (using the same algorithm as the **vimports** tool mentioned in Section 4.2.5), and for each model, to emit a + pattern. The resulting set of patterns is then passed to the basic replication algorithm. Because this feature conveniently replicates everything needed to build a particular package version, it is used far more often than individual + and - patterns are.

For some organizations with multiple repositories, a natural time to invoke the replicator occurs when new package versions are checked in. Rather than build this into the repository server, Vesta provides for optional replication in the **vcheckin** tool, as described in the next section. Organizations will likely want to replicate packages at other times as well, and it is a simple matter to set up scheduled executions of **vrepl** for this purpose. Of course, the replicator may also be run manually as needed.

### 4.3.4 Cross-Repository Check-out

When two sites running separate repositories are closely cooperating, users at one site may want to check out packages whose master copies are in the other site's repository. This section outlines how the development cycle tools described in Section 4.2 support development across sites.

Nearly all the work required to support cross-repository operation occurs in **vcheckout**, as shown in Figure 4.6. The source repository, where the package being checked out is mastered, is shown at the top; the destination repository, in which the user doing the check-out wants to work, is shown at the bottom. Notice that the actions in the destination repository are similar to the single-repository case in Figure 4.2. The steps in cross-repository check-out, whose numbers are circled in the figure, are:

1. Examine the master replica in the source repository to find the highest version number. In Figure 4.6, this is version 3 of the `thread` package.
2. If this version does not exist in the destination, call the replicator to copy it in.
3. Create the reservation stub (for version 4) and the empty session directory in the source repository, just as in the single repository case.
4. Call the replicator to copy them to the destination repository.
5. Transfer mastership on them from the source to the destination.
6. Insert version 0 in the session directory and create the working directory at the destination.

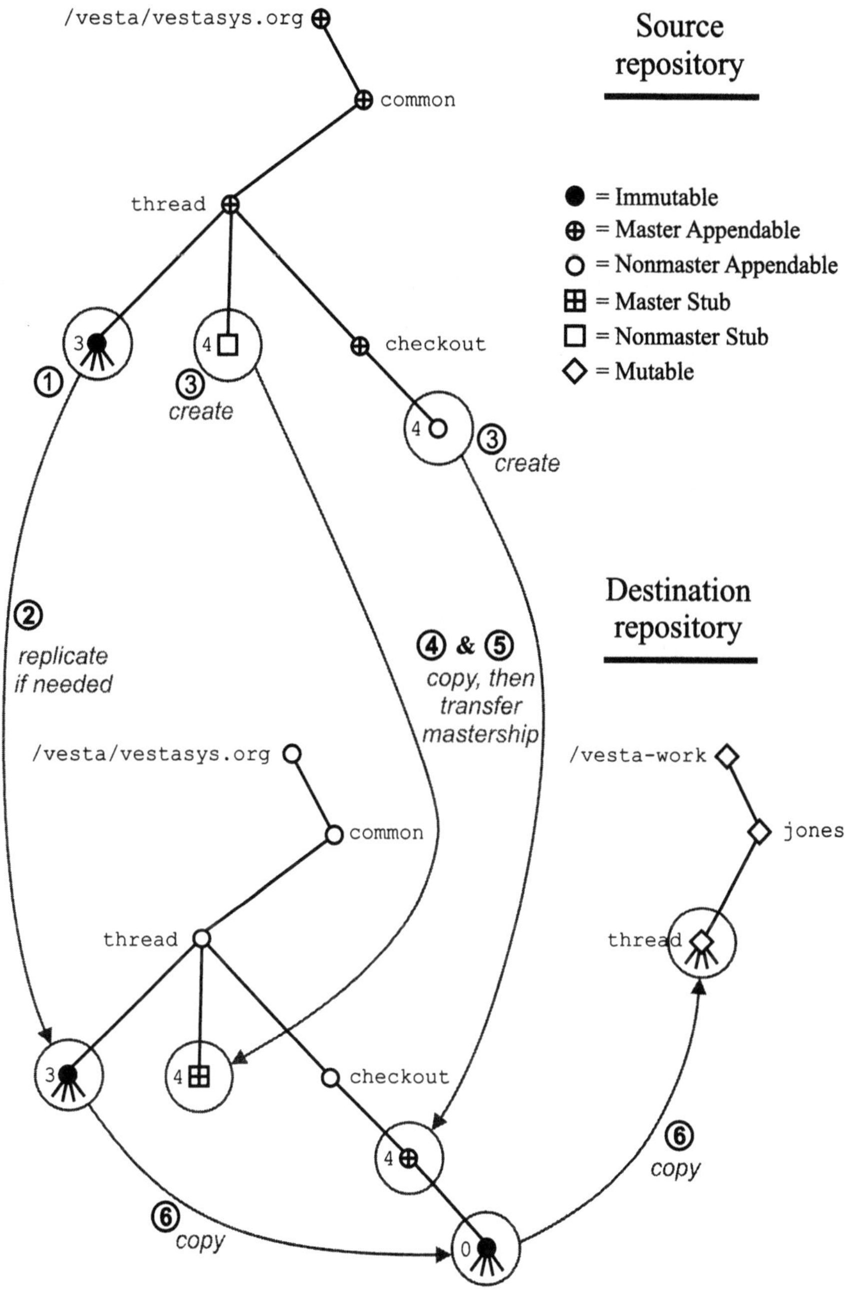


**Fig. 4.6.** Cross-repository check-out.

Once the package is checked out, **vadvance** operates in exactly the same way as it would after a local check-out, since it needs to access only the working and session directories, both of which are in the destination repository.

Similarly, **vcheckin** can do its job strictly within the destination repository, since **vcheckout** moved mastership of the reservation stub there. However, it is likely that the source repository will need to have a copy of the new version soon, so for convenience **vcheckin** completes the check-in locally, then calls the replicator to copy the package back to the source repository. Mastership does not change.

The Vesta tools for creating new packages (**vcreate**), branching the version sequence (**vbranch**), finding the latest version (**vlatest**), and finding who has packages checked out (**vwhohas**) also require minor modifications in order to work properly across repositories. The changes required are similar to those applied to **vcheckout** but considerably simpler.[10]

## 4.4 Repository Metadata

Like most file systems, the Vesta repository stores more than just files and directories. A certain amount of information about the files and directories, or *metadata*, proves useful for a number of purposes. This section describes the repository's general mechanism for managing metadata as well as some specific applications of that mechanism, notably for access control.

### 4.4.1 Mutable Attributes

A source control system typically needs to store auxiliary information about sources beyond just their names and contents. For example, the Vesta repository tools need to know whether each appendable directory is a check-out session, a package, or something else, and they need to know the connections between stubs, sessions, and working directories. Users often want to know when and by whom a package was created, checked out, or checked in, and on what previous versions a new version was based.

The Vesta repository provides *mutable attributes* to serve these purposes and others. Conceptually, a source object's attributes are a total function $F$ from string names to sets of string values. If a name $n$ has never been bound to any value, $F(n)$ is the empty set. There are operations to set the value of $F(n)$ to a singleton set or to clear it to the empty set, and operations to add or remove an element from $F(n)$. Setting $F(n)$ to a singleton is equivalent to clearing it and then adding the value,

[10] One problem remains with the cross-repository tools. In the single-repository case, each tool uses a simple transaction mechanism provided by the repository server to make its complete action atomic. However, since this mechanism is local to a repository, it does not achieve atomicity across multiple repositories, so the tools become non-atomic in this case. With **vcheckout**, steps 3 and 6 (on page 50) are individually atomic, but if there is a failure between them, the check-out is left in an incomplete state. The recovery from this state is not presently automated, but it is a straightforward manual action.

atomically. There are also several operations to query values of $F$. This functionality is available through an RPC interface, and the repository tool **vattrib** provides a general purpose command-line interface to it.

By design, attributes are not visible to the Vesta evaluator or the tools it invokes. Repeatable builds require that the inputs to an evaluation be immutable; hence, attributes, which are mutable, are never queried by the evaluator. Equivalently, changing an attribute cannot change the result of an evaluation.

Each source object has attributes unless its parent directory is immutable. Thus in Figure 4.1, the immutable version `common/thread/3` has attributes, but its files and subdirectories `thread.c`, ..., `doc` do not. While this limitation is imposed to simplify the implementation, it does not pose a problem in practice, because each package version (that is, each versioned directory) is a conceptual unit of development rather than a collection of files with individual properties.

The repository development cycle tools make extensive use of mutable attributes. For example, the **vcheckout** tool adds attributes on the stub, the session, and the working directory it creates so that any one can locate the other two. The **vadvance** and **vcheckin** tools use these attributes and record some of their own. In addition, **vcheckout** and **vcheckin** record the previous version, the user requesting the operation, the time, and other information. Figure 4.7 shows some sample attributes applied by the tools, most of which are self-explanatory. Note the `message` attribute on `vesta/repos/30`; it is a change log entry solicited from the user by **vcheckin**.

A few attributes have meanings interpreted by the repository itself. For example, if a stub is created with an attribute named `symlink-to`, the repository manifests it through the NFS interface as a symbolic link (see Section 2.1.3) whose value is the value of the attribute.[11] The development cycle tools (**vadvance** and **vcheckin**) use this feature to maintain, within each appendable directory that contains versions, a symbolic link named `latest` referencing the newest version. The example directory tree in Figure 4.1 (page 39) would include several such links (not shown in the figure). Specifically, there would be a link named `/vesta/vestasys.org/common/thread/latest` that refers to its sibling named `3`, and one named `/vesta/vestasys.org/common/thread/2.fast/latest` that refers to its sibling named `2`.

One can imagine extensions of the repository tool set that would use mutable attributes in other ways. For example, a `release-status` attribute might be used to mark a particular version as internally released, externally released, or withdrawn from release due to bugs. It would then be natural to extend the **vupdate** tool, which mechanically updates the `import` clauses in a Vesta system model to newer versions, to alter its behavior based on the setting of the `release-status` attribute.

Attributes are also used to store access control information for files and directories in the Vesta repository, which is the subject of the next section.

[11] The `symlink-to` feature cannot compromise the repeatability of builds. The evaluator always sees stubs only as stubs, and as noted earlier, any build that encounters a stub simply fails without producing a result. The build tools invoked by the evaluator do not see stubs at all.

```
% vattrib /vesta/vestasys.org/vesta/repos
#owner
        mann@west.vestasys.org
type
        package
creation-time
        Thu Aug 22 17:41:35 PDT 1996
created-by
        heydon@west.vestasys.org

% vattrib /vesta/vestasys.org/vesta/repos/30
session-dir
        /vesta/vestasys.org/vesta/repos/checkout/30
old-version
        /vesta/vestasys.org/vesta/repos/29
message
        Added code to gather usage statistics.
content
        /vesta/vestasys.org/vesta/repos/checkout/30/12
checkin-time
        Tue Nov  4 14:10:22 PST 1997
checkin-by
        mann@west.vestasys.org
#owner
        mann@west.vestasys.org

% vattrib /vesta-work/mann/repos
session-ver-arc
        0
session-dir
        /vesta/vestasys.org/vesta/repos/checkout/31
old-version
        /vesta/vestasys.org/vesta/repos/30
new-version
        /vesta/vestasys.org/vesta/repos/31
checkout-time
        Wed Dec  3 09:55:12 PST 1997
checkout-by
        mann@west.vestasys.org
```

**Fig. 4.7.** Sample attributes on some directories.

### 4.4.2 Access Control

The Vesta repository's access control model is based on that of Unix (see Section 2.1.4), but the Unix access control model does not work across multiple administrative domains, because the naming of principals (that is, users and groups) is strictly local. Since Vesta supports replication and other forms of remote access between repositories that are under separate administration, some extensions to the basic Unix access control scheme are necessary. These extensions make it possible for repositories that are cooperating closely to replicate all their access control information, while still allowing those with less mutual trust to interoperate sensibly.

The Vesta repository uses text strings to name principals and access control lists (ACLs) to grant permission. Principal names are global, of the form `user@realm` or `^group@realm`. The *realm* is a name for an administrative domain chosen by its administrator, while the user and group names are the local names for users and groups within the realm. By convention, a realm is an Internet domain name; thus a user's principal name may be the same as his email address, although Vesta does not rely on this property.

Each repository object has an owner ACL listing one or more user principals, a group ACL listing one or more group principals, and a set of nine mode flags that indicate whether the owners, groups, and others are granted read, write, and/or directory search access.[12] Unlike the Unix model, the owner and group are sets of global names rather than single local names, chiefly so that an object can be given different owners in different realms if desired. This generality cannot be represented through the NFS interface, so when asked through this path for a file's owner or group, the repository provides one from the local realm, if possible. The repository also maps between global principal names and the numeric user/group ids in which NFS and Unix traffic by examining the local user and group registries and building up a translation table.

Access control lists and mode flags are stored in mutable attributes named `#owner`, `#group`, and `#mode`.[13] Because not all repository objects have attributes, and to save space, the repository uses a form of inheritance: if an object does not have a particular access control attribute, it implicitly inherits the value from its parent directory. Hence, changing the access control on a directory can effectively change the access control on other directories and files below it in the tree, a departure from conventional Unix semantics.

---

[12] As in the basic Unix scheme, user and group names cannot be mixed on the same ACL or anywhere else within the system; thus the leading caret in group names is present only for clarity, not to avoid ambiguity.

[13] The names of all access control attributes begin with an identifying character ("#") to mark them as requiring stronger privileges to change than other attributes. Ordinary attributes of an object can be changed by any user who has write permission on the object, but most access control attributes can be changed only by the object's owner, and some require even stronger privileges. The identifying character also makes it easy to separately control the replication of these attributes across repositories.

In order for the repository server to perform an access control check, the identity of the principal requesting the access must be authenticated. For this purpose the repository implements several authentication methods. A configuration file supplied by the repository's administrator specifies which user names it should accept, from which hosts, using which authentication methods, and whether to grant normal or read-only access. The *trusted unix* authentication method is provided to support local NFS access to the repository. A request submitted using this method includes a numeric Unix user id as a principal identifier. The repository deems such a request authentic if it comes from a trusted host (listed in the table), and translates the numeric id to a user name in the local realm. A request submitted using the *trusted global* authentication method includes a global user name, which the repository deems authentic if it comes from a host that is trusted for the name's realm. These authentication methods clearly offer rather weak security. More secure authentication methods based on Kerberos or other cryptographic protocols have been designed but, at this writing, not yet implemented.

The repository does not treat groups as first-class principals that are individually authenticated; a request coming into the repository does not list or authenticate the group identities that are to be checked against group ACLs. Instead, once the request's user identity has been authenticated, the repository determines for itself the groups to which that user belongs and checks for the presence of those groups on group ACLs. For this purpose, the repository uses a combination of local operating system information and additional data supplied by the repository administrator. For principals whose names are in the local realm, the repository maps user names to their corresponding numeric IDs and checks for local group membership. For principals from other realms, the repository uses data provided by the administrator.[14]

As with any access control system, special privileges must be granted selectively for administrative purposes. The repository recognizes three different administrative principals. The system administrator (Unix user `root`) has blanket permission to perform any operation, except operations that could cause a violation of the replica agreement invariant (Section 7.3.2). There is also a non-root Vesta administrator (typically Unix user `vadmin`) that can perform nearly all the repository operations that `root` can, but is unable to gain privileged access to other system resources or impersonate other users. Finally, there is a special wizard user (typically Unix user `vwizard`) that is permitted to do all repository operations, even those that could potentially violate the agreement invariant. This back door exists primarily for emergency repairs. It is not needed in normal operation except to create names directly under `/vesta`.

[14] The repository doesn't provide any machinery for replicating such data; this would be a useful addition. However, the repository does permit a user or group name to be designated an alias for another, which is useful when the same person has a login in two different realms or when two cooperating realms each have a group that is working on the same project. In such circumstances, replicated data can be accessed by "cross-aliasing" principal names in the two realms, eliminating the need to synchronize access control lists across cooperating realms.

### 4.4.3 Metadata and Replication

The repository's metadata and its replication machinery interact in two ways. First, because of the importance of metadata in the operation of the repository tools, it must be propagated appropriately by the replicator. Second, since the actions of the replicator cross administrative domains, special attention must be given to controlling those actions, which is accomplished with access control lists represented as repository metadata.

The first of these topics, the propagation of mutable attributes, is conceptually straightforward. Section 4.3.3 outlined the replicator's basic algorithm, which examines a specified collection of names in a source repository and copies each one into a destination repository if it isn't already there. In addition, the replicator updates the mutable attributes of every name it considers by merging updates from the source repository into the destination. (See Section 7.3.4 for details of the updating mechanism.) Strictly speaking, this updating is not necessary since mutable attributes play no part in the agreement invariant. Nevertheless, preserving them as part of replication is necessary to enable the cross-repository features of the repository tools, as described in Section 4.3.4.

The other interaction between metadata and replication involves the security of the replication primitives themselves, for which a few special access control lists exist. Why are these lists needed? Suppose repository X attempts to transfer mastership of some directory D to repository Y. However, repository X is misbehaving and does not actually have mastership of D; the true master for D is repository Z. If Y implicitly trusts X, it will accept mastership of D improperly, causing it to come into disagreement with Z. For similar reasons, a transfer of mastership from Y to rogue repository X must be avoided. In general, a repository must not accept data from a rogue repository that might maliciously supply incorrect values.

Conceptually, every object in a repository has ACLs that control replication. As with other ACLs, if an object does not have its own replication access control lists, it inherits them from its parent directory. The `#mastership-to` access control list for an object lists the repositories that mastership on the object can be ceded to, `#mastership-from` lists the repositories that mastership can be accepted from, and `#replicate-from` lists the repositories that replicas can be taken from. In addition, if an object has a `#replicate-from-noac` access control list, it will accept replicas of the object's data from the repositories listed, but it will not accept replicas of their access control attributes (that is, those attributes whose names start with `#`). No special ACL is needed to control giving replicas; read access by the requesting user is sufficient for that. Administrative access is required to change these replication-related ACLs.

Vesta allows any user to replicate data into his local repository as long as: (1) the user has read permission for the data in the remote repository, (2) the user has search permission on the directories involved in the local repository, and (3) the remote repository is on the proper access control list. Because replicating data does not change it, there would be no sense in requiring the user to have write permission in the local repository.

## In Summary

This chapter has covered the major facilities of the repository as they appear to a developer using the Vesta system. These facilities support the development cycle, both for an individual developer (the inner loop) and for the developer's local organization (the outer loop). The repository and repository tools also support an expanded development cycle across geographically separated groups via replication. In the next chapter, the focus shifts from the storage facilities supporting the development cycle to the system description language used to describe how files are put together to form systems, preparatory to an examination of the actual building process in Chapter 6.

# 5

# System Description Language

There are two inputs to the construction of a software system: the *sources* and the *instructions* for producing the system from those sources. For small code bases, simple instructions generally suffice. However, for even moderately large systems, the build instructions become complex and subtle, and the simple, script-like facilities of conventional build "languages" such as Make therefore become inadequate. For this reason, Vesta's *system description language* (SDL) supports complete, hierarchical build instructions, which enable all the details of a build to be specified in a modular form consistent with the overall system structure. Moreover, SDL supports functional abstraction, which makes it possible to encapsulate low-level building. As a result, complex details can be hidden from the view of end users, simplifying the system descriptions they write.

This chapter describes the essential features of the Vesta system description language in preparation for examining in Chapter 6 how those features are used in practice. Appendix A presents the language's complete syntax and semantics.

## 5.1 Motivation

In Vesta, the instructions for building a system are contained in *system models*. System models are programs written in SDL. They describe how to build a software system from sources, that is, from scratch. As the system models are being evaluated, *tools* such as compilers and linkers are invoked to build the program, and their outputs are combined according to the instructions provided by the system models to form the result of the build.

A few essential requirements dictate the structure and functionality of SDL:

- The builder (that is, the SDL evaluator) must be able to construct systems repeatably, incrementally, and consistently.
- The complexity of a software description should, in some sense, be proportional to the conceptual complexity of building the system it describes.
- The language must be practical for developers to use. It must be adaptable to a variety of software development methodologies and organizational processes.

Consideration of these requirements quickly leads to some desirable properties of the description language and building system. They should be designed so that repeatable and consistent builds can't be compromised by errors in system models. Moreover, the language should support incremental building as the norm, so that good performance is the rule, not the exception. Also, the core language facilities should be as basic and "methodology-neutral" as possible, and support for particular styles of system construction or organization should be programmed in the language, not built into the language or the builder.

These requirements and consequent properties establish the major characteristics of the Vesta language and build system:

- Repeatability and consistency give rise to two properties: all information required to build a system from sources is captured in system models and all sources are immutable.
- Incrementality leads to the choice of a functional language, because each function invocation then represents a unit of work that can be conveniently cached.
- Correctness implies that the incremental builder must determine automatically which components of a system need to be rebuilt, not impose on users the responsibility of correctly specifying dependencies.
- "Proportional complexity" is achieved by providing a flexible modular structure in which reusable abstractions can be easily defined.
- Methodological neutrality compels a careful choice of basic data types and primitive operations.

Before examining the specifics of Vesta's SDL, we should pause and consider where these requirements and their consequences are leading us. The properties above are attractive, to be sure, but they must be weighed against the inherent disadvantage of burdening system developers with an additional programming language. The shortcomings of conventional system description languages are familiar to developers, yet many would prefer the devil they know to the devil they don't. The semantics of those languages contribute substantially to their deficiencies. For that reason, Vesta offers a new language, even though that inherently raises a barrier to its adoption. Chapter 12 evaluates the significance of that barrier in the light of experience.

## 5.2 Language Highlights

Unlike many languages used to describe software construction, SDL is a complete (though spartan) programming language with a well-defined syntax and semantics. In a nutshell, it is a scripting language that is functional, modular, lexically scoped, and dynamically typed.[1] Its value space contains booleans, integers, text strings, lists,

[1] All values are typed and operations are type-checked at execution (interpretation) time. Static typing is optional; that is, there are simple provisions in the syntax for annotating the types of variables and function results, but these annotations serve only as comments, and the current Vesta evaluator ignores them.

closures, and bindings. Bindings are ordered lists of name-value pairs, closures are functions with bound values for non-local variables, and the remaining data types are the familiar ones from C-like languages and LISP. Like every scripting language, SDL depends on an extensive collection of built-in and library facilities, so that programmers can write their scripts economically. Accordingly, the language contains about sixty built-in functions for arithmetic and boolean operations, for basic manipulations of texts, lists, and bindings, and for invoking external tools. There is also a built-in function for applying a closure to a list of values in parallel, which is used to achieve coarse-grained parallel compilation.

Why use a functional programming language as the basis for software descriptions? A functional language forms a tractable basis for caching of actions (function calls), and that caching is the foundation for Vesta's incremental building mechanism. However, functional languages are alien to most programmers so although SDL has functional semantics, it adopts a C-like syntax and preserves C semantics wherever practical in order to be more accessible to the average developer.

Whatever the form of the language, it must not force the system developer to write a build script as a monolithic entity. That is, the language must enable the system developer to organize the instructions for building a system as a set of modular units. SDL therefore allows one system model to reference, or *import* another, thereby creating a hierarchical structure that can reflect the component structure of the software system itself. The individual component models are often similar in structure, as shown in the next chapter, and can frequently be constructed by filling in the blanks in a standard template. In essence, this is "programming by copying", a time-honored technique, especially with scripting languages.

Modular structure is intended to help localize information, which is generally a wise methodological principle for organizing software systems. However, the nature of the build process frequently requires broad, systematic alterations of default behavior, and the description language must accommodate these situations gracefully. For example, a customized action may apply to an entire build ("build this program and all the libraries it uses with debugging symbols") or to a large part of it ("build the graphics library with optimization level 2"). In practice, this means that the functions for building a system must be sufficiently parameterized that the construction of the individual components can be sensibly customized by the callers of those functions.

A moment's thought reveals that conventional function parameters are inadequate to this task. Consider invoking the C compiler. It accepts a number of explicit parameters on its command line, including the source file to be compiled, but it has implicit parameters as well. In fact, every file in the file system that the compiler can access as a consequence of C's `#include` directive is a potential parameter, not to mention environment variables and other information supplied by the operating system. This is a potentially vast state space that can and frequently must change subtly from one compilation to the next. Since repeatability requires a precise description of this state, SDL must provide a way to represent and manipulate it. Clearly, passing as an explicit parameter each and every file that might be needed by a compilation is not practical.

How then, is this potential chaos of customization controlled? Individual system descriptions are, indeed, parameterized extensively. This makes it possible to localize the setting of the actual, customized values of parameters near the root of the hierarchy of system description modules. But assigning all these parameters individual names in a flat name space is impractical. Instead, the current construction parameters are collected together in a single composite value called the *environment*. In addition to parameters that control how tools like the compiler and linker are invoked, the environment passed to each such tool contains a complete representation of the file name space in which the tool is to run. That is, when run under Vesta's control, compilers, linkers, and other development tools access all of their data as named entities in a Vesta environment rather than the actual file system. (How this works will be described soon.) SDL's *binding* type is used to represent environments.

The Vesta notion of environment is central. A precisely specified build is nothing more than a series of tool invocations (e.g., compiles and links) in a controlled naming environment. That environment changes subtly but crucially on each tool invocation, and the process of constructing these many slightly different environments must be both convenient to express and efficient to implement. So, SDL provides:

- a mechanism by which the current environment is easily passed between functions,
- a *binding* data type used to represent naming environments (including build customizations and file directories), as well as language facilities for easily creating and modifying bindings,
- a language primitive for executing a tool in a particular environment, and
- a *closure* data type for delaying tool invocations until the files they produce are needed.

The sections that follow consider these particular aspects of SDL in more detail.

### 5.2.1 The Environment Parameter

Since bindings used to represent environments play such an important role in system descriptions, SDL treats them specially. Every Vesta function takes an implicit final parameter named "`.`" (pronounced "dot") denoting the current environment. That is, a function declared with $n$ explicit formal arguments actually has $n+1$ arguments, the last being the implicit formal parameter named "`.`". The name "`.`" is a legal Vesta identifier, so it can be used as any other identifier would be. A function with $n$ formal arguments can be called with either $n$ or $n+1$ actual arguments. In the former case, the current value of "`.`" is bound to the implicit formal parameter "`.`"; in the latter case, the last actual parameter is bound to the implicit formal parameter "`.`". The first of these turns out to be the overwhelmingly common case, that is, "`.`" is usually "inherited" by a callee from its caller.

The name "`.`" was chosen to suggest "current naming environment" by analogy with Unix's use of "`.`" for the current directory. However, the reader who is familiar with Unix should not take the analogy too far. When a tool runs under Vesta, the file system name space that the tools sees is indeed specified by the current naming environment, but the environment is not literally handed to the tool as its working directory. Section 5.2.3 explains this point in detail.

### 5.2.2 Bindings

Because of its use to represent the naming environment for tools (including build customizations and the file name space), the *binding* is perhaps the key data type in SDL. A binding is an ordered mapping from names (text strings) to arbitrary Vesta values and is expressed with the following syntax:

$$[\, name_1 = value_1, \ldots, name_n = value_n \,]$$

Bindings can be nested, giving rise to a hierarchical name space. For example, Figure 5.1a shows a binding that might be used to specify the options for compiling and linking C++ programs. Figure 5.1b shows its representation as a tree. The hierarchical structure arises because a binding is itself an SDL value.

```
[ Cxx= [ switches= [ compile= [opt="-O1"], link= [strip="-s"] ]]]
```

(a)

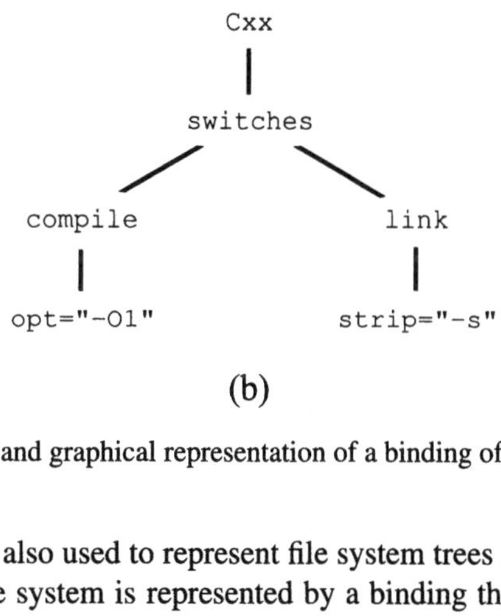


(b)

**Fig. 5.1.** Code and graphical representation of a binding of build options.

Vesta bindings are also used to represent file system trees in a natural way. Each directory in such a file system is represented by a binding that maps each name in the directory either to a subdirectory (a nested binding) or to a file (a text value).[2] Hence, a directory $d$ containing files named $f_1$ and $f_2$ with corresponding contents $c_1$ and $c_2$ would be represented by the binding $d = [f_1 = c_1, f_2 = c_2]$.

SDL includes syntax and operators for creating bindings, selecting a binding element by name, merging two bindings, and subtracting elements from a binding. Bindings are constructed using the syntax we have just seen. The value named

[2] A brief implementation aside: Because file contents are treated in SDL as text values, the implementation must be able to handle large text values that are read and written as files are; it does this by representing such values internally as pointers to files stored in the repository. These pointers are described in Section 7.1.1.

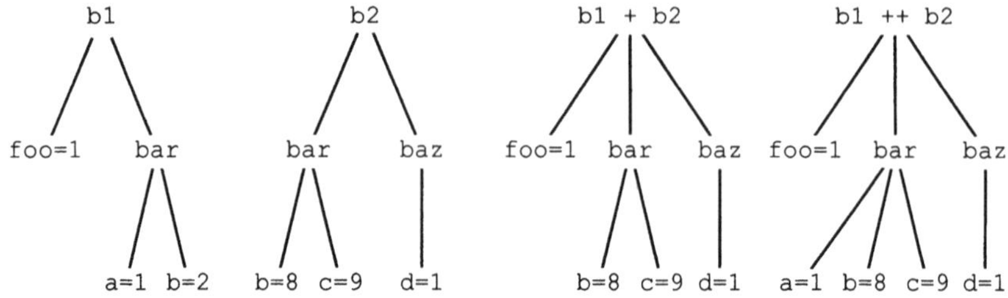


**Fig. 5.2.** The results produced by overlaying (+) and recursively overlaying (++) two bindings, $b_1$ and $b_2$. Notice that in $b_1 + b_2$, the *bar* component of $b_1$ is ignored, while in $b_1$ ++ $b_2$, the *bar* components of $b_1$ and $b_2$ are overlaid recursively, with the values from $b_2$ taking precedence.

*n* in the binding *b* is selected by writing *b*/*n*. For example, if the binding in Figure 5.1 were named `options`, the compiler switches would be selected by writing `options/Cxx/switches/compile`, which evaluates to the singleton binding `[ opt = "-O1" ]`. The use of "/" to descend a binding's name hierarchy corresponds directly to the similar use in the Unix file name space and makes it particularly natural for the writer of Vesta system models when representing directory trees with bindings.

SDL includes syntax that makes it easy to construct bindings including files from the same package directory as the system model that refers to them. Consider the following example.

```
files
  h_files = [ Lex.H, Scan.H, Index.H ];
```

This clause, placed at the top of a system model, introduces the identifier `h_files` and binds it to a binding of three elements named `Lex.H`, `Scan.H`, and `Index.H`. Each of these elements is a text value defined by the contents of the correspondingly named file in the directory in which the system model resides.

Bindings are combined (that is, merged) using the *overlay* (+) and *recursive overlay* (++) operators. The expression $b_1 + b_2$ is the binding containing the union of the names in $b_1$ and $b_2$; for those names that appear in both bindings, the value bound to the name in $b_2$ takes precedence. The binding $b_1$ ++ $b_2$ is like $b_1 + b_2$, except that where both bindings contain the same name, and when that name is bound to a nested binding in each, the nested bindings are overlaid recursively. Figure 5.2 shows an example use of the + and ++ binding operators.

The overlay and recursive overlay operators provide the basic machinery for applying customizations and for modifying a binding that represents a directory tree. For example, if "`.`" is a binding denoting the current environment, and "`./root`" is the root of a file system, then the environment can be extended to include the extra directories and files contained in the binding `fs` by writing:

```
. ++= [ root = fs ];
```

As in C, "a *op*= b" is shorthand for "a = a *op* b".

The overlay operators are also handy for overriding compilation options. Suppose we wanted to alter the build options shown in Figure 5.1 so as not to use optimization (by setting the compiler flag "-O0"). We could write:

```
options ++=
  [Cxx = [switches = [compile = [opt = "-O0"]]]];
```

This kind of modification, in which one wishes to alter an element of a binding nested several levels in the naming hierarchy, occurs so commonly that SDL includes a syntactic shorthand to express it conveniently. The same overlay can thus be written:

```
options ++= [ Cxx/switches/compile/opt = "-O0" ];
```

By definition of the recursive overlay operator, this assignment leaves the binding `Cxx/switches/link` unchanged, but it binds the `opt` element of the `compile` binding to "-O0". As another example, the following fragment of SDL adds three files to a specific point in a file system tree represented by a binding

```
. ++= [ root/lexer_h_files = h_files ];
```

where `h_files` is as defined above.

These examples demonstrate how selected subtrees of the environment can be changed by a single source statement in a Vesta model. More generally, they illustrate how easily new naming environments can be constructed in SDL. The implementation of the Vesta evaluator makes binding manipulations inexpensive, so the traversal and manipulation of these "directory" structures is extremely efficient compared to conventional file systems. Thus, customized naming environments, which are in effect entire file system name spaces, can be created for the particular needs of each tool invoked during a Vesta system build.

The ability to create custom naming environments easily and cheaply has a profound effect on the way developers think about system building. In traditional development environments, creating such customized file systems would be unthinkable because the name space, being implemented by the file system, is stored on disk and is expensive to modify. Therefore, rather than collecting files in one conveniently organized binding, Unix environments use search paths (see Section 2.3) to guide tools to find the files they need, which are located in various places in the file system. In essence, a development environment needs to group files in a variety of ways for different purposes, but a file system directory is only capable of representing one of those groupings efficiently. Vesta's bindings escape this limitation by making it easy and inexpensive to construct a custom file system for each tool invocation.

### 5.2.3 Tool Encapsulation

The purpose of a scripting language is to provide machinery that permits easy combination of large blocks of work performed outside the language. In the case of software construction, and therefore the Vesta language, those blocks of work are carried out by external tools like compilers and linkers. Consistent with the functional nature of SDL, invocations of external tools are expressed as function calls. Those invocations occur through a built-in primitive called `_run_tool`, which enables an arbitrary tool to be used under Vesta without modification and invoked in an execution environment defined through the scripting language.

What is that execution environment? It consists of the complete file name space available to the tool, its standard input `stdin`, the command line arguments with which it was invoked, and the Unix environment variables. Because this execution environment is controlled by the scripting language and therefore by the Vesta user, the environment is said to be *encapsulated*. The encapsulation is performed in such a way that the Vesta system can automatically track and record the values that the tool uses from its execution environment. Knowledge of these dependencies on the environment is essential for proper caching of the results of tool invocations, which in turn is essential for consistent incremental building. Chapter 8 examines this subject in detail.

The `_run_tool` primitive takes parameters that identify the tool to run, the platform on which it is to execute,[3] its command line, and the values that should be placed in the encapsulated environment in which the tool executes. It returns a binding whose elements represent the tool's outcome, including any files created by the tool. The `_run_tool` primitive also takes some arguments that specify what to do about caching the result of the tool invocation in exceptional cases (for example, if the tool returns a Unix error code or if it writes anything to its standard error output). The complete specification of `_run_tool` appears in Section A.3.4.8.

The environment parameter "`.`" is a key argument to `_run_tool`. It defines both the tool's environment variables (that is, the Unix environment variables described in Section 2.3) and the file system name space in which the tool is to run. If the value `./envVars` is defined, it is taken to be a binding that defines the names and values of environment variables to be set for the tool's execution. If the value `./root` is defined, it is taken to be the root of the file system that the tool will be able to access while it executes. More specifically, an absolute pathname referenced by the tool is looked up in `./root`, while a relative pathname is looked up in the nested binding `./root/.WD`. This lookup occurs through the cooperation of the `_run_tool` machinery, the Vesta repository, and the Vesta evaluator. Section 3.1.2 touched on this briefly, and Part III examines it in greater detail.

Although the `_run_tool` function provides a flexible means for invoking external tools, it is a low-level primitive. Few user-written system models need to call it directly. Instead, most calls of `_run_tool` are "wrapped" in functions that are more convenient for a developer to use. Such functions can hide platform-specific details of tool invocation, enable multiple compilations to be performed together (or in parallel), and so on. These wrapper functions are part of Vesta function libraries called *bridges*, which are discussed in the next chapter.

---

[3] The `_run_tool` implementation maps the platform name to a list of suitable machines, using a site-specific configuration table, then selects a machine from the list based on its current load characteristics.

### 5.2.4 Closures

A *closure* is a function paired with a mapping (also called a context) that supplies values for all of the unbound variables appearing in the function's body. In SDL, closures are first-class values; that is, they can be passed as parameters, bound to names, or embedded in data structures just as any other value can.

Consider the SDL fragment in Figure 5.3. When evaluated, this fragment returns a binding with two elements named `f` and `g`, each of which is a closure. The name `f` is bound to a closure whose body is the SDL expression `return x + b/count;` and whose context maps the name `b` to a binding of two components, an integer named `count` with value 3 and a text string named `label` with value "abc". This closure, when invoked with an integer parameter, returns an integer whose value is 3 greater than the parameter. Similarly, in the binding computed by this SDL fragment, the name `g` is bound to a closure whose body is the SDL expression `return str1 + b/label + str2;` and whose context maps the name `b` in the same way as the closure `f` does. The expression `g("xyz", "pqr")` evaluates to the text string "xyzabcpqr".

```
{
  b = [ count = 3, label = "abc" ];

  f(x) { return x + b/count; };
  g(str1, str2) { return str1 + b/label + str2; };
  return [ f = f, g = g ];
}
```

**Fig. 5.3.** Closures defined by SDL functions.

A closure is generally created by an explicit SDL function definition. As the example above illustrates, closures created in this way may have an arbitrary list of formal parameters. Closures are also created implicitly by Vesta system models. In particular, each system model implicitly defines a function whose body is the text of the model and which takes a single parameter, "`.`". The closure consists of this function and an empty context, since no free variables are permitted in the body of a system model.

Closures of either sort are invoked using the normal function call syntax. The expression `g("xyz", "pqr")` is an example for a closure defined by an explicit function definition. The next section shows an invocation of a closure defined by a system model.

To begin an evaluation, the Vesta evaluator invokes the closure defined by the model to be evaluated. This closure expects a single argument, and the evaluator passes an empty binding as that argument.

Closures have several uses. A collection of callable functions can be represented by a binding that maps function names to closure values, as in Figure 5.3. If the name `intf` were bound to the result of evaluating the system model in this figure, then the

```
{
  app1 = build_app(/* args1 */);
  app2 = build_app(/* args2 */);
  app3 = build_app(/* args3 */);
  return [ app1, app2, app3 ];
}
```

**Fig. 5.4.** System model that builds three applications.

```
{
  app1() = { return build_app(/* args1 */); };
  app2() = { return build_app(/* args2 */); };
  app3() = { return build_app(/* args3 */); };
  return [ app1, app2, app3 ];
}
```

**Fig. 5.5.** System model with three closures that build applications.

closure `g` could be invoked by writing `intf()/g("xyz", "pqr")`. This is a convenient idiom for representing abstract interfaces.

Closures can also be used to delay evaluation until it is certain that the evaluation is required. For example, a system model might contain the instructions for building several applications. If the model is structured as a simple binding, as in Figure 5.4, then evaluating the model unconditionally builds all three applications. However, if each application's construction is a closure, as in Figure 5.5, then the evaluation of the system model merely produces a binding containing three closures.[4] The system model that uses (imports) this binding, say using the name `build_apps`, can then selectively build the application(s) it wants, e.g., `build_apps()/app2()`, and avoid the cost of unnecessarily building the others.

### 5.2.5 Imports

The *import* clause enables one system model to refer to another and therefore, ultimately, to invoke the closure it creates. More precisely, the import clause binds a local identifier to the closure corresponding to the model being imported. Here is a small example:

```
import
  sample = /vesta/vestasys.org/sample/21/build.ves;
{
  // assume that sample returns a binding with members
  // named a and b, each of which is a closure that
  // accepts an integer parameter and returns a binding.

  return sample()/a(1) ++ sample()/b(23);
}
```

[4] The binding constructor `[ a, b ]` is syntactic shorthand for `[ a = a, b = b ]`.

This system model begins with an import clause binding the name `sample` to the closure corresponding to the model stored in the Vesta repository under the given file name. This closure is then invoked twice. The two components `a` and `b` of the result are selected and are themselves invoked, each with an integer parameter, yielding two bindings. The bindings are then combined with the recursive overlay operator to form the result of evaluating the model.

This is a nonsensical example, but it bears some resemblance to the way in which the closures of imported models are generally used. In particular, such closures often return bindings consisting of a number of other closures, which are then selectively invoked by the importing model as appropriate. Because closures are first-class values, they need not be invoked immediately, as in this example, but may be held in a data structure (typically a part of the environment binding) and invoked subsequently. This technique is used extensively in realistic system models.

## In Summary

The Vesta system description language provides a semantically precise scripting facility with a few key features — bindings, closures, flexible parameterization — that are well-matched to the needs of developers writing instructions for repeatable, incremental, consistent, and scalable builds. However, it is a big step from the rather simple language described above to a practical set of facilities for writing such instructions conveniently. We take that step in the next chapter.

# 6

# Building Systems in Vesta

The preceding chapter provided the motivation behind Vesta's system description language and presented its primary constructs. This chapter focuses on the use of SDL to express complex build instructions. Of course, there are many ways to do this and, as noted in the preceding chapter, SDL strives to be "methodology-neutral". This chapter presents a particular set of choices — a methodology, or a style — that has worked well in practice. Before getting into the details, however, we need to examine some of the considerations that motivated the specific choices this methodology embodies.

The previous chapters mentioned several times the importance of repeatable construction. The desire for repeatability gave rise to Vesta's immutable source files coupled with versioning as the mechanism to represent change. System models, like all Vesta sources, are contained in packages in the Vesta repository and are versioned, immutable, and immortal. Hence, the instructions for building a particular version of a software artifact are never lost.

System models are also complete. This means that the result produced by carrying out the instructions embodied in a system model depends only on the information in that model and the other models it imports either directly or indirectly. No file, environment variable, or other aspect of the surrounding system on which Vesta is being run can implicitly affect the evaluation of a system model. Thus, an evaluated model and the models it imports form a complete record of the sources, instructions, and tools contributing to a build.

Together, immutability and completeness imply that a system model must specify the particular version of each source file and model that contributes to a build. At first blush, this would seem impractical, since the process of creating a new version of a package could involve updating the version number of every source file referenced within a model. However, the burden of referring to correct source versions from a system model is mitigated by four factors.

- Sources are versioned and imported at the granularity of packages (directory trees), not individual files.

- Due to the hierarchical arrangement of packages, updating the version of a single high-level import can indirectly import new versions of many packages lower in the hierarchy.
- A model directly references only source files that exist in the same package as the model itself, though it may import models inside or outside the package. References to source files (including models) within the package version do not require an explicit version specification because the package is versioned as a whole. That is, these file references are implicitly bound to files in the same package version as the referencing model itself.
- Tools can help the developer to revise a system model's imports. Vesta provides such a tool, called **vupdate**, that creates a new model from an existing one by updating the versions of imported models according to the setting of command-line parameters.

Since by the completeness and immutability principles, everything needed for a build must be explicitly named in a system model, that model (including transitively everything it imports) must either provide the rules for building a component from its constituent pieces or must deliver the component already constructed. The latter case frequently applies when the component is a tool (e.g., a compiler) or a licensed software library for which no source code is available. In such cases, the binary files are the "source" for the purposes of system construction, and they are stored as source files in the Vesta repository. The system models that describe them do no construction at all, but simply name these previously built files. On the other hand, a tool or library for which sources are available is described by a system model that defines its construction from constituent parts. Thus, a Vesta system description references all the components, including construction tools, needed for a build, whether those components exist as pre-built binaries or are constructed from simpler pieces.

This last observation highlights the necessity of organizing a potentially large amount of build-related information in a way that is manageable both by an individual developer and by the development organization as a whole, which is the primary subject of this chapter.

## 6.1 The Organization of System Models

A system model is the building block in a Vesta system description. A complete build description of a system is a collection of system models that refer to each other via `import` clauses and define every aspect of the build to be carried out. As the system is developed, these system models must change; they are not written once and then left untouched. So, just as the architecture of the software system requires careful organization to accommodate its evolution, so does the build description. It is therefore appropriate to ask: How should the collection of system models that form a build description be structured? What principles or methodology should be followed to create a collection of understandable and usable models? The particular example developed throughout this chapter embodies specific answers to these questions that derive both from the overall Vesta requirements and from the following observations about software development.

**Separate environment.** Files in a package under development change more frequently than the environment in which that package is built. Consequently, it is useful to separate the description of the package from the description of the environment for building the package.

**Standard templates.** From the perspective of system construction, many packages have a similar form. For example, a package may build either a complete program or a body of code intended to be linked into other programs. The former is an *application* and the latter is a *library*. Generally, the system models for applications look quite similar to one another, as do the models for libraries. The development environment should take advantage of this similarity by providing standard templates for these models and by minimizing the amount of "boilerplate" in each. In effect, these standard forms of models are institutionalized in the development environment. Of course, they can be modified or entirely bypassed in exceptional cases.

**Extensive parameterization.** Occasionally, a developer will need a customized environment. The customization might include special versions of libraries, or libraries compiled in a special way or with a special version of a compiler. Consequently, the system description for the construction of the environment must be parameterized to permit an individual developer to create the custom environment needed to develop a package. Moreover, examining the space of sensible customizations quickly yields the conclusion that the parameterization required is extensive.

**Library hierarchy.** Any constructed system is linked together from a collection of components, typically derived object files and library archives. The dependencies between these components induce an abstract hierarchy, the library hierarchy. Some tools used during the build process, notably the Unix program linker, require the libraries they process to be presented in a total order that is consistent with the library hierarchy's partial order. Since the library hierarchy is distinct from the package naming hierarchy, system models must represent the library hierarchy explicitly.

**Defaulting.** Systems are built by executing tools (e.g., compilers and linkers), which generally have extensive options that are needed only for specialized purposes. These options must be accessible from Vesta models, but most users of the tools never need to be aware of them. Consequently, the mechanisms for compiling and linking package components must hide these rarities by default, without compromising a developer's ability to exploit the full power of the tools when necessary.

These considerations guided the organization of a particular *standard construction environment*, one largely based on the notion of a hierarchy of library descriptions. The remainder of this chapter examines that environment as it is used by a developer.

## 6.2 Hierarchies of System Models

To understand concretely how a build description is organized as a package hierarchy, we will examine an extended example: a hypothetical email system. Figure 6.1 shows the hierarchy of packages comprising the complete release of our mail system. A directed arrow in the figure links a system model in one package to a model it imports from another package. At the lower right of the figure are two library packages named *mail/send_rcv* and *mail/index*, for transporting and indexing mail, respectively. The release consists of two application packages named *mail/inc* and *mail/search*, which respectively build applications that incorporate newly received mail into an inbox and carry out queries on mail messages. (A more realistic mail system would, of course, have additional application and library packages, but two of each will suffice for the purposes of this chapter.)

At the root of the tree is the release package itself. The *mail/release* package does not contain any source code. Instead, its model imports the standard environment (*common/std_env*), the packages for the two application programs, and an *umbrella library* package named *mail/lib_umb*, which itself imports the two mail-related libraries.

As shown in Figure 6.1, the standard environment imports two kinds of models:

- the "bridge" models that export interfaces for invoking collections of tools, such as language-specific compilers and linkers, and
- the standard libraries required by client applications (in this example, only two standard C libraries are shown).

Looking at the subtree rooted at the *mail/lib_umb* package, we see that library packages themselves may be arranged in hierarchies. In fact, the standard construction environment supports three kinds of libraries: *leaf libraries*, which are libraries built from source, *pre-built libraries*, which are libraries that exist only in binary form, and *umbrella libraries*, which are collections of other libraries (any combination of

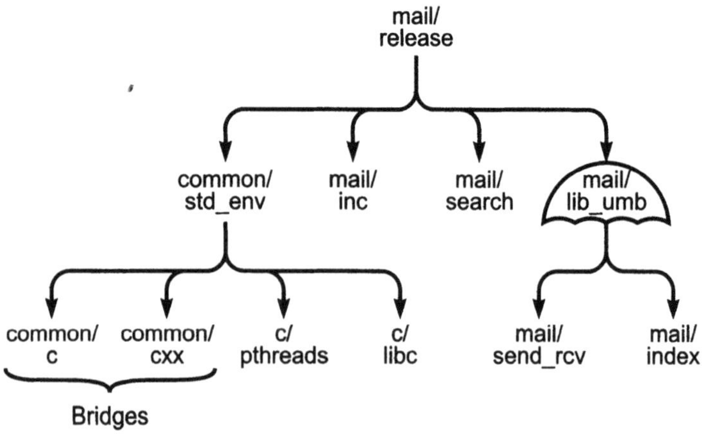


**Fig. 6.1.** The packages of a hypothetical mail system and their imports.

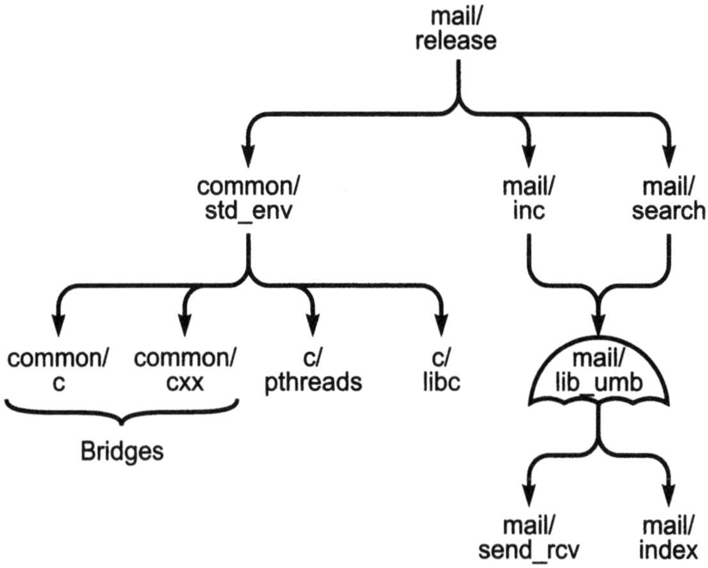


**Fig. 6.2.** An alternative arrangement of package imports for the mail system of Fig. 6.1.

umbrellas, leaves, and pre-builts). In Figure 6.1, *mail/lib_umb* is an umbrella library, *mail/send_rcv* and *mail/index* are leaf libraries, and *c/pthreads* and *c/libc* are pre-built libraries.

Umbrella libraries are a convenient way to gather up a collection of related libraries into a single conceptual entity.[1] In this example, the umbrella enables the release package to import one library package rather than two. In larger software systems — such as the release model for the Vesta system itself, which contains nine leaf libraries — the use of umbrella libraries makes client models simpler and more succinct.

To emphasize that the particular arrangement of import relationships shown in Figure 6.1 is a methodological choice rather than a correctness requirement, Figure 6.2 gives an alternative arrangement. The essential difference in the two arrangements is the way in which the umbrella package is imported. In the first arrangement, the umbrella package is named once, by the *release* model, while in the second arrangement, it is imported twice, by the *inc* and *search* packages. Both are logically correct, in the sense that they completely capture the information necessary to build our example mail system. However, the first arrangement is more convenient operationally because only one import statement needs to be updated when a new version of the umbrella package becomes available. While the difference is relatively minor in this simple example, it becomes more compelling when the umbrella is used in many places, as it would be if the mail system had many applications in addition

[1] Umbrella libraries also provide the place to express the order in which the child libraries are given to the program linker so that they link correctly. This is the order noted in the previous section, a total order consistent with the partial order induced by the library hierarchy.

```
import
  std_env =
    /vesta/vestasys.org/common/std_env/9/build.ves;
{
  // build the current environment
  . = std_env()/env_build("AlphaDU4.0");

  // instructions for building the complete mail system
  // would come next...
}
```

**Fig. 6.3.** The initial part of the hypothetical *mail/release* system model.

to *inc* and *search*. For concreteness in the subsequent discussion, our example mail system will use the structure shown in Figure 6.1.

We can now look inside the *mail/release* model, to see how it establishes the building environment for the mail system components. It begins as shown in Figure 6.3.

The SDL code bears a structural resemblance to the example we saw in Section 5.2.4. The `import` clause binds the identifier `std_env` to the closure corresponding to version 9 of the standard environment model. That closure is invoked by the expression `std_env()`. This invocation returns a binding that contains a number of closures. One of them is bound to the name `env_build`; its job is to build and return a suitable construction environment for a target platform named by its argument. We see this closure being invoked to build an environment for the DEC Alpha platform running Digital Unix version 4.0. The environment (a binding) thus created is bound to the Vesta identifier "`.`" for use by the rest of the mail system build. The choice of "`.`" is not arbitrary; it means that the environment will be passed by default as a parameter to any other closures that the *mail/release* model invokes (recall the special properties of "`.`" as explained in Section 5.2.1). Thus, once the environment is set up by the first two statements of the release model, the rest of the system building instructions never need to mention it explicitly. Nevertheless, it is completely and immutably specified, because of the explicit version number included in (and required by) the `import` clause.

Before we can understand the remainder of the *mail/release* model, we must look into the four models it imports, shown in Figure 6.1.

### 6.2.1 Bridges and the Standard Environment

As Figure 6.1 suggests, the *std_env* model imports a collection of *bridge models*. Each bridge model exports an interface (in the sense of Section 5.2.4) to a collection of related tools. Vesta bridges are models written in SDL, and they are interpreted by the Vesta evaluator just like any other model. They are not hard-wired into the Vesta system in any way.

Bridge models must handle the complexities of interfacing to external tools and supporting customized builds, so they tend to be much more complicated than the models that use them. The `std_env` model and the seven bridge models comprising the standard construction environment total roughly 1,800 lines of SDL code. Approximately two-thirds of that code is in the bridges for C/C++ and Modula-3 programs. These bridges export functions (closures) for building programs, pre-built libraries, leaf libraries, and umbrella libraries from code written in their respective languages. (For concreteness, we limit the discussion here to the C/C++ bridge. The facilities of other bridges are similar.)

Strictly speaking — and this is a crucial point — the closures for building the three types of libraries don't actually do the building! The complete information necessary to build a library is not available, in general, until the program in which the library will be used is built. The system model that builds that program supplies the needed information, at which time the library can be properly constructed. Hence, the closures provided by the bridge for each library type do little more than embed the library source files in a binding that serves as part of a set of *instructions* for constructing the library later.

This approach differs sharply from the conventional one, in which particular versions of standard libraries are constructed and placed in standard locations in the file system hierarchy. The Vesta standard environment places *highly parameterized construction recipes* at the developer's disposal rather than particular, previously built versions. This is an essential distinction, and the resulting differences in flexibility and development ease are enormous. We'll see some of that flexibility later in this chapter.

So, the C++ bridge supplies three functions named `leaf`, `prebuilt`, and `umbrella` that simply collect the values passed to them into a binding that represents (parameterized) instructions for building the library.

The `program` function defined by the C++ bridge does the real work of building an application. Its parameters include the source code of the application and the values representing the libraries that the application requires. These values are, of course, the bindings returned by the library-creating functions above. The `program` function also takes parameters that define the customizations that control the details of the construction process.

We will cover some additional details of these bridge functions as we see them in use in our mail system example.

### 6.2.2 Library Models

Let's now look at the mail system's library models, beginning with the *mail/index* library, whose model is shown in Figure 6.4. The model starts with a `files` clause that binds local variable names to local files and directories within the package; the paths in a `files` clause are interpreted relative to the directory containing the model itself. In this case, the first four lines of the model introduce three local identifiers (`c_files`, `h_files`, and `priv_h_files`) whose values are bindings that associate the listed names with the corresponding local file contents. For example, the identifier `priv_h_files` names a binding that associates the name `IndexRep.H` with the contents of that local file. Thus the source files are arranged in three groups:

```
// This is mail/index/3/build.ves
files
  c_files = [ Lex.C, Scan.C, Index.C ];
  h_files = [ Lex.H, Scan.H, Index.H ];
  priv_h_files = [ IndexRep.H ];
{
  return ./Cxx/leaf("libMailIndex.a",
    c_files, h_files, priv_h_files);
}
```

**Fig. 6.4.** The model for building the leaf library of the hypothetical *mail/index* package.

(1) C++ source files that must be compiled to produce object files, (2) header files that are provided to clients of the library, and (3) private header files that are required only by the implementation.

The body of the model consists of a single function call. It invokes the C++ bridge function `leaf` to build a leaf library from the files mentioned just above. We learned in the preceding section that this function simply collects the files into a single binding that will be passed to the `program` function when an application (in this case, `inc` or `search`) is built. The `leaf` function gives the library binding the name `libMailIndex.a`.

The structure of the model for the *mail/search* library is similar, so let's proceed to the umbrella model *mail/lib_umb*, shown in Figure 6.5. The first three lines of this model import the two top-level models of the umbrella's component libraries, binding those models to the local identifiers `send_rcv` and `index`. The body of the model first assigns the name `libs` to a list of the libraries comprising the umbrella. (A list is denoted by a comma-separated sequence of values enclosed in angle brackets.) Note that the list of libraries also includes the standard *pthreads* and *libc* libraries. These libraries do not have to be imported, but instead are accessed from "`.`", where they were installed by the standard environment. Including these standard libraries in the umbrella obviates the need for application models to mention them; in effect, all library code for the mail applications, regardless of its location, is made available through the umbrella. The model's final line invokes the C++ bridge's `umbrella` function, which collects the supplied libraries in an umbrella with the name `libMailUmb`. As with the leaf library above, this umbrella represents the *instructions* for building the set of libraries under the umbrella, not the result of carrying out those instructions. That will happen later when an application program that uses the umbrella is built.

The library hierarchy provided by umbrella models greatly simplifies the developer's job in specifying which libraries are needed to link a complete program and the order in which they must be listed on the linker's command line. Rather than having to determine and explicitly specify in order the set of all necessary library files, as is generally required in the Unix environment, the developer specifies a small number of higher-level umbrellas. (In the mail system example, it's a single one.) Consequently, the developer's models are simpler and more robust against changes

```
// This is mail/lib_umb/18/build.ves
import
  send_rcv =
    /vesta/vestasys.org/mail/send_rcv/1/build.ves;
  index =
    /vesta/vestasys.org/mail/index/3/build.ves;
{
  libs = < send_rcv(), index(), ./C/libs/c/pthreads,
           ./C/libs/c/libc >;
  return ./Cxx/umbrella("libMailUmb", libs);
}
```

**Fig. 6.5.** The model for building the umbrella library of the hypothetical *mail/lib_umb* package.

in the structure of libraries. The C++ bridge function `program` handles the complexities of constructing a suitable command line for the Unix linker by "flattening" the umbrella hierarchy.

Our mail system doesn't have any pre-built libraries, only an umbrella and two leaves. However, the *std_env* umbrella incorporates two libraries that are pre-built: *c/libc* and *c/pthreads*. These models are quite similar in structure to a leaf library, but they deliver binary data rather than source code and, of course, are not subject to later customization during execution of the `program` function.

Now that we've seen what library models look like, we can turn to the application models that use them.

### 6.2.3 Application Models

Figure 6.6 shows the system model for building the hypothetical application package *mail/search*. The model begins with an enumeration of the sources comprising the application. The actual construction occurs when the `program` function of the `Cxx` bridge is invoked. This function first builds the libraries specified by its `libs` argument, which in this case lists a single umbrella library taken from the environment. It then augments the current environment to include the header files in the `h_files` argument, compiles each of the files in the `c_files` argument, and links everything together. The value returned by the function is a binding that maps the name `mailsearch` to the resulting executable.

Notice that the package expects to get the mail umbrella library `libMailUmb` from its environment ("`.`"). This reflects the structure shown in Figure 6.1, where a release model imports particular versions of the standard environment and the mail umbrella, adds them to "`.`", and then imports and builds the two mail applications in this environment. Had the mail system been structured as in Figure 6.2, an explicit import of *mail/lib_umb* would appear at the start of this model.

```
// This is mail/search/6/build.ves
files
  c_files = [ QueryAST.C, ParseQuery.C, Search.C ];
  h_files = [ QueryAST.H, ParseQuery.H, Search.H ];
{
  // build program
  libs = < ./Cxx/libs/mail/libMailUmb >;
  return
    ./Cxx/program("mailsearch", c_files, h_files, libs);
}
```

**Fig. 6.6.** The model to build the search application of the hypothetical *mail/search* package.

### 6.2.4 Putting It All Together

We can now return, finally, to the model at the root of the package tree that defines our hypothetical mail system. The beginning of this model appeared in Figure 6.3. Based on the structure of the mail system (Figure 6.1), we would expect the release model to import four packages (the standard environment, the mail umbrella, and the two mail applications), build the environment, put the umbrella into it at the point in the naming hierarchy expected by the applications, then build the two applications. This would indeed be a possible structure (see Figure 6.7), but there are other considerations.

```
import
  std_env =
    /vesta/vestasys.org/common/std_env/9/build.ves;
  umb =
    /vesta/vestasys.org/mail/lib_umb/18/build.ves;
  inc =
    /vesta/vestasys.org/mail/inc/4/build.ves;
  search =
    /vesta/vestasys.org/mail/search/6/build.ves;
{
  // bind the standard environment to '.'
  . = std_env()/env_build("AlphaDU4.0");
  // add umbrella to environment
  . ++= [ Cxx/libs/mail/libMailUmb = umb() ];
  // build and return applications
  return [ progs = inc() + search() ];
}
```

**Fig. 6.7.** A possible but impractical release model for the hypothetical mail system.

A release model organized in this way would be complete and self-contained. This would be an advantage for the developer of the mail system, whose work is then isolated from external influences. However, suppose that developer were part of an organization that provides a suite of applications as a single release. That is, the release of the mail system does not occur in isolation, but rather in conjunction with the release of many other applications and libraries. If the mail system's release model is self-contained, then consistent construction of the larger release that includes the mail system and the many other programs will be difficult, as there will be no way to ensure that they are all using the same version of the standard environment.

It's easy to see where this observation leads: another level of models and parameterization. That is, the mail system release model is not actually the "root" of a build. It doesn't explicitly import the standard environment itself, but instead assumes it has been set up by its invoker. Moreover, instead of building the umbrella and applications, it provides its invoker with closures that do so. The actual building of the mail system and the other packages is done by a "master" release model. With these alterations, the mail system release model looks approximately as shown in Figure 6.8. (Figure 6.9 contains a semantically equivalent but structurally more realistic version, which exploits some additional SDL features to produce a more easily maintained set of building instructions.)

```
// This is mail/release/21/build.ves
import
  inc =
    /vesta/vestasys.org/mail/inc/4/build.ves;
  search =
    /vesta/vestasys.org/mail/search/6/build.ves;
  umb =
    /vesta/vestasys.org/mail/lib_umb/18/build.ves;
{
  // This closure builds two applications:
  progs() { return inc() + search(); }

  return [ lib = umb, progs = progs ];
}
```

**Fig. 6.8.** A model for building the release of the hypothetical mail system.

This structure will enable the development organization as a whole to build its "master" release consistently, but it would seem to leave the mail system developer without a way to build and test that component individually, since the mail system release model is no longer self-contained. However, the Vesta system does provide a way — one that has other benefits as well — which we call *control panel* models.

### 6.2.5 Control Panel Models

Once a developer has organized the release model as shown in Figure 6.8, there are only a few details that need to be specified in order to build the component.

```
// A more maintainable version of
// mail/release/21/build.ves
from /vesta/vestasys.org/mail import
  mail_pkgs = [ inc/4, search/6 ];
  umb = lib_umb/18;
{
  // This closure builds all application programs:
  progs() {
    pkg_results = [];
    foreach [ pkg_name = pkg_model ] in mail_pkgs do
      pkg_results += [ $pkg_name = pkg_model() ];
    return pkg_results;
  }
  return [ lib = umb, progs = progs ];
}
```

**Fig. 6.9.** A more realistic release model for the hypothetical mail system.

Chiefly, these are the version of the standard environment to be used and any build customizations (e.g., optimization or debugging switches). These details are properly viewed as external to the component and are frequently more transient in nature than the instructions for building the component itself. For that reason, it is convenient to put them in a separate model, which is called a *control panel* model.

The rationale for this name is simple. Such a model is truly the "top-level" model from the developer's perspective, who presents this model to the Vesta evaluator in order to get an instance of the mail system built (say, for debugging purposes). This action would naturally be performed from a graphical user interface, or control panel, which could provide a way to view and modify the transient details (such as standard environment version or debugging options) and to invoke a specified version of the component's release model in a suitably constructed environment. But how, exactly, would that environment get constructed? By a Vesta model, of course — one that imports the specified standard environment and alters it according to the specified options. That model, which is of a highly stylized form, can be "written" by a control panel, using a simple template into which the information provided by the developer through the control panel's GUI is substituted at appropriate points.

Despite their name, there is nothing special about control panel models. Indeed, most development under Vesta has occurred in the absence of a control panel GUI; control panel models are simply written by hand.[2] Writing such models is very straightforward. By convention, they are named *.main.ves*. They are highly stylized, and usually on the order of 10 to 20 lines long, depending on the number of customizations specified. After creating a suitable environment by importing a specified version of the standard environment and adjusting parameters to suit the developer's

[2] The initial users of Vesta (other than its implementers – see Section 12.1) did build a simple control panel GUI, but it had somewhat more specialized functionality than the general-purpose control panel envisioned by the previous paragraph.

needs, a control panel model invokes another model in the same package. Typically, this is the release model, conventionally named *build.ves*, which then customarily compiles and links the package's source code in the prepared environment. As the previous section showed, the *build.ves* model is designed to be independent of the version of the standard environment in use, so it can also be called from elsewhere (notably, the "master release" model) to build the same package in different environments.

One other factor influences the structure of control panel and release models. A package may produce several different categories of derived files. For example, a package may produce executables meant to be exported to clients, test programs, libraries, and documentation. A developer may not wish to produce each of these artifacts on every build. So by convention, a package's *build.ves* model returns a binding that contains a separate closure for building each category of derived file. The control panel model then invokes only those closures in the binding that are currently of interest to the developer. In essence, each category is built lazily.

Figure 6.10 shows a control panel model for our mail system example. The initial lines import the package's local *build.ves* model (that is, either Figure 6.8 or 6.9) and version 9 of the standard environment model, binding them to the names `self` and `std_env`, respectively. Line (1) invokes the `env_build` function of the `std_env` model to build an environment targeted to Alphas running the Digital Unix 4.0 operating system. Line (2) evaluates the local *build.ves* model, binding the result to the local name `b`. Line (3) puts the building instructions for the libraries into the environment where the application models (of which Figure 6.6 is representative) expect to find them. Finally, line (4) selects the `progs` field out of the binding `b` and invokes it. `progs` is a closure of one argument: the all-important implicit argument "`.`", which was just set up on lines (1) and (3). The result of invoking `b/progs` is returned in a singleton binding as the overall result of the package build.

As should be evident, most of this control panel model is highly stylized, meaning it could easily come from a template. There are really only three pieces of vari-

```
// This is mail/release/21/.main.ves
import
  self = build.ves;
  std_env =
    /vesta/vestasys.org/common/std_env/9/build.ves;
{
  // bind the standard environment to '.'
  . = std_env()/env_build("AlphaDU4.0");                // (1)

  b = self();                                           // (2)
  . ++= [ Cxx/libs/mail/libMailUmb = b/lib() ];         // (3)
  return [ progs = b/progs() ];                         // (4)
}
```

**Fig. 6.10.** A control panel model for the hypothetical mail system.

able information — the package name, the standard environment version, and the target platform — which can be easily inserted by hand-editing or by a control panel GUI if one exists. However, without compromising its template-like nature, a control panel model can accommodate additional customization, which is naturally inserted between lines (1) and (2) of Figure 6.10. An example appears in the next section.

One final note: the structure describe in this section and the previous one can be repeated to any number of levels required. That is, for each organizational level at which applications are aggregated, a pair of models — *build.ves* and a control panel model — can be created. This is Conway's Law in action: systems resemble the organizations that build them.[3]

## 6.3 Customizing the Build Process

The standard construction environment includes several different mechanisms for performing customized builds, that is, builds in which default choices are *overridden* in some way. The available customizations range from building against a specified version of an entire package to compiling a single file of a library with individualized compiler options. In most cases, as a result of the parameterization used throughout the standard construction environment models, a developer can override a default by editing a single line of a package model.

The overrides supported by our standard environment can be divided into two classes: *general overrides* and *named overrides*. A *general* override is used to alter the standard environment by adding or replacing bindings in one or more locations. Since the standard environment is a naming hierarchy, a general override is a binding that defines new values for selected names in some portion of that hierarchy. A general override is effected by recursively overlaying (using the ++ operator described in Section 5.2.2) the overriding value at some point in the standard environment. A *named* override is a binding (possibly containing other bindings) that is interpreted like a table, with the names in the binding(s) being the keys. Typically, the names specify the entities to which the override applies, such as a source filename or a library name.

We now consider three uses for overriding supported by our standard construction environment. These cases arose often in our experience with Vesta, so we found it useful to institutionalize them in the standard environment. However, others can certainly be imagined and could be implemented by altering the standard environment models.

**Build-Wide Overrides.** As its name implies, a *build-wide override* applies to an entire build. It is effected in a control panel model by applying a general override to the current environment after the environment has been constructed, but before the package's own *build.ves* model is called.

[3] As originally formulated, Conway's Law states "Organizations which design systems are constrained to produce systems which are copies of the communication structures of these organizations." [16]

For example, consider Figure 6.11. It is the control panel model of Figure 6.10 with the addition of two lines of code that alter the switch settings for C++ compilations. This build-wide override causes all C++ files to be compiled with debugging symbols and optimization. The override applies to all programs built as a result of evaluating this control panel model, which of course includes all of the libraries they import, either from within the mail system or from the standard environment.

```
// This is mail/release/22/.main.ves
import
  self = build.ves;
  std_env =
    /vesta/vestasys.org/common/std_env/9/build.ves;
{
  // bind the standard environment to '.'
  . = std_env()/env_build("AlphaDU4.0");

   // build-wide override
  comp_switches = [ debug = "-g3", opt = "-O1" ];
  . ++= [ Cxx/switches/compile = comp_switches ];

  b = self();
  . ++= [ Cxx/libs/mail/libMailUmb = b/lib() ];
  return [ progs = b/progs() ];
}
```

**Fig. 6.11.** A control panel model with a build-wide override.

This example shows how parameters can be passed to bridge functions through the environment (that is, through "`.`"). Because the environment is passed implicitly on every function call, parameters stashed inside it are available to every bridge function. The documentation of the bridge interface specifies which parts of the environment are accessed by each of its functions.

**Package Overrides.** A second kind of override, a *package override*, is commonly employed when a package (or package tree, such as our hypothetical mail system) needs to be built with a non-standard version of a package it acquires from the standard environment. For example, consider the developer of the mail system who in the course of adding functionality to the *mail/index* application discovers a small but debilitating bug in the *c/libc* library, which is buried deeply in the standard environment. Must he wait until a new version of the standard environment with a repaired *c/libc* is built? No! Instead, he checks out that package himself and fixes the bug, then incorporates his newly corrected version in his mail system build in order to test the fix. He does this by specifying in his control panel model that *c/libc* is to be overridden with his checked-out version, as shown in Figure 6.12. Note that this model differs from the one in Figure 6.10 only in the extra `pkg_ovs` parameter passed to the `env_build` function. This parameter specifies that checkout version 7/1 of the *c/libc* package should be used.

```
// This is mail/release/23/.main.ves
import
  self = build.ves;
  std_env =
    /vesta/vestasys.org/common/std_env/9/build.ves;
  libc =
    /vesta/vestasys.org/c/libc/checkout/7/1/build.ves;
{
  // package override
  pkg_ovs = [ c/libc = libc ];
  // bind the standard environment to '.'
  . = std_env()/env_build("AlphaDU4.0", pkg_ovs);

  b = self();
  . ++= [ Cxx/libs/mail/libMailUmb = b/lib() ];
  return [ progs = b/progs() ];
}
```

**Fig. 6.12.** A control panel model overriding the *libc* package version used in the build.

Once the developer has convinced himself that the fix works properly, he will check in the *c/libc* package. Eventually, someone will create a new version of the standard environment that incorporates it, at which point the mail system developer can forgo the override and simply import the new standard environment. But, in the meantime, because the structure of the standard environment supports package overriding, the developer needed to make only a simple local change to his control panel model in order to include the repaired library and continue testing his mail system. It's worth contrasting this with systems less flexible than Vesta in which the developer would have been blocked because he lacked the authority or the knowledge to rebuild the entire standard environment with one changed component. In such systems, the developer typically faces two unattractive alternatives: submit a bug report to the appropriate organization and wait for a new version to appear (in days or perhaps weeks) or combine his changed *c/libc* with other necessary components of the standard environment in a way that bypasses checks that they were built consistently. Vesta replaces these alternatives with an attractive one: build the whole system consistently without interfering with the development activities of the group responsible for the standard environment. The mail system developer can still submit his bug report so that the problem is eventually fixed in the "official" version of the standard environment, but he need not wait for that version to be built and released.

**Library Overrides.** We saw that a build-wide override enabled non-default options to be used for all compilations in the course of a build. The standard construction environment also includes a mechanism called *library overrides* to change the way a particular library or even a particular file within a library is compiled. This type of override, unlike the two we have already seen, is a *named* override, since it must name the library archive(s) or source file(s) to which the override applies. In the case that the override applies to an umbrella library, the override also affects all descendants of the umbrella.

A library override, like a build-wide override, is achieved by recursively overlaying part of the current environment, typically in the control panel model. For example, suppose we wanted only the *c/pthreads* library to be built with debugging information included. Figure 6.13 shows a control panel model to do this.

```
// This is mail/release/24/.main.ves
import
  self = build.ves;
  std_env =
    /vesta/vestasys.org/common/std_env/9/build.ves;
{
  // bind the standard environment to '.'
  . = std_env()/env_build("AlphaDU4.0");

  // library override
  . ++= [ lib_ovs/libc.a =
            [ ovs/Cxx/switches/compile/debug = "-g3" ]];

  // build selected components
  b = self();
  . ++= [ Cxx/libs/mail/libMailUmb = b/lib() ];
  return [ progs = b/progs() ];
}
```

**Fig. 6.13.** A control panel model overriding the *libc* library construction used in the build.

How does this override work? Inside the `./Cxx/program` function, there is a point at which the libraries are built. At that point, prior to the construction of each library, the name of the library (here, `libc.a`) is "looked up" in `./lib_ovs`. If the name is present, as in our example, its value (or, more precisely, the value of its `ovs` field) is overlaid on `./Cxx`. Of course, a fresh "`.`" is used for the building of each library, so the override affects the construction of the specifically named library only.

Recall that the construction of each library is delayed until it is needed. Consequently, each library is built according to the overrides *in force at the time the application using it* is built. Hence, different application programs in a release could be built using different customizations of the same library. This, however, would imply a significantly more elaborate control panel model, since it would require constructing different environments (that is, values of "`.`") for the individual applications built by the mail system release model.

## 6.4 Handling Large Scale Software

For Vesta to accommodate the construction of large scale software, the naming used by the standard construction environment must be designed to handle a large number of named artifacts. The standard construction environment addresses this problem by providing various hierarchical name spaces. There are two in particular worth mentioning.

First, the names used to specify packages in a package override are hierarchical, using a name space that (by convention) parallels the repository's package name space. Notice that in the package override example of Figure 6.12, the `pkg_ovs` parameter binds the two-level name `c/libc` to the new version of the package.

Second, the C/C++ bridge of the standard construction environment provides an option for naming libraries in library overrides using hierarchical names. We have already seen that umbrellas can be used to organize libraries hierarchically. As long as the number of libraries is small, a flat name space suffices to name them (and, in most Unix environments, this is conventionally what is used). We've assumed a flat name space in Figure 6.13 in specifying the name of the library (`libc.a`) to be overridden. However, a flat name space is insufficient if the same name is used for two leaf libraries under different umbrellas. To accommodate such a situation, the bridge has a mode in which libraries are named hierarchically. In this mode, a library is named in a library override by its *path* in the library hierarchy, thereby avoiding a naming ambiguity.

## In Summary

This chapter showed how Vesta system description language is used in practice to construct substantial systems, using the example of a simplified email system. It described a particular way to arrange the code of substantial systems to facilitate incremental development by individuals within a larger organizational context. The presentation emphasized the overall structure of the system models written by developers and touched on the facilities provided by the standard environment. However, the discussion stopped short of a look inside the C/C++ bridge and, in particular, the internals of the bridge's `program` function. The reader who seeks to understand the Vesta system at this level of fine detail can study the actual bridge code on the Vesta public web site (see Appendix B). In addition, Section 8.7 presents call graphs for the construction of an actual system. which give a more execution-oriented view of the bridge models discussed in this chapter.

# Part III

# Inside Vesta

The next three chapters explore aspects of Vesta's implementation. These chapters emphasize novel or unusual aspects instead of giving a comprehensive survey of the entire implementation. The treatment assumes considerable familiarity with standard techniques for constructing compilers and operating systems. The reader who wishes only to understand how Vesta appears to its users can skip this material.

Chapter 7 begins by presenting specialized features of the repository that help to implement the exhaustive dependency tracking required for tool encapsulation during Vesta evaluations. It then examines the repository implementation, including the details of replication. Chapter 8 discusses how the Vesta evaluator and function cache server implement fine-grained dependency analysis and caching, which form the core of Vesta's incremental building machinery. Chapter 9 concludes Part III by describing how the weeder supports largely automated management of derived file storage.

# 7

# Inside the Repository

Chapter 4 described the functionality of the Vesta repository as seen by a developer. This chapter examines additional features of the repository, including those used by other components of the Vesta system, and the way in which notable aspects of the repository functionality are implemented.

## 7.1 Support for Evaluation and Caching

The interactions of the Vesta evaluator, function cache, and repository are substantial and occasionally subtle. This makes it difficult to describe any one of them without first describing the others. But since an order is unavoidable, we begin by examining some of the features of the repository that exist especially for the use of the other two subsystems, then return in the next chapter to consider how those systems use these features and provide others required by the repository. The reader seeking to follow this thread may skip to Chapter 8 after reading Section 7.1.

### 7.1.1 Derived Files and Shortids

Like most file systems, the Vesta repository uses a machine-sensible identifier to name the files it stores, and it provides a separate data structure (directories) to map human-sensible names to these machine-sensible identifiers. The latter are 32-bit integer values called *shortids*, and the files they name are ordinary disk files called *shortid files*. The repository provides an interface for allocating a new shortid and creating a corresponding file, and for opening an existing file given its shortid.

From the repository's perspective, a *source file* is simply a shortid file that has a name in the repository's source name space. That is, the shortid is stored in the repository's human- to machine-sensible name mapping. A *derived file*, on the other hand, is a shortid file that the repository is storing on behalf of the Vesta function cache.

Running the Vesta evaluator on a model creates derived files such as object modules, libraries, and executable programs. These files do not acquire permanent names within the repository's name space but do have temporary human-sensible names *within the context of the evaluation in which they are created*, that is, within a running program written in Vesta's system description language. This means that names (identifiers in SDL) may be bound to shortids by the Vesta evaluator, and embedded in bindings or more complicated SDL structures. Most significantly, the Vesta evaluator may, and typically does, write function cache entries that refer to derived files via their shortids. Thus, both ongoing evaluations and persistent function cache entries refer to derived files by shortid.

Because shortids appear in data structures (such as the function cache) that the repository does not manage, it cannot unilaterally delete files. Instead, the Vesta system as a whole adopts an approach called "weeding" (similar to garbage collection) for managing shortid files. (We touched briefly on the operation of the weeder in Section 3.1.3.) When the Vesta weeder deletes a function cache entry, some or all of the deriveds referenced in the entry's result value may become garbage (that is, no cache entries referencing them remain). As the weeder scans the cache using a mark-and-sweep collection algorithm, it assembles a complete list of shortids that are referenced by cache entries being retained. The weeder passes this list and a timestamp to the repository, which augments this list with the shortids it discovers by walking over its own directory tree. The repository can then delete any shortid file that is not on the augmented list and whose contents predate the specified timestamp.[1]

It may seem surprising that sources and deriveds are pooled together by the repository and both are garbage collected during the same weeding process. Why not treat them separately? The main reason is that a source can become a derived, and vice versa. A source becomes a derived (in the sense that a shortid is written into a cache entry) if a function returns a source as part of its result. This happens quite often. Later, the original source's name might be deleted (rebound to a ghost), but the shortid file in which that source was stored will be kept as long as a cache entry still refers to it. A derived becomes a source if an RPC client calls the repository and asks for the derived to be inserted (linked) into a source directory.

The repository also assigns a shortid to every distinct immutable directory. (Two immutable directories that are identical except for their name and parent directory are not considered distinct; they usually have the same shortid.) This feature lets the evaluator and function cache refer to a whole tree of sources with one shortid, allowing a more compact, coarse-grained representation of dependencies on files in the tree. However, this optimization adds another step to the repository's garbage collection algorithm, since for each directory shortid that the weeder asks it to keep, the repository must walk the subtree rooted at the corresponding directory and keep the subdirectories and files there as well.

### 7.1.2 Evaluator Directories and Volatile Directories

The repository provides two special kinds of directories (called *temporary build directories* in Section 3.1.2) specifically for use by the `_run_tool`primitive (Sec-

[1] The timestamp used is the time just before the start of weeding. This ensures that deriveds created by evaluations running in parallel with the weeder are not deleted. See Chapter 9.

tion 5.2.3). Recall that `_run_tool` executes tools (compilers, linkers, etc.) in an environment in which all their file references are intercepted by the Vesta system, which then supplies appropriate, immutable contents. *Evaluator directories* and *volatile directories* implement this restricted file name space.

An evaluator directory serves two purposes at once. It forces file references from a tool to obtain their data from the environment of the Vesta evaluation that invoked the tool, and it enables the evaluator to maintain a record of the specific values on which the tool invocation depends. The former ensures that only immutable files are accessed, while the latter supports the automatic dependency detection that is at the heart of incremental building.

An evaluator directory is an immutable directory whose contents are defined by a binding in the value space of an in-progress Vesta evaluation. A binding, being a name-to-value mapping, can naturally represent a file system directory. If the name $N_1$ in the binding $B$ refers to a value $V_1$ of type Text, then the name $N_1$ in the corresponding evaluator directory $D$ refers to a file with $V_1$ as its contents. If the name $N_2$ in the binding $B$ refers to a nested binding $V_2$, then the name $N_2$ in the directory $D$ refers to a subdirectory whose contents are defined by $V_2$, recursively.[2] An evaluator directory is immutable because it is created and used only while an evaluation is within a call to the language's `_run_tool` primitive, during which time $B$ cannot change.

How is an evaluator directory actually used during a `_run_tool` invocation? When the repository receives an NFS request to list an evaluator directory or look up a name in it, the repository passes the request through to the evaluator via an RPC. When the evaluator receives such a request, it records a dependency on the given name and returns its value (see Section 8.4.2). The value can be either a shortid, representing a file, or a handle for another binding, representing another evaluator directory. The repository then generates the appropriate NFS reply. The repository keeps a cache for each evaluator directory to avoid repeated RPCs for the same name. The immutability and short lifetime of evaluator directories make this cache straightforward.

Evaluator directories hold files (SDL text values) that exist before `_run_tool` is invoked. An external tool also typically creates new files or makes changes to existing ones. Such changes cannot be made directly to the binding backing the corresponding evaluator directory, since that would amount to a side-effect. Instead, the repository records all such changes in *volatile directories*. At the completion of the `_run_tool` call that launched the tool, the changes recorded in the volatile directory are reported back to the caller as part of the `_run_tool` result. (For details, see Section A.3.4.8.)

A volatile directory consists of a pointer to an evaluator directory, called its *base*, and a list of changes. As in a mutable directory, one can create new files or (with copy-on-write) edit existing files in a volatile directory.[3]

---

[2] Unix experts will recognize the need to include I/O devices, especially `/dev/null`, in an evaluator directory, and the repository does indeed provide a way to do that.

[3] See Section 7.2.3 for restrictions.

To summarize, here is how the evaluator, repository, and runtool server interact to run a tool in an encapsulated naming environment.

- An evaluation invokes the `_run_tool` primitive with the arguments described in Section 5.2.3, including the binding that is to supply the initial contents of the tool's root directory.
- The evaluator calls the repository to set up two directories: an evaluator directory backed by the binding and a volatile directory based on the evaluator directory.
- The evaluator invokes the runtool server, which starts the tool with the root directory name "`/`" rebound to the new volatile directory. (On Unix, this step uses the `chroot` system call.)
- Whenever the tool attempts to look up a name in a directory, the volatile directory first consults its list of changes to see if the file was created or modified previously by the tool. If not, it delegates the operation to its base evaluator directory, which in turn passes the request to the evaluator to be recorded as a dependency (as described earlier). Similar delegation is performed when listing a directory's contents.
- After the tool finishes running, the evaluator calls the repository to find out what changes the tool made to its volatile directory and uses this information to construct a result binding. If the tool created or edited any files, their new shortids are returned as part of the change list, and they become deriveds.
- The evaluator deletes the directories it created in the repository, freeing the resources they were consuming.

It should be pointed out that volatile directories are so named not for any fundamental reason, but merely because the repository implementation does not record them on disk and they are lost if the repository crashes and restarts. Any shortid files created are of course recorded on disk; they are later garbage-collected, if necessary, through weeding. This volatility is tolerable because a volatile directory needs to exist only as long as it takes a single tool to run, so the only negative effect is that on the rare occasions when the repository server crashes, any in-progress evaluations fail. In compensation, the task of reclaiming resources after a crash is simplified.

### 7.1.3 Fingerprints

The Vesta function cache employs special 128-bit checksums called *fingerprints* [10, 52] as compact abbreviations for values. Fingerprints are computed in such a way that they are essentially unique. That is, the probability that two different values will have equal fingerprints is vanishingly small. (See Section 8.2 for further details on the use of fingerprints.) As a service to the function cache and evaluator, the repository keeps fingerprints for certain kinds of files and directories and makes them available though an RPC interface.

Every immutable directory and immutable file in the tree rooted at `/vesta` has a fingerprint, because an evaluation can refer to such files and directories as sources. Ghosts, stubs, and appendable directories do not have fingerprints, because a successful evaluation can never refer to one. The repository also supplies fingerprints for files in volatile and evaluator directories, because an evaluation can produce and cache such a file as a derived. Volatile and evaluator directories themselves do not require fingerprints; their existence is ephemeral and the function cache never contains a reference to one.

The implementation of fingerprints is conceptually straightforward but is complicated somewhat by performance considerations. As a result, Vesta uses several different methods of fingerprinting files and directories, and characterizes files as "small" or "large" for fingerprinting purposes. More on this distinction shortly.

Each large immutable file and each immutable directory has a fingerprint based on the full hierarchical name under which it is first placed into the repository. That fingerprint stays with the source as it acquires new names via the check-out/advance/check-in cycle. Fingerprinting based on the name provides the required uniqueness semantics because the repository guarantees that a name is never reused for a different source.

Each large new derived (that is, each large new file in a volatile directory) has a fingerprint based on a unique identifier that is generated when the file is created. That fingerprint is reported back to the evaluator, stored with any function cache entry that points to the file, and supplied again to the repository if the file later appears as an existing file in a new evaluator directory. Fingerprinting based on a unique identifier provides the required semantics because the identifiers are never reused. It gives better performance than fingerprinting the file contents because the identifiers are much shorter than the average large file.

Each small file has a fingerprint computed from its contents. This method of fingerprinting has some interesting consequences. For example, if a user "touches" a source file in a working directory (that is, performs a write to the file that does not actually change the contents), source fingerprinting based on a unique identifier would cause the file to be recompiled and everything that depends on it to be rebuilt. With fingerprinting based on contents, however, the file will be recognized as unchanged and nothing will be rebuilt. Further, suppose a user edits the comments in a source file but does not change the code. This always causes the file to be recompiled, but if the compiler is fully deterministic, the recompilation will generate a derived object file with exactly the same contents as the previous version. With derived fingerprints based on contents, the new derived file will be recognized as identical to the old one, and subsequent build steps that use the compilation output, such as a link step, will not be executed again since they will get a hit in the Vesta function cache. (Unfortunately, some C and C++ compilers insert timestamps into the object files they produce, negating the benefits of fingerprinting these files by contents.)

Because these various types of fingerprinting give equally correct results, the choice between them is based on performance. The threshold that distinguishes "small" and "large" files is therefore dynamically configurable. By default, the threshold is one megabyte; smaller files are fingerprinted by contents, larger ones by unique identifier.[4] Note that changing the size threshold between the fingerprint-

[4] On the hardware described in Chapter 11, a file can be fingerprinted at roughly 1 MB/sec (elapsed time).

ing methods does not cause a correctness problem. The cache and evaluator require only that two files or directories with different contents always have different fingerprints. It is not essential that two files or directories with the same contents always have the same fingerprint, though it is advantageous that they do as often as possible, since that will yield more function cache hits.

Although fingerprinting is chiefly intended to support the Vesta function cache, it has benefits for optimizing the repository implementation as well. The repository includes an internal table that allows any file or directory to be looked up by its fingerprint. This table has two important uses. First, if a user adds a small file to the repository (via **vadvance**) that is already present with the same contents but a different name, the repository looks up the new file's fingerprint in the table, finds that a copy is already present, and arranges for the two files to share storage, thus saving disk space. Second, the replicator (Sections 4.3.3) uses the table to avoid making redundant copies when copying files and directories from one repository to another. The table is not kept on disk, as the repository server is able to rebuild it from other data structures when it starts up.

## 7.2 Inside the Repository Implementation

This section explores selected aspects of the repository implementation, which will be of interest chiefly to readers familiar with file system and file server internals.

### 7.2.1 Directory Implementation

The repository keeps all of its directory structure in virtual memory. This includes all five directory types described previously (appendable, immutable, mutable, evaluator, and volatile), plus stubs and ghosts. File data is of course stored separately in shortid files; directory entries for these files point to them by shortid.

Every directory is implemented as a *base pointer* (possibly null) to another directory plus a *list of changes*. Conceptually, the contents of a directory are the contents of the directory referenced by the base pointer (recursively), augmented and potentially overridden by the change list. This representation is convenient in many commonly occurring situations. For example:

- When a package is checked out, the repository creates a mutable directory whose initial contents are the same as a given immutable directory. This can be done very quickly, since the mutable directory is represented with a base pointer to the immutable directory and an initially empty change list.
- Similarly, when the runtool server is creating a volatile directory to serve as a tool's working directory, it represents it with a base pointer to an evaluator directory that defines the initial contents plus an empty change list.
- A package version and its successor often have many files in common, since generally only a few files change with each revision. Thus, the later version is com-

pactly represented as a pointer to the earlier one together with a list of changes relative to it.[5]

As a result of this representation, the externally visible directory tree is actually stored as a directed acyclic graph, saving a great deal of memory. It is worth noting that, internally, directories do not have parent links. This saves additional space in the common case that a package version and its successor share a subdirectory since, without parent links, there need only be a single copy.

The repository packs its in-memory structure tightly to keep memory consumption down. The goal is to keep the structure small enough to stay resident in physical memory at all times, so that directory access will not be slowed by paging. To this end, references between parts of the structure use 32-bit array indices instead of pointers (which are 64 bits wide on Alpha, the architecture on which Vesta was first implemented), and record fields are arbitrarily byte-aligned. Section 11.3.2 quantifies the effectiveness of this compaction.

To keep the directory data stable, the repository uses a simple logging and checkpointing technique [7]. Whenever a repository client requests an operation that alters the directory data structure, the server appends a record of the operation's name and parameters to a log file and forces it to disk before modifying the in-memory data and returning to the client. If the repository crashes, upon restart it replays the log to restore its state. (Operations on volatile directories are not logged.) To make recovery faster, the repository occasionally makes a *checkpoint* by dumping its state to a file. The next recovery then begins from the most recently committed checkpoint.

The checkpoint code incorporates a special-purpose compacting garbage collector, so checkpointing has the useful side-effect of reducing memory fragmentation. The algorithm is designed for minimal memory usage. First, it writes the compacted checkpoint directly to a file, not to a second ("to-space") memory region as an ordinary copying garbage collector would. Second, when it copies an object, it puts the forwarding pointer to the object's new address (which is needed to keep the object from being copied more than once if there are many pointers to it) into the first few bytes of the object's old location. Thus the algorithm is destructive, necessitating an immediate recovery from the checkpoint file when it is complete.[6] This recovery is transparent to the rest of the system, an effect achieved by including even volatile directory structures in the checkpoint. The volatile structures are written at the end of the checkpoint and are ignored when recovering from a real crash.

This log-and-checkpoint machinery is sufficiently general-purpose that the function cache server uses it as well. The logging mechanism permits an arbitrary number of bytes to be appended atomically, even if the underlying file system and disk controller hardware reorder writes to disk, by including a version number in every disk block. The log packs data tightly into disk blocks, yet ensures that committed data is not lost even if a hardware failure corrupts the block currently being written. It

[5] In principle, this kind of sharing can lead to long base-pointer chains, but this hasn't been a practical problem. Section 11.3.1 shows that lookup performance is adequate.

[6] If the repository server crashes while writing a checkpoint, it will recover from the most recent successful checkpoint and the succeeding operation log.

achieves this by alternately writing two different blocks when adding more data at the tail of the log, like the ping-pong algorithm [22] but avoiding the occasional need to perform the last write twice. The facility also supports fuzzy checkpointing; that is, making a checkpoint in parallel with appending more data. The repository server does not require this feature, but the cache server uses it to enable weeding to proceed in parallel with normal operation.

### 7.2.2 Shortids and Files

The repository server stores shortid files in an ordinary (Unix) file system provided by the underlying operating system, under a fixed directory established when Vesta is installed.[7] Each file's name is derived from its 32-bit shortid. For example, a file with shortid 0x12345678 would have a name like `/vesta-sid/123/456/78`. Intermediate directories such as `/vesta-sid/123` and `/vesta-sid/123/456` are created only when needed and are deleted when they become empty.[8] Vesta users never see these filenames. The `/vesta-sid` directory and all files and directories beneath it have their access permissions set so as to be directly accessible only to the repository server, the function cache server, and the evaluator. Immutable shortid files (those corresponding to immutable source files or to deriveds that have been completely written and are referenced by cache entries) have their write permission bits turned off.

Why do processes other than the repository server itself have direct access to the `/vesta-sid` directory tree? This is a performance consideration. A process that knows a file's shortid can read or write it directly though the underlying file system, thereby avoiding the overhead of passing data through the repository NFS interface while offloading work from the repository server. A further optimization permits processes to create shortid files without contacting the repository for each one. The repository provides an RPC interface that allocates new shortids in blocks of 256. The blocks have leases; that is, ownership of a block times out if it is not periodically renewed, enabling the repository to reclaim blocks allocated to processes that have crashed. A layer of library code provided by the repository implementation hides the complexity of block allocation and lease renewal from client programs.

This efficient route for accessing shortid files unfortunately sees little use. Nearly all accesses to shortid files are through the repository NFS interface. Users of course access sources through NFS. Encapsulated tools read existing sources and deriveds, and write new deriveds, using the repository's NFS interface to volatile directories.

---

[7] Embedding in a file system is not conceptually necessary — implementing on a raw disk makes sense too. While the latter might have enabled some modest performance gains, it would have been considerably more effort and would have made installation and configuration more complicated.

[8] There is no inherent reason for the directory substructure. In principle, a single flat directory of shortids would work. However, in practice, the underlying file system performance degrades with the size of the directory, so some scalable scheme for using multiple directories to hold the shortid files is necessary. The one described here is simple to implement and achieves satisfactory results in practice.

Only a few accesses by the evaluator itself and by the weeder bypass the repository NFS server. In hindsight it would have been simpler to omit this access path, instead making the `/vesta-sid` directory tree a private data structure that is hidden from all processes but the repository server itself.

To conserve memory, the repository server avoids keeping any sort of in-memory structure indexed by shortid. It keeps a record only of which 256-shortid blocks are currently leased. When some process holds a lease on a block, that process maintains a bitmap of unused shortids in the block. The initial value for this bitmap is computed when the block is allocated, by looking at the `/vesta-sid` directory tree and seeing which shortids in the block are currently bound to files. When allocating new blocks, the repository tries to choose empty ones in order to maximize the value of the block to its client, but does not guarantee to do so every time.

The repository does need to keep an index that maps from immutable directory shortids to the actual directory structure in memory. The index is stored as a hash table in memory. The index is infrequently used, so there should be no serious performance problem if it falls out of the repository's working set and needs to be paged back in from disk when used. It would have been more attractive to eliminate this index by invertibly computing a directory's shortid from its memory address, but this was impractical because the repository's checkpointing machinery moves directories to different addresses. At any rate, the index does not take up much space. See Section 11.3.2.

### 7.2.3 Longids

To operate as an NFS server [49, 54], the repository must assign a 32-byte *NFS file handle* to every file and directory it stores, and it must be able to look up a file or directory by its handle. For proper NFS semantics, the meaning of a handle must remain stable across repository crashes and restarts, and a handle for a deleted object must not be reused (at least not soon). To keep from using too much memory, the repository must avoid having a large table that maps from handles to memory addresses, yet it cannot use memory addresses directly as handles because checkpointing moves directories to different addresses.

Another problem the repository faces is how to implement the parent links in a Unix-like directory tree when the internal representation does not store such links. As noted in Section 7.2.1, several externally visible and apparently distinct directories with different parents may share the same internal representation.

The repository solves both these problems with a single mechanism, the *longid*. A longid is a 32-byte value that encodes the path through the externally visible directory tree that was used to reach an object. Each component of the pathname is represented as an index number. The low-order bit of this index number indicates whether the entry is in the mutable change list of the directory or in the immutable base, while the other bits give the entry number within the indicated list. Index number 0 is reserved for use as a pathname terminator. The index numbers are packed into the longid using a variable-width encoding in which the low-order seven bits of each byte carry data and the eighth (high-order) bit, if set, indicates that more bytes follow. Thus small index numbers, which are common, take up less space in the encoding, leaving room for more pathname components. If the encoded longid needs fewer than 32 bytes, the remainder is filled with pathname-terminating zeroes.

Longids have the major properties necessary to implement the NFS file handle semantics. Every object in the externally visible directory tree has its own longid, which remains stable across repository restarts. Longids are not reused, because directory entries are not reused or deleted.[9] The repository looks up the referent of a longid by traversing the directory tree much as if it were looking up the corresponding name. This traversal is fast because the entire tree is kept in memory. Given an object's longid, one can determine its parent's longid simply by truncating the final component.

Longids do not quite provide a perfect implementation of the expected NFS semantics, but the repository is able to paper over the difference effectively. In particular, if an object is renamed, its NFS handle is expected to remain the same. In the repository, an object that is renamed gets a new longid, but the repository replaces its old directory entry with a forwarding pointer to the new one so that its old longid can continue to work also. The old longid stops working if the object's old parent directory is deleted, however. Also, the existence of two handles for the same mutable file will cause an NFS cache coherence problem in the extremely unlikely event that the same client has the file open twice, once under the old handle from before it was renamed and once under the new name and new handle. Even though both opens are done by the same client and thus would normally be coherent, in this case the client sees two different handles, so it will cache the file twice and fail to keep the two copies coherent. In practice, this situation does not arise.

However, longids as described so far have one major drawback. When the evaluator creates a new volatile directory tree to provide an encapsulated environment for a tool, all the files and directories in the tree acquire new, unique longids. But when the evaluator runs several tools in succession in the course of a build, many shortid files are accessed repeatedly. For example, standard C header files are often read by many compilations, and object files that are written by a compilation are normally read by a subsequent link. For good performance, tools should get NFS client cache hits when they access files that other tools have recently accessed, but this is impossible when the same file is seen as having a different file handle each time a new tool is run.

To solve this problem, files in volatile directories are usually given a *shortid-based longid*, a variant of longid that encodes the file's shortid and fingerprint instead of its pathname. Thus, the same shortid file has the same file handle every time any tool encounters it, and the tools see good NFS cache performance.

At first glance, it might appear that shortid-based longids are unconditionally superior. However, shortid-based longids have two drawbacks that keep them from universally displacing pathname-based longids.

---

[9] In directory types that permit deletion, the repository keeps an invisible placeholder for each deleted entry to prevent its index number from being reused.

First, shortid-based longids sacrifice a level of indirection, making copy-on-write (Section 7.2.4) impossible. That is, with a pathname-based longid, there are two levels of indirection; the longid specifies a path through the directory tree, at the end of which is a shortid. Therefore, copy-on-write is achieved simply by changing the shortid in the directory, in particular, replacing an immutable shortid file with a new, mutable copy of the same file with a different shortid. But a shortid-based longid specifies the shortid directly, so its meaning cannot be changed this way. This makes shortid-based longids unsuitable for files in mutable directories, so the repository does not use them there. It also means that tools cannot be allowed to modify existing files in volatile directories because that also requires copy-on-write. This is an inconsequential limitation for most tools, but to accommodate a few tools that need to be able to modify existing files, Vesta makes this functionality selectable by a boolean parameter to the evaluator's `_run_tool` primitive, which is in turn passed to the repository's volatile directory creation primitive.

Second, shortid-based longids sacrifice the ability to find a source object's parent directory. This makes shortid-based longids unsuitable for directories. It also means that a file's access control cannot be inherited from its parent directory, which makes these longids poorly suited for files in immutable and appendable directories. (Recall Sections 4.4.1 and 4.4.2.) One can imagine living with the access control limitation by making all immutable files world-readable and relying on directory access controls to protect them when necessary, but this option would be unattractive.

Fortunately, pathname-based longids provide adequate NFS cache performance in mutable, immutable, and appendable directories because such directories are not created and deleted frequently.

### 7.2.4 Copy-on-Write

The repository uses copy-on-write to save disk space. The basic technique is evident from the representation of directories as a base pointer plus a list of changes. For example, in the case of a **vcheckout** operation, the repository makes a mutable directory based on an immutable one, with an empty change list. Thus, all of the files initially in the mutable directory are actually immutable. When a user tries to write one of these files, the repository copies the data from the immutable file to a new mutable file with a new shortid, adds an entry to the change list of the mutable directory to point to it, and writes the user's data to the new file instead.

Pathname-based longids add an extra complication here. In the situation just described, the new entry has a different index number than the old one, so although the new copy of the file has the same name as the old one, it has a different longid! The repository fixes this problem by setting a flag in the new directory entry to indicate that the old longid should continue to be used, not the new one. When the repository looks up a name to find a longid, if it encounters an entry with this flag set, it looks for another entry containing the same name in the directory's immutable base and uses that entry's index number in the longid. When the repository looks up an object by longid, each time it encounters an index number that points into the immutable base of a mutable directory, it extracts the name from the directory entry found and checks to see if there is a flagged entry in the change list with the same name. This solution uses minimal space but does slow down name and longid lookup somewhat.

The repository also implements copy-on-write for directories. A new mutable directory may be based on an immutable directory with immutable subdirectories. If a user tries to edit a file or make any other change in such a subdirectory, the repository copies the old immutable subdirectory to a new mutable one, and adds an entry to the mutable parent directory to point to it. In this case, of course, the copying itself is optimized by creating the copy as a new directory based on the old one with an initially empty list of changes. If the user's first edit is several levels deep in the directory structure, the copying process is carried out recursively.

### 7.2.5 NFS Interface

The repository NFS server runs entirely in user space. It is simply a software layer on top of the basic repository functionality which, as we have seen, is layered on top of an ordinary file system. The layered, user-space approach makes for simpler implementation and debugging than a kernel-resident approach, but it incurs additional overhead in data copying and context switching. Section 11.3 quantifies repository performance and shows that although the repository provides poorer file system performance than a standard kernel-resident NFS server, it is still fully adequate for Vesta's overall needs.

The NFS server implementation uses a modified version of Sun's ONC (Open Network Computing) RPC library [56,57]. The original library was designed for use only in single-threaded programs; in particular, its server-side duplicate suppression machinery assumes there can be only one outstanding request at a time. But because NFS is built on a simple request/response protocol with no data streaming, NFS implementations generally perform badly unless many NFS reads and/or writes can be in flight simultaneously between the same client and server in separate threads. Therefore, Vesta includes a custom version of the duplicate suppression machinery that enables multithreading and removes this performance bottleneck.

The repository cheats slightly in its implementation of NFS version 2 semantics for mutable files. The NFS2 protocol requires a server to make sure that a write is stable (either on disk or in nonvolatile memory) before acknowledging it to the client. Otherwise, if the server should crash and restart with some data acknowledged but not stable, the client's cache would become incoherent with the server's state and the data would never be written. The repository does not implement these semantics. Instead, it passes writes on mutable files to the underlying operating system before acknowledging them to the client, but it does not wait for the operating system to make them stable. Therefore, if the machine that the repository server is running on (not just the repository process itself) crashes while a client is actively writing to it, a write that the client believes has been done may actually be lost. This case is rare, and it typically should do nothing worse than cause some user who is working at the time of the crash to lose a few edits.

Still, it would still be preferable to resolve this issue in the future. The best fix would be to upgrade the repository's NFS implementation to NFS version 3 [12], which does not require writes to be stable before they are acknowledged; however, this protocol is much more complex than NFS version 2. A simple fix within the NFS2 framework would be to make a Unix `fsync` system call to force each write to be stable before acknowledging it back to the client, but this change would significantly harm the repository's NFS write performance.

The repository does force all writes to a newly created *immutable* file to be stable before acknowledging creation of the file to the requesting client or making it available to other clients for use. It also forces all writes to a derived that is created by a `_run_tool` call to be stable before the evaluator can ask the cache server to write a cache entry referencing it. Thus, since only immutable files and deriveds participate in replication and builds, the repository's loose NFS2 implementation cannot cause disagreement between replicas or inconsistent builds.

### 7.2.6 RPC Interfaces

In addition to the NFS interface, the repository has two RPC interfaces, one for access to shortid files and one for access to the directory structure. These include the operations used by the repository tools to optimize common development cycle operations, as described in Chapter 4. For example, **vcheckout** uses the latter of these interfaces to create a mutable directory based on an immutable one, as described above. Similarly, **vadvance** uses the same interface to efficiently create an immutable directory from the mutable working directory by copying the base pointer and the change list, then marking each entry in the change list as immutable.

The significant repository features available through these interfaces have already been discussed. These interfaces are invoked using the SRPC (simple RPC) package described briefly in Section 11.6.

## 7.3 Implementing Replication

Section 4.3 described the repository's replication facility from the viewpoint of a developer using Vesta. Two aspects of the replication implementation deserve closer attention: the way in which agreement between repositories is preserved and the details of attribute propagation. First, however, we must elaborate on the concept of mastership.

### 7.3.1 Mastership

Section 4.3.1 briefly introduced mastership, explaining its use for appendable directories and stubs. However, the notion applies to every source object in a Vesta repository, including files, directories, stubs, and ghosts. Every such object has a boolean *master* flag that, when true, identifies a master copy. The agreement invariant, to be formalized in the next section, specifies that there is at most one master copy of each object; that is, an object's master flag is true in at most one of the replicas in which it appears. The setting of the master flag affects the operations that are permitted on an object.

For appendable directories, the master copy is the synchronization point for the addition of new names. Arbitrary new names can be freely added to a master appendable directory, but new names can be added to a non-master appendable directory only by copying them from another repository. When an appendable directory is mastered at a particular repository, a complete copy of the subtree rooted at that directory need not be stored in that repository. However, the master repository needs to keep a complete record of bound names to prevent clashes when new names are inserted. To do so it uses stubs and ghosts.

A master stub is a placeholder for data that has yet to be created, and a non-master stub is a placeholder for data that may exist in another repository but is not currently replicated locally. A master stub can be freely replaced with a freshly created master source of any object type, but a non-master stub can be replaced only with a non-master source created by copying from another repository. The reservation stubs described in Section 4.2 are master stubs.

Both master and non-master ghosts indicate that a previously existing source has been deleted. Either type of ghost may be replaced by a copy of the source taken from another replica, with no change in mastership, except that a master ghost cannot be changed to a master appendable directory or master stub. The replicator prohibits the former because it cannot guarantee to restore all the names that were bound in the directory at the time it was deleted. The replicator prohibits the latter because the master stub could in turn be replaced by an arbitrary object different from the name's original, pre-ghost value, thereby violating Vesta's immutability guarantee.[10]

For immutable directories and files, the "at most one master" requirement of the agreement invariant still applies, but mastership has no other enforced meaning. Because an immutable directory can contain only immutable subdirectories and files, never stubs or ghosts, all replicas (whether master or non-master) are necessarily identical. Thus, in each repository, every tree rooted at an immutable directory is either completely present or completely absent. In terms of packages and versions, if any file or directory from a package version is present in a given repository, then that entire version must be present there. Mastership is meaningful for immutable objects only by convention: the master copy is considered the "main" copy, which should not be deleted or replaced with a ghost without thinking twice.

### 7.3.2 Agreement

We can now define Vesta repository agreement formally. Recall the informal definition of agreement (Section 4.3.1): no name is bound to different values in different repositories. Thus, agreement is a global predicate on the combined state of all repositories. A natural way to formalize this is first to define a pairwise agreement

[10] The repository design could have been simplified slightly by eliminating both master and non-master ghosts and using non-master stubs for deleted items instead, at the cost of losing information about whether a source was explicitly deleted or is simply not present locally.

predicate, then to assert that global agreement exists when the pairwise predicate holds for all pairs of repositories.

In the definitions below, let $A$ and $B$ be Vesta source objects, let $A.master$ denote the master flag of $A$, let $A.repos$ denote the repository where $A$ is stored, and if $A$ is a directory, let $A.names$ denote the list of names that are bound in it. Let $A \simeq B$ (read "$A$ agrees with $B$") denote pairwise agreement. Then $A \simeq B$ if and only if the following recursively defined conditions hold:

1. $A.master \wedge B.master \Rightarrow A.repos = B.repos$ and
2. At least one of the following holds:
   a) $A$ and $B$ are files with identical contents.
   b) $A$ and $B$ are immutable directories where
      i. $A.names = B.names$, and
      ii. $\forall n : n \in A.names \Rightarrow A/n \simeq B/n$.
   c) $A$ and $B$ are appendable directories where
      i. $\forall n : n \in A.names \wedge n \in B.names \Rightarrow A/n \simeq B/n$,
      ii. $A.master \Rightarrow B.names \subseteq A.names$, and
      iii. $B.master \Rightarrow A.names \subseteq B.names$.
   d) $A$ and $B$ are both master stubs.
   e) $A$ or $B$ (or both) is a non-master stub.
   f) $A$ or $B$ (or both) is a ghost.

In addition, we say two *repositories* agree when their replicas of the root directory `/vesta` agree.

Condition 1 effectively says that the same source is not mastered in more than one repository (and that agreement is reflexive — a repository agrees with itself). Condition 2d is also needed only for reflexivity. Conditions 2a and 2b require replicas of immutable files and directories to be identical.

Conditions 2c and 2e make partial replication possible. By 2c, two appendable directories can agree even if one or both have only a subset of the complete set of names defined in the directory across all repositories. But the master replica has a complete list of names; thus, the master can coordinate the creation of new names, assuring that the same name is never bound in different replicas to sources that do not agree. By 2e, two appendable directories can agree even if one has a non-master stub where the other has some other object.

Conditions 2d–2f reflect the way stubs and ghosts are intended to be used, as described in the previous section. A master stub agrees only with itself or with a non-master stub, because a master stub represents a source that is to be checked in later. If the master stub is still present, the actual source has not yet been checked in, so it cannot exist in a different repository. A non-master stub, however, agrees with anything. A ghost also agrees with anything, because an object can be deleted from one repository but remain present in others.

Notice that the agreement relation is not transitive; pairwise agreement between $A$ and $B$ and between $B$ and $C$ is not sufficient to guarantee agreement between $A$ and $C$. This nontransitivity is an unavoidable property of partial replication. Replicas are considered to agree when their overlapping portions do not clash, but $A$ and $C$ may overlap and clash in a portion that does not overlap with $B$. For example, suppose that `/vesta/foo` is mastered at repository $A$, and that `/vesta/foo/bar` is an immutable directory in repository $A$, absent in repository $B$, and an immutable file in repository $C$. Then $A \simeq B$ and $B \simeq C$, but the directory at $A$ clashes with the file at $C$, so $A$ does not agree with $C$.

### 7.3.3 Agreement-Preserving Primitives

Given the preceding definition of agreement, it is easy to establish initial agreement among repositories, since a new repository that contains only an empty copy of the root directory `/vesta` agrees with every other repository. Thereafter, each repository operation that alters the agreement-related state must preserve the agreement invariant. For an operation that modifies only one repository $A$, it is sufficient to show that for all repositories $B$, if $A \simeq B$ holds initially, then it still holds after the operation. For an operation that modifies two repositories $A$ and $B$, it is sufficient to show that for all repositories $C$, if $A \simeq B \wedge B \simeq C \wedge C \simeq A$ holds initially, then it still holds after the operation. (Due to the nontransitivity of agreement, all three terms in the postcondition must be proved, and all three in the precondition must be given.)

The repository semantics and the agreement invariant have been carefully designed so that most operations that modify repository state can be safely carried out by one repository acting alone, and no operation requires more that two repositories to participate, while agreement is still preserved. Seven essential primitives underlie all repository operations that can affect agreement-related state.

1. Create a new master appendable directory in `/vesta`, using a unique Internet domain name.
2. Create a new child object of any immutable or appendable type in a master appendable directory.
3. Replace a master stub with a new immutable object.
4. Replace any child of an appendable directory with a ghost that has the same mastership status as the old child.[11]
5. Copy any child into an appendable directory from another repository, possibly replacing an existing ghost or non-master stub. If the original is an appendable directory, the copy is an empty non-master appendable directory. If desired, its children can be copied by further applications of the primitive. If the original is immutable, however, it is copied in full, including all its descendants.
6. Create a non-master stub in an appendable directory, if another repository has that name defined.
7. Transfer mastership on an object from one repository to another, at the same time adding stubs to the new master for any missing children of the old master. (This primitive is used by cross-repository check-out; see Section 4.3.4.)

[11] There are alternative formulations of this functionality that are also safe, such as using a non-master stub in place of a ghost, or completely removing the child if the parent is not master.

As an exercise, the reader may want to check that each of these operations preserves the agreement invariant of the preceding section.

The repository implements these primitives using a series of simpler operations that add and replace single objects. To achieve the necessary atomicity, the repository server uses a mechanism, already implemented to support other features, that provides short atomic transactions on persistent storage within a single repository. Primitives 1–4 run at a single repository; their implementation is straightforward using the transaction mechanism.

Primitives 5 and 6 require consulting another repository, but a multi-site atomic transaction is not required. It is sufficient to read the data from the source repository, then atomically insert a copy into the destination. No lock on the source repository is needed while reading the original, since it cannot change; at worst, it can be replaced with a stub or ghost while the read is in progress, but this simply causes the primitive to return an error without changing the destination.

As mentioned at the end of Section 7.1.3, the destination repository optimizes the copying process in primitive 5 to avoid making redundant copies of objects, such as multiple objects that have the same content but different names. Specifically, each repository keeps an in-memory table in which each locally stored immutable file and immutable directory tree can be looked up by its fingerprint. When an object is to be copied, the destination repository first looks up its fingerprint in the table to find whether a copy is already present. If so, the repository links the existing copy into its name space instead of making another. In addition, if a directory being copied is encoded in the source repository as a list of changes relative to a base directory (Section 7.2.1) and the destination repository already has a copy of the base directory, then the destination encodes the copy in the same way.

Primitive 7, mastership transfer, is the most complex. The implementation guarantees that agreement between repositories is preserved, avoids blocking either repository during the transfer protocol, minimizes the likelihood of a failure resulting in neither repository being master, and keeps a location hint with each non-master object for its associated master repository.

In barest outline, the implementation consists of two separate atomic operations. First, the repository ceding mastership on an object makes a complete list of its children and turns off its master flag. Second, the repository acquiring mastership inserts any missing children into its copy as non-master stubs and turns on the master flag. The implementation also updates the master location hints and keeps a stable record of in-progress transfers at both repositories, persistently retrying them until they are complete. With this implementation, the agreement invariant cannot be violated, and the object can be left without a master only if one repository crashes permanently or the network link between the repositories is permanently severed while a transfer is in progress.

In more detail, the implementation works as follows. Steps carried out by the repository trying to acquire mastership are numbered starting with A1. Steps carried out by the repository ceding mastership are numbered starting with C1 and are indented. Request/grant identifiers and master location hints are stored in mutable attributes (Section 4.4.1).

A1. Check that the requesting user has the necessary access permissions and that the current master repository can be reached over the network; quit if not.
A2. Choose a unique request identifier and record it on the local copy of the object.
A3. Ask the current master to cede mastership, supplying the request identifier.
    Do steps C1–C4 atomically:
  C1. Check that the requesting user has the necessary access permissions; refuse to cede mastership if not.
  C2. Form a grant identifier. If the object is an appendable directory, do this by appending a list of its children to the request identifier; otherwise use the request identifier. Record it on the local copy of the object.
  C3. Change the object's type from master to non-master, and record the new master repository's location on it. This location is of course only a hint, since mastership could move to yet another repository later.
  C4. Return the grant identifier to the caller.
A4. If the current master refused to cede, erase the request identifier and quit.
A5. Atomically fill in any missing children listed in the grant identifier (creating them as non-master stubs), change the object's type from non-master to master, record this repository in the object's master location hint, and record the grant identifier in place of the request identifier.
A6. Ask the old master to erase the grant identifier.
  C5. Erase the grant identifier.
A7. Erase the grant identifier.

The repository that is trying to acquire mastership tries persistently to complete these steps, even if it crashes and restarts during the transfer, until step A7 is finished. Thus mastership will not be lost unless one of the repositories permanently fails (or the network is permanently severed) between steps C4 and A5, and even in this case there will be a record of the incomplete transfer in whichever repository continues running.

### 7.3.4 Propagating Attributes

The definition of repository agreement includes nothing about mutable attributes; two replicas of a source may agree but have entirely different attributes. Each repository can change the attributes of both master and non-master sources, and there is no requirement to propagate attribute changes to other repositories. However, in many cases such propagation is desirable, so the repository includes a feature in the attribute facility to support it.

Section 4.4.1 described attributes as a total function $F$ from names to sets of values, but this is only the user's view. At a lower level of abstraction, an object's attributes are recorded as a history of state changes $H$, represented as a set of timestamped tuples. Each of the four write operations on attributes (`set`, `clear`, `add`, and `remove`) takes a timestamp argument, which can be any value but defaults to the time at which the operation was requested. Applying one of these operations inserts a new tuple into $H$ consisting of the name of the operation and its arguments.

$F(H)$ is then computed whenever needed by starting with an empty mapping, sorting $H$ into timestamp order (with ties broken by taking the operation, name, and value as secondary sort keys), and operating on the mapping as dictated by the resulting sequence of operations.

In addition to the high-level operations that query $F$, there is also a low-level operation to query $H$. This operation does not necessarily return $H$ itself. Instead, it returns a history $K$ that is *equivalent* to $H$, in the following sense. Histories $H$ and $K$ are equivalent if for any history $L$, $F(H \cup L) = F(K \cup L)$. That is, $K$ may as well have been the real history, because one cannot tell the difference by observing either the present state of $F$ or its future states as more operations are applied. The implementation does not store $H$ itself, but stores an equivalent $K$ that is generally smaller. For example, if the same attribute is set twice in succession, only the second operation is retained in $K$. $K$ is represented as a list sorted in timestamp order, which makes the time to compute $F(K)$ or to insert a tuple in $K$ with one of the four write operations linear in the size of $K$.

The representation of attributes using histories provides a way to reconcile the results of attribute operations performed independently on two replicas of the same object in different repositories. If the history $K_A$ at repository $A$ is propagated to repository $B$, $B$ can combine it with the history $K_B$ simply by forming $H = K_A \cup K_B$; the new $F(H)$ then gives a well-defined and reasonable final state for the object. This technique is adapted from Grapevine [6].

To summarize: Vesta propagates attribute changes from one repository to another by sending the timestamped change tuples of the source repository to the destination repository, then forming the union with the second repository's change history.

## In Summary

In this chapter we have examined several aspects of the repository's inner workings, chiefly those that present a significant implementation challenge or strongly influence performance. We also considered the specifics of the replication algorithm, focusing on the underlying machinery required to preserve its invariants with only moderate complexity.

With this knowledge of the repository's internals, we can now look into the implementation of Vesta's most complicated and subtle components, those that support incremental building.

# 8

# Incremental Building

Vesta builds systems by interpreting programs (system models) written in Vesta's system description language. Most aspects of that interpretation are straightforward, since the language is fairly spartan with no semantically complex constructs. However, to achieve essential performance, Vesta implements incremental building. To do this effectively and with maximum benefit for the developers of a large software system presents a significant implementation challenge.

The core issues for incremental building are the accurate detection of fine-grained dependencies and the maintenance of an efficient shared cache of SDL function evaluations. In this chapter, we examine how the Vesta evaluator and function cache do this, assisted by the repository (Section 7.1) and the weeder (Chapter 9).

## 8.1 Overview of Function Caching

Section 3.1.2 explained the basics of Vesta's function caching. When the evaluator interprets a function invocation, it keeps track of every value on which the result depends and records those dependencies with the result in the function cache. When the evaluator is about to invoke a function, it first checks the cache to see if there is a usable cache entry and if so, skips the function invocation and uses the cached result instead.

When is it safe for the evaluator to reuse a cached result? Only when the evaluation context at the current call site agrees with those parts of the context on which some previous call to the same function depended. It is, of course, essential not to omit any dependencies, otherwise the use of the cached result would be unsound.[1] However, it is also important not to err by introducing overly *coarse-grained* dependencies, or the cache will be ineffective, sometimes failing to return a result when it should: a *false miss*.

[1] Vesta's dependency recording and analysis does not make use of any specific knowledge about the workings of the build tools; it is thus *semantics-independent* in the terminology of Gunter [24].

False misses arise because the cache has recorded an unnecessary dependency on the calling context. False misses do not produce incorrect results, but they do create inefficiency. In fact, a false cache miss can be quite costly because it can trigger a cascade of subsequent cache misses. For example, if one source file is recompiled unnecessarily, then all subsequent commands that use the resulting object file (e.g., building a library that contains the file and programs that use the library) may be unnecessarily repeated as well, since a constituent object file will appear to have changed. Hence, the Vesta evaluator works very hard to avoid false cache misses, which means it attempts to record each function call's dependencies as precisely as possible.

For example, consider the following simple function:

```
f(x, y, z) {
  return (if x > 0 then y else z);
}
```

Because of the conditional expression, the arguments on which this function depends vary *dynamically* from call to call. For example, in the call $f(1,2,3)$, the result depends only on the values of $x$ and $y$; the value of $z$ is irrelevant. Hence, the subsequent invocation $f(1,2,7)$ should be able to use the cached result of calling $f(1,2,3)$, since both calls supply identical values for $x$ and $y$.

In this particular example, the observant reader will notice that the exact *value* of $x$ is also unimportant. What matters is simply whether or not $x$ is positive. Hence, to get the most effective caching, dependencies must be expressed as *predicates* on values rather than the exact values themselves.

The problem of recording precise dependencies is further complicated by Vesta's composite value types: lists and bindings. For example, consider a slight modification to the previous example, in which the $y$ argument is a binding:

```
f(x, y, z) {
  return (if x > 0 then y/a else z);
}
```

In this case, the result of the call $f(1,[a=2,b=5],3)$ depends only on $x$ and $y/a$. A subsequent call $f(1,[a=2,b=9],7)$ should produce a cache hit, but recording a dependency on the entire binding $y$ would cause the second call to get a false cache miss. This example demonstrates that the dependencies calculated with respect to composite values should be as *fine-grained* as possible.

From these two examples, we see that the Vesta evaluator faces two challenges in dealing with dynamic, fine-grained dependencies. First, the evaluator needs algorithms to represent, compute, and propagate dependencies with sufficient precision to minimize the costs of false misses. Second, the caching mechanism must work effectively even though the dependencies of a function invocation, being dynamically determined, cannot be known when the cache is consulted at the moment the function is called. The remainder of this chapter explores each of these difficulties in more detail, beginning with the second.

## 8.2 Caching and Dynamic Dependencies

To understand the problem introduced by dynamic dependencies, consider the prototypical case of caching a compilation. Assume that a compilation is invoked by a function call like this:

`compile(`*filename, options,* `.);`

Here, *compile* is the name of a bridge function that uses the `_run_tool` primitive to invoke the C compiler, *filename* is the name of the file to compile, *options* is a binding denoting the command-line options to be passed to the compiler, and "`.`" is the current environment. (The normally implicit parameter "`.`" appears explicitly for emphasis.)

The current environment "`.`" is a binding value that includes a representation of a file system directory tree. This directory tree contains all the files necessary to perform the compilation. As described in Section 5.2.2, SDL makes it easy to construct and extend bindings, so a custom file name space can be constructed quite cheaply for each build.

Figure 8.1 shows a sample environment. Two paths in "`.`" are special: `root` and `root/.WD`. As described in Chapter 3, external tools such as compilers and linkers are run in an encapsulated environment in which all references to files are trapped by the repository and serviced by the evaluator. To service a file request from the repository, the evaluator looks up the file in the current environment. Absolute pathnames are looked up in the `root` subtree, while relative pathnames are looked up in the `root/.WD` subtree.

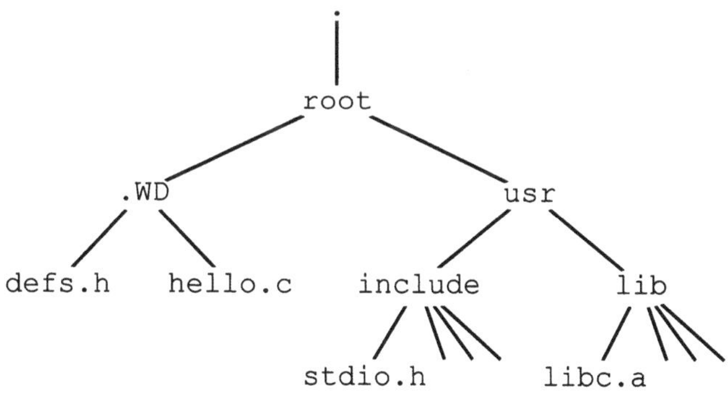


**Fig. 8.1.** The file system directory trees of a sample environment.

Now consider the following invocation of the *compile* function:

```
compile("hello.c", [debug = "-g"], .);
```

Let "`.`" be the binding shown in Figure 8.1. When invoked, this function returns the singleton binding that maps the name "`hello.o`" to the derived object file produced by compiling the file bound to `./root/.WD/hello.c`.

To cache the result of this call, the evaluator computes the fine-grained dependencies and discovers that the call depends on the definition of the *compile* function itself, the values of the first two arguments, and the following parts of the environment:

```
./root/usr/lib/cmplrs/cc
./root/.WD/hello.c
./root/usr/include/stdio.h
```

It would then seem straightforward to write a cache entry consisting of the function (the compiler) and a set of pairs (name and value) representing the dependencies, plus the result computed by the function call. The cache entry would be indexed in the cache by applying a hash function to the sequence of dependency pairs.

Unfortunately, such a cache entry would be useless. For the evaluator to locate this cache entry at the time of a subsequent call of the same function, it must compute a hash of the dependencies, but since these are determined dynamically, the necessary information isn't available at the call site. That is, in order to perform the cache lookup, the evaluator first must determine all the dependencies, which can be determined only by evaluating the function, which renders the cache useless.

To see how to solve this chicken-and-egg problem, consider for a moment the following obviously inefficient caching algorithm. Before performing a function call, the evaluator exhaustively enumerates the cache entries and, for each one, compares the value associated with each name in its dependency set with the value of the corresponding name in the current execution environment. If it gets a match, then the evaluator uses the result value from the matching cache entry instead of invoking the function.

While this brute-force algorithm is obviously impractical, it contains the germ of the idea needed to solve the dynamic dependency problem. Separate the dependencies into two groups, those that can be statically determined at the function invocation site and those that cannot. Call the former the *primary key* and the latter the *secondary key*.[2] Cache lookup then becomes a two-step process. The evaluator computes the primary key and hashes it to access the cache. This yields a small number of candidate cache entries, each of which has its secondary key compared against the call site environment for a possible match. By applying the brute-force algorithm to a few entries only, it becomes efficient.

In reality, some additional modifications are necessary to make this two-step algorithm practical. These modifications add a bit of operational complexity in exchange for reasonable performance.

To begin with, the evaluator does not store in cache entries the values associated with dependencies, since these values may run to thousands or even millions of bytes. Instead of storing the individual values, the evaluator substitutes for each one its *fingerprint*. A fingerprint is a small, fixed-size hash of an arbitrary byte sequence. Fingerprints come with a mathematical guarantee bounding the probability of a collision, so by choosing long enough fingerprints, the probability of a collision can be

[2] This is a slight simplification. Section 8.4 examines more closely the precise way in which the Vesta evaluator distinguishes primary and secondary dependencies.

made vanishingly small.[3] [10,52] So, in effect, $FP(a) = FP(b) \iff a = b$; that is, fingerprinting can be used to test equality of values.

Fingerprints have another attractive property that makes further space economies possible. A fingerprint can be *extended*, either by a byte sequence or another fingerprint, producing a new fingerprint with the same probabilistic guarantee. We write extension with the non-commutative operator $\oplus$, e.g., $fp_3 = fp_1 \oplus bytes$ and $fp_3 = fp_1 \oplus fp_2$. The latter version is particularly relevant for cache key computations.

The primary key (PK) of a cache entry is formed by combining the fingerprints of the primary dependency values, using $\oplus$. Each secondary dependency consists of a name and the fingerprint of the corresponding value. Together, these secondary dependency names and fingerprints form the cache entry's secondary key (SK). Overall, then, a cache entry is a triple of the following form:

$\langle$ primary-key, secondary-key, result-value $\rangle$

Here, the primary key is a single fingerprint, the secondary key is a set of (name, fingerprint) pairs, and the result value is the function's full result value, suitable for use by the evaluator in the event of a cache hit.

Figure 8.2 shows the primary and secondary keys computed for the example compilation above. First, the fingerprint $Q$ of the *compile* function itself and the fingerprints $R$ and $S$ of the first two function arguments are computed. These fingerprints are then combined to form a new fingerprint $A$, the primary key. As the function is evaluated, three references to "`.`" are noted. Their names and the fingerprints $B$, $C$, and $D$ of their corresponding values are recorded as secondary dependencies. The cache entry formed for this function evaluation is a triple consisting of the primary key, secondary dependency names and fingerprints, and the result value of the evaluation.

It is common for multiple cache entries to have the same primary key. In particular, this occurs whenever a source file is edited and recompiled. Figure 8.3 shows an example. In that figure, the two columns of fingerprints on the right denote two different cache entries. Both cache entries correspond to the compilation of a file named "`hello.c`" with the same compilation switches, so both entries have the same primary key $A$. However, between the two compilations, the source file "`hello.c`" has been edited, so the fingerprint for the corresponding secondary dependency has changed from $C$ to $E$.[4] Since the secondary dependencies for the two evaluations are different, two different entries are stored in the cache.

An important consequence of using dynamic fine-grained dependencies is that the set of secondary dependency *names* may differ from one cache entry to the next,

[3] Vesta uses 128-bit fingerprints. Based on an overall system size of 20 million source lines (see page 30) and some conservative estimates about the number of versions of each source file, the probability of a collision occurring over the expected lifetime of the Vesta system is much less than $2^{-42}$.

[4] Of course, `hello.c` hasn't really been "edited", since Vesta source files are immutable. More precisely, the name `hello.c` is now bound to a different version of the source file than was the case when the initial cache entry was constructed.

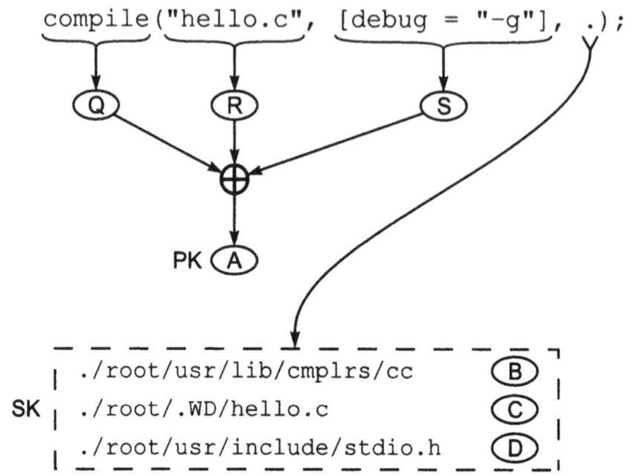


**Fig. 8.2.** The primary key (PK) and secondary key (SK) of a single cache entry.

| | | Entries 0 | Entries 1 |
|---|---|---|---|
| | Primary Key (PK) | A | A |
| SK | ./root/usr/lib/cmplrs/cc | B | B |
| SK | ./root/.WD/hello.c | C | E |
| SK | ./root/usr/include/stdio.h | D | D |

**Fig. 8.3.** Two cache entries with the same primary key (PK).

| | | Entries 0 | 1 | 2 | 3 | X |
|---|---|---|---|---|---|---|
| | Primary Key (PK) | A | A | A | A | A |
| SK | ./root/usr/lib/cmplrs/cc | B | B | B | B | B |
| SK | ./root/.WD/hello.c | C | E | F | F | F |
| SK | ./root/usr/include/stdio.h | D | D | | | J |
| SK | ./root/.WD/defs.h | | | G | H | H |

**Fig. 8.4.** Multiple cache entries with the same primary key (PK), but with differing sets of secondary dependency names.

even among entries with the same primary key. (By definition, the set of names contributing to the primary key is statically determined, so there is no need to include them in the PK calculation.) An example is shown in Figure 8.4, where cache entries 1 and 2 have different sets of secondary dependency names because the file "`hello.c`" was edited to include (in the sense of the C preprocessor's `#include` directive) a file named "`defs.h`" instead of "`stdio.h`". The difference between entries 2 and 3 is that the file "`defs.h`" was changed.

Figure 8.4 also illustrates an important property of the Vesta caching strategy. Correct (i.e., sound) caching requires that all cached functions be functional and deterministic; that is, the same (possibly dynamic) inputs always produce the same output.[5] This means that cache entries like the one labeled "X" in the figure cannot be created. Note that the fingerprints of cache entry X agree with those of cache entry 3 for those secondary dependencies shared by the two entries, but entry X has an additional secondary dependency on the file "`stdio.h`". A little thought shows that this cannot occur in a functional, deterministic program. All external tools (compilers, linkers, etc.) invoked from Vesta evaluations as well as functions written in SDL behave properly in this respect.

## 8.3 The Function Cache Interface

Having examined primary and secondary dependencies, we can now consider the two-step cache lookup process in detail. Figure 8.4 helps illustrate how lookups in the cache are performed. We continue with the function call from our running example:

```
compile("hello.c", [debug = "-g"], .);
```

The cache lookup protocol involves two remote procedure calls (RPCs) from a client evaluator to the function cache server.

1. In the first RPC (the "SecondaryNames" step), the evaluator computes the primary key from the function call site (as shown in Figure 8.2), and passes it to the function cache. In response, the cache returns a set of names that is the *union* of all secondary dependency names associated with cache entries having the designated primary key. In our example, the secondary dependency names are the four pathnames shown in Figure 8.4.
2. In the second RPC (the "Lookup" step), the evaluator computes the fingerprints of the values associated with each of those secondary dependency names in the current evaluation context and sends them to the function cache. The function cache then compares those fingerprints to each of the entries with the designated primary key, looking for a match between the fingerprints from the evaluation context and those in a cache entry. In our example, the received fingerprints are compared to the columns of Figure 8.4. If any column matches, a cache hit is reported and the result value from the selected cache entry is returned. Otherwise, a cache miss is reported.

In the event of a cache miss, the evaluator proceeds to execute the function, recording dynamic fine-grained dependencies along the way (as described in Section 8.4 below). It then forms the primary key, secondary key, and result value for a new cache entry, and calls a method of the function cache interface that adds this new entry to the cache.

[5] This requirement is stated more strictly than is actually necessary. For example, some compilers embed a timestamp in the object files they generate, so strictly speaking, the contents of generated object files depend on when the compiler is run. However, such embedded timestamps are semantically irrelevant to the use of the object files, so it is safe to treat the compiler as a functional tool.

This two-step protocol minimizes the amount of data that has to flow between client and server during a cache lookup, which is important for performance. However, because the lookup process requires two steps, it is possible that other cache operations may occur between them. In particular, what should be done if another client adds a new cache entry that includes some new secondary names, that is, names that did not appear in the set returned by the SecondaryNames step? Locking the cache against updates between the two RPCs would eliminate the problem, but is unappealing. Instead, the protocol uses optimistic concurrency. The Lookup step may return a result indicating that the set of names returned from the SecondaryNames step is stale, in which case the client restarts the protocol afresh.

## 8.4 Computing Fine-Grained Dependencies

Now that we have seen the process by which cache lookups occur, we can turn our attention to the other major complexity of incremental building, the computation of fine-grained dependencies. We begin with a brief description of the technique used by the evaluator to represent dependencies, then examine in turn the three major cases it must handle.

### 8.4.1 Representing Dependencies

As noted earlier, dependencies in general are predicates on the evaluation context. In order for a cache hit to occur, these predicates must hold. Consequently, a dependency that is too coarse-grained corresponds to a predicate that is unnecessarily strong. The evaluator's goal is to record dependencies that are as weak as possible but strong enough to capture the relevant aspects of the state.

In practice, the dependencies recorded by the evaluator are not the weakest possible predicates. Sometimes, unnecessarily strong dependencies are deliberately used because they can be represented more compactly and are therefore easier and cheaper to manipulate and check. Inevitably, there is a tradeoff between the strength of the recorded dependencies and the cost of a cache miss. Of course, the evaluator must never record a dependency that is too weak, since that would produce false cache hits and incorrect builds.

In balancing this tradeoff, the Vesta evaluator avoids representing arbitrary predicates. Instead, it uses a small, fixed collection of predicates, encoded as *dependency paths*. It is these dependency paths that are passed to the function cache as the names in a cache entry's secondary key.

The following grammar gives the syntax of a dependency path:

$$
\begin{aligned}
\mathit{dpath} &::= t\!:\!\mathit{path} \\
t &::= V\,|\,X\,|\,D\,|\,T\,|\,L\,|\,E \\
\mathit{path} &::= \varepsilon\,|\,\mathit{id}/\mathit{path}
\end{aligned}
$$

A dependency path thus takes the form $t$:*path*, where $t$ denotes the dependency type, and *path* specifies the component of the evaluation context on which the evaluation depends. $\varepsilon$ denotes an empty path; a path of the form *id*/$\varepsilon$ or $\varepsilon$/*id* is equivalent to the path *id*.

The *type* is a single-character code that selects a predicate on the path's value that must be satisfied for the dependency to match. The *path* is a hierarchical name that is meaningful in the context of the function call being evaluated. However, despite its appearance, *path* should not be confused with an SDL expression that selects a member from a (possibly nested) binding. Indeed, if *a* is a binding containing a field *b*, then the path used for dependency recording purposes is *a*/*b*, which looks just like the Vesta language expression for selecting the field. However, if *a* is a closure, the path *a*/*b* represents for dependency purposes the value of *b* in *a*'s context. The corresponding SDL expression is erroneous.

Associated with each dependency path is a value whose fingerprint is passed to the cache on a lookup operation or when a new cache entry is created. The rules for computing the value associated with a dependency path vary depending on the dependency type and the kind of function being evaluated. These rules are described in the sections that follow.

We can now look in detail at the algorithms used by the evaluator to collect and store dependency information for the three kinds of function calls that produce cache entries: tool invocations (i.e., calls of `_run_tool`), user-defined function calls, and system model evaluations.

### 8.4.2 Caching External Tool Invocations

Calls to the `_run_tool` primitive are the leaves of a Vesta evaluation's call graph. Caching these calls is fairly straightforward. The primary key for the cache entry is formed by combining a fixed fingerprint for the `_run_tool` primitive with the fingerprints of all of the function's arguments except the implicit "`.`" argument.[6] As described in Section 5.2.3, the tool's file name space is supplied via the binding `./root`. Obviously, recording a dependency on the complete file name space represented by `./root` would be too coarse-grained, since it is very unlikely that the tool will access all the files in that directory tree. Instead, references into this file name space during the tool's execution form the cache entry's secondary key. As described in Sections 3.1.2 and 7.1.2, the tool's file system references are intercepted by the repository, sent to the evaluator, and satisfied by the evaluator by doing lookups in the binding `./root`.

Actually, the repository distinguishes two different kinds of requests from the tool, and the evaluator can record several different types of secondary dependencies based on the kind of request and its outcome. A *lookup* request occurs when the tool looks up a name in a binding that represents a filesystem directory. A *list* request

[6] To be strictly correct, the primary key also includes the environment variables, which are passed to `_run_tool` in `./envVars`. This is a matter of expedience. It would be preferable to record dependencies on only those environment variables read by the tool, but there is no mechanism for intercepting such references in Unix. Since, in practice, few tools require any environment variables to be set, the coarser-than-necessary dependencies on environment variables have made no discernable difference.

occurs when the tool enumerates the entries in such a binding. Table 8.1 lists the dependencies that the evaluator creates in response to repository requests during a tool execution. We look at these in turn.

| Operation | Dependency Path | Value |
|---|---|---|
| lookup(*dir*, *file*) ⇒ success | $V$:*dir*/*file* | Value(*dir*/*file*) |
| lookup(*dir1*, *dir2*) ⇒ success | $T$:*dir1*/*dir2* | "t_binding" |
| lookup(*dir*, *name*) ⇒ failure | $X$:*dir*/*name* | FALSE |
| list(*dir*) | $D$:*dir* | domain(*dir*) |

**Table 8.1.** The dependency types recorded by the evaluator during external tool invocations.

When a name lookup succeeds and returns a file, the evaluator passes the file's shortid (see Section 7.1.1) back to the repository and records a *value* ($V$) dependency. The dependency's associated value is the fingerprint of the file supplied by the repository (see Section 7.1.3).

When a name lookup succeeds and returns a directory, the evaluator passes a handle for the directory back to the repository. The tool now knows that the directory exists, so the evaluator records a dependency reflecting this fact. Since the evaluator treats directories as bindings, it records a *type* ($T$) dependency on the directory's pathname, with value "t_binding". If the tool does nothing else with the directory, this is the dependency that will be recorded. However, in most cases, the tool will subsequently look up a name in the directory; that is, it will perform a lookup using a path that has the directory name as a prefix. The result of this lookup yields a new dependency path, per the table, which replaces the type dependency on the parent directory. That is, a dependency of any type on the path *d*/*n* implies that the value of $T$:*d* is "t_binding". This situation arises very often, making the optimization, which ultimately omits a secondary dependency in the cache entry, highly worthwhile.

When a name lookup fails, the evaluator returns a "not found" result to the repository and records an *existence* ($X$) dependency on the path. Since the path does not yield a value, the dependency's associated value is (the fingerprint of) FALSE.

Finally, if the evaluator receives a request to list a directory, it records a *domain* ($D$) dependency. To obtain the dependency's value fingerprint, the evaluator combines the fingerprints of the names defined by the corresponding binding, in a canonical order. The values bound to those names are not included in the fingerprint. This procedure reflects the semantics of listing a directory, since the result depends only on what names are defined and their order, not on what the names are bound to.

Table 8.2 shows some of the secondary dependencies that might be recorded for a simple compilation of a file named "hello.c". The fingerprints listed are those supplied by the repository for the corresponding files (except, of course, for *FP*(FALSE)).

Correctness requires that the evaluator record a FALSE existence ($X$) dependency when a lookup request fails, as in the third line of Table 8.2. Consider the following common situation, illustrated by the table. A compiler typically searches

| Type | Path | Fingerprint |
|---|---|---|
| *V* | `./root/usr/lib/cmplrs/cc` | *FP*(`cc`) |
| *V* | `./root/.WD/hello.c` | *FP*(`hello.c`) |
| *X* | `./root/.WD/stdio.h` | *FP*(FALSE) |
| *V* | `./root/usr/include/stdio.h` | *FP*(`stdio.h`) |
| ⋮ | ⋮ | ⋮ |

**Table 8.2.** Some of the secondary dependencies for a simple compilation of the file "hello.c". *FP* denotes the fingerprint function.

several directories for header files (using a search path, described in Section 2.4). In our example, it searches the working directory (`.root/.WD`), then a standard location (`./root/usr/include`). Assume, as in this case, that the file `stdio.h` is found in the standard location rather than the working directory. Suppose that the evaluator failed to record a dependency on the non-existence of the file in the working directory. This would result in a cache entry with the secondary dependencies listed in the table *but omitting the third line*. Now, consider a subsequent compilation in an identical environment except that the working directory now contains a file named `stdio.h`. Obviously, this compilation should miss in the cache, but, because of the way secondary dependencies are processed, it will incorrectly hit. Why? Recall from Section 8.3 that the function cache server will send to the evaluator a list of names of secondary dependencies whose fingerprints are to be obtained from the current evaluation context. That list will include `./root/usr/include/stdio.h`, and when the evaluator returns its fingerprint, there will be a match with the one in the cache entry, implying a dependency match. But the new evaluation should not depend on that file, since, were the compilation to be carried out, it would access `./root/.WD/stdio.h` instead. Thus, the evaluator's failure to record the first evaluation's dependence on the non-existence of this file has produced an erroneous cache hit, which of course, is unacceptable.[7] It is easy to see that including the non-existence dependency causes a cache miss, as required.

### 8.4.3 Caching User-Defined Function Evaluations

Computing fine-grained dependencies for calls to `_run_tool`, described above, is relatively straightforward, since those dependencies are limited to file system accesses. But handling the general case of caching a call to a user-defined function written in SDL is considerably more complex; indeed, it is the most complicated and subtle part of the evaluator.

We define the rules for dependency calculations during the evaluation of a user-defined function by induction on the grammar for the language constructs that can

[7] It is worth noting that some popular build systems do not handle this situation correctly. For example, ClearCASE [4] records dependencies only on existing files. Makefiles generated by the Unix Makedepend tool have this problem as well. In both cases, this deficiency can produce inconsistent builds.

| | |
|---|---|
| $e ::=$ | |
| $\mid a$ | literal (constant) |
| $\mid x$ | variable (identifier) |
| $\mid \lambda x.e$ | lambda (closure) |
| $\mid$ **if** $e_1$ **then** $e_2$ **else** $e_3$ | conditional |
| $\mid [n_1 = e_1, n_2 = e_2, \ldots, n_k = e_k]$ | binding constructor |
| $\mid e/n$ | binding selection |
| $\mid e!n$ | binding domain test |
| $\mid e_1 + e_2$ | binding overlay |
| $\mid$ **let** $x = e_1$ **in** $e_2$ | variable introduction |
| $\mid e_1(e_2)$ | function application |

**Table 8.3.** The syntax of a semantic subset of SDL.

appear in a function body. To keep the case analysis manageable, the discussion here is restricted to a semantic subset of SDL whose syntax appears in Table 8.3. This subset includes the core parts of SDL and all the features that significantly affect the calculation of fine-grained dependencies. The subset language omits SDL's sixty-plus primitive functions, the iteration construct, and the `import` clause, for which dependency calculations are straightforward. The grammar in the table uses the following conventions: $a$ is any constant (that is, any member of *Literal*, the set of all possible constants in the language), $x$ is a variable (that is, any member of *Id*, the set of all possible identifiers), $e$ is an expression, and $n$ is a name. The constructs of the subset language should all be familiar except perhaps the boolean-valued expression $e!n$, which tests whether the name $n$ is bound in the binding $e$.

As it interprets a Vesta expression (that is, a syntactic construct), the evaluator computes both a value and a set of dependencies for that value. Every expression is evaluated in some *evaluation context*, which is a function from variable names (identifiers) to values. $Eval(e,c)$ denotes the result of evaluating the expression $e$ in the context $c$ and $Dpnd(e,c)$ denotes the dependency paths resulting from evaluating $e$ in $c$. Thus, the dependencies are precisely the values of $Dpnd(e,c)$, where $e$ ranges over the syntactic forms in the subset language of Table 8.3.[8]

Before diving into the details of the dependency rules, we need to consider more closely the workings of the evaluator as it prepares and uses cache entries.

## The Composition of Cache Keys

We saw earlier the separation of dependencies into primary and secondary groups and the way these groups appear in the two-step cache lookup protocol. We observed that the primary key should include only information available at the call site, but how does the evaluator decide specifically what information that should be? The obvious approach of using all the function arguments produces too coarse-grained a result, as we saw. The other extreme, using none of the arguments, groups too many

[8] Rules for evaluation of the complete language appear in Section A.3.3.

cache entries under the same primary key (e.g., all invocations of the `compile` function, regardless of the file being compiled) with poor lookup performance as the result.

The evaluator adopts a middle course. For the primary key, it combines the fingerprint of the function being invoked (which is actually a fingerprint of its parse tree) with the fingerprints of "simple" arguments (that is, booleans, integers, and texts). The evaluator records fine-grained secondary dependencies for everything else, specifically lists, bindings, and closures. This is a natural strategy based on the need for fine-grained dependencies, since all the values whose fingerprints form the primary key have no fine structure.[9]

### The Interaction of Caching and Evaluation

We noted that the evaluator computes a pair for each syntactic construct it interprets. This pair consists of the value as defined by the SDL semantics (that is, the value as perceived by the user) and the dependencies of that value. The dependencies are invisible to the user, but are an implementation necessity. In reality, it is this value-dependency pair that is stored in a cache entry as the result of a function call. Thus, when the evaluator encounters a function call, it can consult the function cache and either obtain the result from the cache (a hit) or proceed to interpret the call (a miss). Either way, it will have both the SDL-defined value and the implementation-required dependencies it needs to continue evaluation.

This interchangeability of function call result and cache result is formalized as a theorem later (page 130); what is important here is the intuition behind it. Assume that the cache contains an entry with primary key *pk* that resulted from evaluating the expression *e* in a context $c_1$. The secondary names associated with this cache entry will be the set of dependencies[10] $\mathit{Dpnd}(e, c_1)$. When the evaluator is interpreting *e* in another context $c_2$, it will consult the cache. It should get a hit on the cached entry only if the values computed in $c_2$ for the dependencies $\mathit{Dpnd}(e, c_1)$ match the values stored in the cache. Note that the values associated with the dependencies in the cache are precisely those computed in $c_1$ for $\mathit{Dpnd}(e, c_1)$.

We therefore define *equivalence* between two contexts with respect to a set of dependencies *d* as follows:

$$\mathit{Equiv}(c_1, c_2, d) \equiv (\forall p \in d : \mathit{Value}(p, c_1) = \mathit{Value}(p, c_2)).$$

---

9 The Vesta language includes a construct (a stylized comment, or "pragma") that enables the writer of a function to indicate explicitly which parameters are to be included in the primary key calculation (see Section A.3.3.17). In practice, this facility is rarely needed, and then only in specialized situations (e.g. in writing a bridge).

10 The previous section mentioned that the cache stores secondary names. In fact, the cache treats these names as uninterpreted strings, and the evaluator exploits this fact to store dependency paths, which are more complex than simple names. Hence, the terms "secondary name", "dependency", and "dependency path" are essentially interchangeable when they refer to the content of cache entries.

In this definition, $Value(p,c)$ denotes the result of "evaluating" the dependency path $p$ in the context $c$. It corresponds to the fingerprint associated with each secondary name in the cache.

Clearly, the cache should produce a hit only if performing the evaluation of $e$ in $c_2$ would yield the same result as the one stored in the cache, that is:

$$Equiv(c_1, c_2, Dpnd(e, c_1)) \Longrightarrow Eval(e, c_2) = Eval(e, c_1).$$

This is essentially the correctness theorem, which is stated in more technical form at the conclusion of this section.

We now are ready to look at the specifics of dependency calculation for user-defined functions.

### Dependency Types

During the invocation of a user-defined Vesta function, the evaluator records six different types of dependencies, shown in Table 8.4. The table also shows in each case the rule that the evaluator uses to compute $Value(t : path, c)$, the value of the dependency path $t{:}path$ in the context $c$.

| Type | Dependency on the component's ... | Computed Value |
|---|---|---|
| $V$ | ...complete value | $Value(V : path, c) = Eval(path, c)$ |
| $X$ | ...existence | $Value(X : path/id, c) = Eval(path!id, c)$ |
| $D$ | ...domain | $Value(D : path, c) = \{n \mid Eval(path!n, c)\}$ |
| $T$ | ...type | $Value(T : path, c) = Eval(typeof(path), c)$ |
| $L$ | ...length | $Value(L : path, c) = Eval(length(path), c)$ |
| $E$ | ...expression (closures) | $Value(E : path, c) = Eval(path, c).body$ |

**Table 8.4.** The meanings of the six dependency types and the rules used by the evaluator to evaluate each type of path in a context $c$.

The first four dependency types are familiar from the previous section's discussion of calls of the `_run_tool` primitive. As before, $V$ denotes a dependency on the entire run-time value. $X$, $D$, and $T$ are broader in scope than previously described, as they apply to named values in SDL, not just file and directory names. That is, $X$ denotes a dependency on the existence (or non-existence) of a name in a binding or closure context, $D$ denotes a dependency on the domain of a binding (i.e., the sequence of names in the binding's domain), and $T$ denotes a dependency on the run-time type of a value, in the sense of the `_type_of` primitive (see Section A.3.4.7).

The $L$ dependency type denotes a dependency on the length of a list or binding. It arises solely from the use of the `_length` primitive.

Finally, $E$ denotes a dependency on the value of a closure *cl*'s expression (that is, its function body), indicated by the notation *cl.body*.[11]

It is perhaps worth repeating that there is nothing fundamental about this set of dependency types. They encode predicates that were chosen based on practical considerations and experience in using the Vesta language. This set of dependency types works well for the standard construction environment (Section 6.2.1) and should work well for many similar environments. It is possible, of course, that a radically different style of use of the Vesta language might reveal a need for additional dependency types to record weaker dependencies in certain situations.

### Dependency Calculation Rules

Armed with the dependency types and (subset) SDL grammar, we can now write the mathematical rules for calculating dependencies. We first define $D(e,c,t\!:\!p)$ where $t\!:\!p$ is a dependency path; $D(e,c,t\!:\!p)$ evaluates to a set of dependency paths. We then define $Dpnd(e,c) = D(e,c,V\!:\!\varepsilon)$. Intuitively, $D(e,c,t\!:\!p)$ is the dependency for just the portion of $e$'s value that is "selected by" $p$, in the sense that a name selects a value from a binding and a path selects a value from a nested collection of bindings. The definition of $D(e,c,t\!:\!p)$ now proceeds by cases on the productions of the SDL grammar:[12]

- If $e = a$ ($a \in Literal$), then $D(e,c,t\!:\!p) = \{\}$. Evaluating a constant has no dependency on the context.
- If $e = x$ ($x \in Id$), then $D(e,c,t\!:\!p) = \{t\!:\!x/p\}$. Evaluating a variable $x$ depends only on the dependency path extended on the left by $x$.
- If $e = \lambda x.e_1$, only the following three cases arise:

$$\begin{aligned} &D(e,c,V\!:\!\varepsilon) = \{V\!:\!n \mid n \in FVs(e)\} \\ &D(e,c,E\!:\!\varepsilon) = \{\} \\ &D(e,c,t\!:\!y/p) = \{t\!:\!y/p\},\ \text{if } y \in FVs(e) \end{aligned}$$

  where $FVs(e)$ denotes the set of $e$'s free variables. In the first two cases, the path is empty. If the type of the path is $V$, the lambda expression depends on

[11] As noted in connection with the `_run_tool` primitive, some dependencies imply others. For example, the value ($V$) dependency implies the other five, meaning that the evaluator could choose to discard one of the others if it encounters a value dependency with the same dependency path. At present, the evaluator does not attempt to minimize the set of dependencies recorded in a cache entry by eliminating those subsumed by others. There are space and time tradeoffs here, which have not been fully investigated.

[12] The dependency calculation explained here is related to earlier work by Abadi, Lampson, and Lévy [1], which uses a labeled $\lambda$-calculus to compute both dynamic and fine-grained dependencies. However, their approach is significantly different. It associates labels with all expressions in a function body, and then develops rules for keeping the labels of only those expressions that are evaluated during a call. As a result, it records only one kind of dependency, analogous to the value dependencies used here. Also, their calculus supports only the selection operation on records. Computing dependencies for the binding operators ! and + complicates the problem significantly.

the whole closure value, that is, the values of $e$'s free variables (excluding the closure argument $x$). If the type of the path is $E$, it depends on only the lambda expression of the closure value, namely, the expression $e$. Here, a shortcut is possible. Since dependency analysis is used for secondary dependencies only and since $e$ is incorporated into the primary key for every call of $e$, there is no need to record a (secondary) dependency on $e$ at all. Hence the empty set in the second case above. Finally, in the third case, the path is not empty and $y$ is a free variable of $e$. It signifies a dependency only on the portion of $y$'s value that is selected by $p$.

- If $e$ = **if** $e_1$ **then** $e_2$ **else** $e_3$, the rule is:

$$\frac{\begin{array}{c} d_1 = D(e_1, c, V\!:\!\varepsilon) \\ v_1 = \mathit{Eval}(e_1, c) \\ d_2 = \text{ if } v_1 \text{ then } D(e_2, c, t\!:\!p) \text{ else } D(e_3, c, t\!:\!p) \end{array}}{D(e, c, t\!:\!p) = d_1 \cup d_2}$$

This rule states that the dependency of a conditional is the union of the dependencies of the guard $e_1$ and the dependency of either $e_2$ or $e_3$, depending on the value of $e_1$. An empty path is used in computing the guard's dependencies because the guard evaluates to a boolean value that has no components.

- If $e = [n_1 = e_1, n_2 = e_2, \ldots, n_k = e_k]$, there are two cases to consider. If $p$ is empty, it signifies a dependency on the entire binding:

$$D(e, c, t\!:\!\varepsilon) = \cup_{i=1}^{k} D(e_i, c, V\!:\!\varepsilon)$$

If $p = t\!:\!n_i/p'$, it signifies a dependency only on the value of field $n_i$:

$$D(e, c, t\!:\!n_i/p') = D(e_i, c, t\!:\!p')$$

- If $e = e_1/n$, then $D(e, c, t\!:\!p) = D(e_1, c, t\!:\!n/p)$. This is binding selection, and the rule says to recursively apply $D$ with the path extended on the left by $n$.
- If $e = e_1!n$, then $D(e, c, t\!:\!p) = D(e_1, c, X\!:\!n/p)$. This is a binding domain test, and the rule says to recursively apply $D$ with the path extended on the left by $n$. Compare this with the preceding rule and note that the new dependency path has type $X$, regardless of the type $t$.
- If $e = e_1 + e_2$, then there are two cases to consider: If $p$ is empty, it signifies a dependency on the entire binding:

$$\begin{array}{l} D(e, c, t\!:\!\varepsilon) = \\ \quad D(e_1, c, V\!:\!\varepsilon) \cup D(e_2, c, V\!:\!\varepsilon) \end{array}$$

If $p = t\!:\!n/p'$, it signifies a dependency only on the binding that supplies the $n$ field. In the case that the $n$ field comes from $e_1$, the semantics of $n$ require adding the dependency that $n$ is not defined in $e_2$:

$$\begin{array}{l} D(e, c, t\!:\!n/p') = \\ \quad \text{if } \mathit{Eval}(e_2!n, c) \\ \quad \text{then } D(e_2, c, t\!:\!n/p') \\ \quad \text{else } D(e_2, c, X\!:\!n) \cup D(e_1, c, t\!:\!n/p') \end{array}$$

- If $e = \textbf{let}\ x = e_1\ \textbf{in}\ e_2$, then

$$\frac{\begin{array}{c} c_1 = c \circ \{x \rightarrow Eval(e_1,c)\} \\ d_2 = D(e_2,c_1,t:p) \\ d_{2a} = \{t':p' \mid t':p' \in d_2 \wedge head(p') \neq x\} \\ d_{2b} = \{t':p' \mid t':x/p' \in d_2\} \end{array}}{D(e,c,t:p) = d_{2a} \bigcup \bigcup_{t':p' \in d_{2b}} D(e_1,c,t':p')}$$

where $\circ$ denotes the operation for extending a context (that is, adding a name-value pair), and $head(p)$ denotes the first element of $p$'s path. The first line of the rule augments the evaluation context with $x$ mapped to $Eval(e_1,c)$. The second line computes $d_2$ as the dependency of $e_2$ in the augmented context. The next two lines partition the dependency paths in $d_2$ into two sets $d_{2a}$ and $d_{2b}$. The set $d_{2a}$ contains paths unrelated to $x$; all of these must be included in the result. The set $d_{2b}$ contains the tails of the paths in $d_2$ starting with $x$; the final line recursively computes $D(e_1,c,p')$ for each path $p'$ in $d_{2b}$.

- If $e = e_1(e_2)$, then

$$\frac{\begin{array}{c} Eval(e_1,c) = <\lambda x.e_3, c_3> \\ d_1 = D(e_1,c,E:\varepsilon) \\ c_1 = c_3 \circ \{x \rightarrow Eval(e_2,c)\} \\ d_3 = D(e_3,c_1,t:p) \\ d_{3a} = \{t':p' \mid t':p' \in d_3 \wedge head(p') \neq x\} \\ d_{3b} = \{t':p' \mid t':x/p' \in d_3\} \end{array}}{\begin{array}{l} D(e,c,t:p) = d_1 \bigcup \\ \quad (\bigcup_{t':p' \in d_{3a}} D(e_1,c,t':p')) \bigcup \\ \quad (\bigcup_{t':p' \in d_{3b}} D(e_2,c,t':p')) \end{array}}$$

As one would expect from the semantics of function application, this rule resembles the rule for the **let** construct, where $e_1$ in the **let** expression corresponds to the argument $e_2$ here, and $e_2$ in the **let** expression corresponds to the closure body $e_3$ here.

### Fine-Grained Analysis: An Example

Here is a simple example demonstrating the workings of some of these rules. Consider the evaluation of the expression

$$e = \textbf{let}\ x = [r = [s = y], t = z]\ \textbf{in}\ x/r/s$$

in the context $c$. It is easy to see by inspection that the value of this expression is the value of $y$ in $c$, that is, $Eval(e,c) = c(y)$. Now let's apply the dependency rules.

$$\begin{array}{l} \quad Dpnd(e,c) \\ \equiv \{\text{ by the definition of } Dpnd\ \} \\ \quad D(e,c,V:\varepsilon) \end{array}$$

Since the expression $e$ is a **let** construct, the **let** rule applies. The main step in calculating the dependencies for the **let** construct involves calculating the dependency set named $d_2$ in that rule, where $e_1 = [r{=}[s{=}y], t{=}z]$ and $e_2 = x/r/s$. Using $c_1$ to denote the augmented context $c \circ \{x \to Eval(e_1, c)\}$, the value for $d_2$ is derived as follows:

$$
\begin{aligned}
& D(x/r/s, c_1, V{:}\varepsilon) \\
\equiv\ & \{\text{ by the binding selection rule }\} \\
& D(x/r, c_1, V{:}s) \\
\equiv\ & \{\text{ by the binding selection rule }\} \\
& D(x, c_1, V{:}r/s) \\
\equiv\ & \{\text{ by the variable rule }\} \\
& \{\, V{:}x/r/s \,\}
\end{aligned}
$$

From the dependency set $d_2$, we compute the partitioned sets $d_{2a}$ and $d_{2b}$:

$$
\begin{aligned}
d_{2a} &= \emptyset \\
d_{2b} &= \{\, V{:}r/s \,\}
\end{aligned}
$$

We can now complete the computation of $Dpnd(e, c)$ as follows:

$$
\begin{aligned}
& D(e, c, V{:}\varepsilon) \\
\equiv\ & \{\text{ by the } \textbf{let} \text{ rule }\} \\
& \emptyset \cup D([r{=}[s{=}y], t{=}z], c, V{:}r/s) \\
\equiv\ & \{\text{ by the binding constructor rule }\} \\
& D([s{=}y], c, V{:}s) \\
\equiv\ & \{\text{ by the binding constructor rule }\} \\
& D(y, c, V{:}\varepsilon) \\
\equiv\ & \{\text{ by the variable rule }\} \\
& \{\, V{:}y \,\}
\end{aligned}
$$

Hence, the evaluation of $e$ in $c$ depends only on the value of $y$, as expected.

### The Correctness Theorem

With the preceding sections as background, the correctness theorem follows.

**Theorem 1 (Caching Correctness)** *If the expression e evaluates to a value v in the context $c_1$, then we can compute $Dpnd(e, c_1)$, and, if every path in $Dpnd(e, c_1)$ evaluates to the same value in contexts $c_1$ and $c_2$, then e also evaluates to v in $c_2$. Formally,*

$$
\begin{aligned}
(\exists v : Eval(e, c_1) = v) \Longrightarrow \\
(\exists d : Dpnd(e, c_1) = d) \\
\wedge\ (Equiv(c_1, c_2, Dpnd(e, c_1)) \Longrightarrow \\
Eval(e, c_2) = Eval(e, c_1))).
\end{aligned}
$$

The proof of the theorem is beyond the scope of this book. However, the proof was mechanically checked with the Nqthm theorem prover [9]. This process exposed some subtle problems in the initial dependency rules, and several iterations of running the prover and correcting the dependency rules were required before the mechanical proof succeeded. Only after a successful proof were the rules implemented in the Vesta evaluator. Because the subset language includes all the complex aspects of SDL that affect dependency calculation, the proof provides considerable confidence in the correctness of Vesta's caching.

### 8.4.4 Caching System Model Evaluations: A Special Case

The preceding section described the evaluator's rules for caching user-defined function calls. Since the evaluation of a system model is a special case of function application (recall from Section 5.2.4 that a system model is a special form of closure), the rules we have just seen apply when caching model evaluations. However, they do not take advantage of some special properties of models, which, as we will see, can significantly enhance cache performance.

When one function calls another, most (secondary) dependencies of the callee typically become dependencies of the caller. Hence, in the absence of special measures, the root function of an evaluation accumulates most of the dependencies of everything in the evaluation, making it costly both to store and to use the corresponding cache entry. It is desirable, therefore, to eliminate some of those dependencies while preserving caching correctness and without losing the benefits of fine-grained dependencies. Some properties that distinguish system models from other user-defined functions make this possible.

In particular, the evaluator can characterize the contents of a system model in two different ways. A system model, considered as a closure, has a body and a set of free variables, the latter being the names introduced and bound in the `files` and `imports` clauses. But a system model is also an immutable file residing in an immutable directory. These two views of a model suggest two different ways to compute its fingerprint for dependency purposes. The evaluator can fingerprint the parse tree of the closure body, just as it would fingerprint any other Vesta closure. Alternatively, the evaluator can fingerprint the entire immutable directory in which the model resides (see Section 7.1.3) plus the file name of the model. Each of these fingerprints then uniquely characterizes the model for dependency purposes, though in significantly different ways.

The evaluator computes both of these fingerprints for a model and constructs two cache entries for its evaluation. A *normal* model cache entry is based on the fingerprint of the model as a closure, and is constructed using the rules of the preceding section, just as for any other closure. This typically means that the secondary dependencies include all the free variables of the function (the `files` and `import` clauses) plus the fine-grained dependencies from the environment ("`.`") parameter. A *special* model cache entry is based on the fingerprint of the model as a file, so the primary key incorporates all of the immutable content of the model's directory, which includes everything named by its `files` clause. The primary key also includes, indirectly, models in other parts of the repository that are referenced through the `import` clause, since the immutable pathname of each such import appears in the text of the system model and thus is "covered" by the directory fingerprint.[13] This means that the secondary dependencies for a special model cache entry come solely from the environment parameter.

Special model entries have two important advantages. First, since they have fewer secondary dependencies than normal model entries, they are faster to look up. Second, and more importantly, special model entries serve as cut-off points that prevent many dependencies from propagating up the function call graph. In particular, individual dependencies on `files` or `imports` of a model are not propagated to cache entries nearer to the root in the function call tree. Without these cut-offs, the root node of the function call graph of a build would contain a separate dependency on every source file contributing to the build.

Because of their coarser-grained dependencies, special model entries inevitably produce some false cache misses. However, they produce frequent cache hits. For example, when an application is built using standard libraries, most of the libraries are generally unchanged from a previous build, so the evaluator will get fast cache hits on their special model entries. This situation occurs quite often. The performance benefits of the special cache entries are sufficiently appealing that developers sometimes create a separate model for a piece of Vesta code, rather than simply wrapping that code in a function definition within an existing model. They thereby obtain better caching performance in exchange for a slightly larger number of model files.

When looking up a model evaluation in the cache, the evaluator naturally checks for a hit on the special model entry first. If that fails, it tries for a cache hit on a normal model entry. It is uncommon for a cache lookup to miss on the former and hit on the latter, but it does happen occasionally, typically when a small cosmetic edit has been made to the corresponding model. Such hits easily save enough work to justify the cost of creating the larger normal entry. Whether a hit occurs or not, the evaluator uses the special model fingerprint in the dependency calculation for the caller of the model.

## 8.5 Error Handling

The preceding section described how the evaluator collects the information necessary to create cache entries. From a purely formal point of view, a function evaluation that produces an error has simply created a result of a particular kind, which could be cached like any other. In practice, however, caching the result of a function with an evaluation error would be undesirable, as we will now see.

Two cases of evaluation errors affect caching: runtime errors that occur while evaluating an SDL expression and failed `_run_tool` calls. The evaluator handles the first of these cases in the expected way, by terminating the evaluation and providing the user with a suitable error message that incorporates a call stack trace.

[13] Unfortunately, the directory fingerprint also includes any files in the model's directory tree that the model doesn't reference, as well as irrelevant elements in the model text such as unused imports, comments, and whitespace.

Naturally, no cache entries are created for any of the function evaluations that were in progress (that is, on the call stack), since their evaluation is incomplete. Cache entries previously produced for completed function evaluations are retained; consequently, if the evaluation were to be performed again, the same error message would be regenerated quickly.

When a `_run_tool` call fails, however, the evaluator does not necessarily abort the evaluation. A failed `_run_tool` call frequently indicates a compilation error. If the build in progress includes many compilations, the user will generally prefer to deal with all the errors at once. So, the evaluator offers a command-line option to continue evaluating even in the presence of tool failures. If the option is not enabled, failed `_run_tool` calls abort the evaluation, just like any other runtime error. However, if the option is enabled, the evaluator outputs an error message and continues. The Vesta bridge functions that invoke `_run_tool` are typically written to detect an error and to return the special value `ERR` to their callers. Any attempt to use this value causes an error that terminates the evaluation, but frequently that doesn't happen until most or all of the compilations involved in a build have been completed.

When a `_run_tool` error occurs, the user can direct the evaluation to continue but the evaluator never caches the result, for two reasons. First, occasionally a tool invocation fails because of a transient condition that is outside Vesta's control, such as a full disk or a network timeout. A failure of this kind violates Vesta's assumption that the result of a function is deterministic. Capturing such a failure in the cache would make it impossible to correct the problem by clearing the transient condition and retrying. Second, even if the error represents a deterministic result, the associated error message that generally is displayed by a Vesta bridge is not incorporated in the result it returns, for practical reasons. That means the error message is essentially a side-effect (something that Vesta functions aren't supposed to have!) and to cache the result would be to lose the ability to recreate that side-effect on a subsequent cache hit. By refraining from caching the error result, the evaluator enables the user to recreate the error message(s) by performing the evaluation again.

There is one additional complexity associated with the evaluator's option to continue in the face of `_run_tool` errors. We have seen that a cache entry for the tool invocation must not be created. Caching any function call higher up in the call graph would be equally bad, since a hit on such an entry would prevent the failed call to `_run_tool` from reoccurring, again suppressing the error messages. To handle this situation, the evaluator records a **cacheable** flag for each runtime value. This flag is true for most values, but false for the value of a failed `_run_tool` call. The evaluator computes the cacheable flag of a value based on the cacheable flags of the values from which it is produced. A cache entry for a function evaluation is created only when its result value is cacheable.

There is also an interaction between error reporting and the existence of closures as first-class values in SDL. Because a closure can be returned as part of a function's result, it can be cached, meaning that its value (the parse tree of its body) is held in a cache entry. If that cached value is subsequently retrieved and the closure invoked, the Vesta evaluator must be able to report an error during the closure's evaluation in just the same way as if the closure had not come from a cache entry. This implies that the evaluator must include in the cached parse tree sufficient information to be able to report the original source location (file name, line number, position) for any construct that might produce an error (which is essentially everything in the language). This extra information increases communication, memory, and disk storage costs in the function cache. However, hard-won experience in debugging system models that use closures confirms the benefit associated with this additional cost, as it is extremely hard to isolate errors in cached closures without source location information.

## 8.6 Function Cache Implementation

We now turn our attention from the evaluator to its partner, the function cache. Section 8.3 briefly introduced the interface that the evaluator uses to perform cache lookups. This section discusses some of the issues that the function cache server faces in implementing that interface. These arise directly from the operational requirements on the server, which must:

- store cache entries persistently,
- tolerate faults and errors, both by clients and in the server itself, while maintaining consistent cache state,
- support fast lookup,
- service multiple clients concurrently,
- support concurrent weeding (the deletion of unwanted derived files and cache entries) without affecting clients adversely, and
- scale.

Let's look briefly at the way the cache server attacks each of these requirements.

**Persistence.** Properly shutting down and restarting the server must not cause any cache entries to be lost. Persistence is achieved by storing older cache entries in disk files and using a combination of logging and checkpointing for newer cache entries. For efficiency, log entries are kept in memory, and the interface to the function cache includes a method for synchronously flushing all pending log entries to disk.

**Fault tolerance.** In the event of a crash or other failure of the server, the function cache must be able to recover in a consistent state. In particular, the various log files and cache entry files must be flushed in an order that allows the recovery algorithm to tolerate failure at any time. Although some recently created cache entries may be lost in a crash, only a relatively small amount of work has to be repeated to recreate them.

The server must also tolerate errors and failures in its clients. For the former, the function cache interface includes run-time checks of its arguments with provisions for an error return code. For the latter, the function cache ensures that any resources associated with interrupted or otherwise incomplete evaluations are eventually reclaimed.

**Fast lookup.** Since disk reads dominate the time required to do a lookup, cache entries are arranged on disk so that most lookups can be performed with at most two disk reads. Moreover, many lookups result in hits on in-memory cache entries, which can be serviced without any disk reads.

**Concurrent client access.** The server is multi-threaded, and its data structures are organized to permit fine-grained locking and thereby to avoid excessive lock contention and serialization of clients.

**Concurrent weeding.** The weeder (Chapter 9) is a special client of the cache server. It must be possible for the weeder to complete its work without affecting other clients adversely. It is impractical to lock out clients while the weeder is running, as it can take minutes to hours to decide what to weed and then to delete it. The cache server enables the weeder to run concurrently by providing a way for it to take a snapshot of the cache and compute the entries to be deleted based on that snapshot. This immediately introduces the need for an additional mechanism to ensure that cache entries created after taking the snapshot are retained.

**Scaling.** The design targets for the Vesta system imply that the function cache must be able to store tens of millions of cache entries. To accommodate that load, a two-level memory hierarchy is used; newly created and recently looked-up cache entries are cached in main memory, while others are stored only on disk. Within each disk file, cache entries are stored in a three-level hierarchy, which we will examine shortly.

### 8.6.1 Cache Lookup

Because the SecondaryNames step of the cache lookup protocol narrows the search down to entries that match a given primary key, it is natural and efficient for the cache server to organize its cache entry storage by primary key. Both in memory and on disk, the server stores entries in groups called *PKFiles*. Each PKFile holds all the entries that have a particular primary key.

If the cache lookup algorithm worked exactly as outlined in Section 8.3, its Lookup step would have to search through all the cache entries in the relevant PKFile. For each such entry, it would have to perform a fingerprint comparison for each of the entry's secondary dependencies. Both the number of cache entries in a PKFile and the number of secondary dependencies in a cache entry can be quite large, on the order of hundreds of each. Hence, if this naive lookup algorithm were used, lookups would require tens of thousands of fingerprint comparisons in the worst case, and hence would be unacceptably expensive.

The cache server avoids this problem by organizing the cache entries in a multi-level hierarchy. First, all entries with the same primary key are grouped together (the PKFile). Then the entries in each group are partitioned in such a way that only a subset of the entries in each group need be examined on any lookup. We now examine how this partitioning is performed.

For any cache entry $e$, let $e.pk$ denote $e$'s primary key, let $e.names$ denote the set of names in $e$'s secondary key, and for any name $n \in e.names$, let $e.val(n)$ denote the fingerprint value associated with $n$ in $e$'s secondary key. We define the following sets:

$$\begin{aligned} Entries(pk) &= \{e \mid e.pk = pk\} \\ AllNames(pk) &= \bigcup_{e \in Entries(pk)} e.names \\ CommonNames(pk) &= \bigcap_{e \in Entries(pk)} e.names \end{aligned}$$

$$CFP(e) = \bigoplus_{n \in CommonNames(e.pk)} e.val(n)$$

The set *CommonNames*($pk$) thus consists of those names that occur in every cache entry with the given primary key. The names in the set difference *AllNames*($pk$) − *CommonNames*($pk$) occur in some, but not all, cache entries with the given primary key; they are called *uncommon*. The value *CFP*($e$), $e$'s *common fingerprint*, is the result of combining the fingerprints of all secondary values of $e$ corresponding to $e.pk$'s common names. Because the $\oplus$ operation is non-commutative, it is necessary to enumerate the names $n$ in a well-defined order. To this end, the function cache maintains a canonical ordering for each $pk$ of the names in *AllNames*($pk$); it uses that ordering when computing *CFP*($e$).

Given these definitions, we can now examine how the cache implements both steps of the lookup algorithm. For each primary key $pk$, the cache maintains the sets *Entries*($pk$), *AllNames*($pk$), and *CommonNames*($pk$) (the last of which is represented by a bit vector with respect to *AllNames*($pk$)). In the SecondaryNames step of the lookup protocol, the cache simply returns *AllNames*($pk$) for the supplied primary key. To perform the Lookup step of the algorithm efficiently, the cache maintains *CFP*($e$) for every entry $e$. It then groups the entries *Entries*($pk$) into equivalence classes according to their common fingerprints (CFPs). For example, Figure 8.5 shows the common names and CFPs for the cache entries of Figure 8.4 (on page 118).

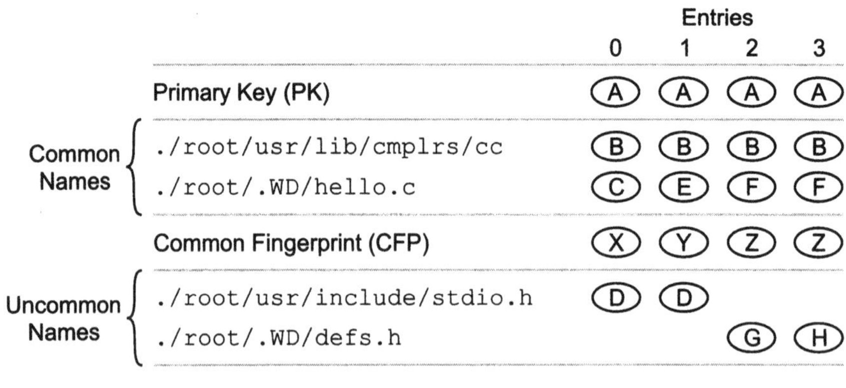


**Fig. 8.5.** The common names and common fingerprints for the cache entries of Figure 8.4.

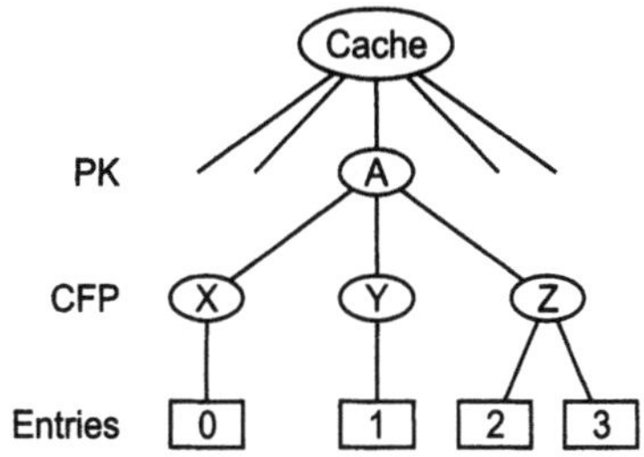


**Fig. 8.6.** The hierarchical division of cache entries first by primary key (PK) and then by common fingerprint (CFP) for the cache entries of Figure 8.5.

The PKFile is then partitioned by CFP value; two entries are in the same partition if and only if they have the same CFP. Figure 8.6 shows the hierarchy that results from the cache entries and common fingerprints shown in Figure 8.5. Multiple entries appear in the same CFP group only when one of the uncommon secondary dependencies changes.

In the Lookup step, the evaluator passes the cache server a primary key *pk* and the fingerprints $f_1, f_2, \ldots, f_k$ of the values corresponding to the names *AllNames*(*pk*) at the call site.[14] Call these fingerprints $f_i$ the *call site fingerprints*. The server first combines the call site fingerprints associated with *CommonNames*(*pk*), thereby producing a common fingerprint *cfp*. Next, the server does a hash table lookup to see if *pk* has *cfp* as one of its associated common fingerprints. If not, the server reports a miss to the evaluator. Otherwise, the server examines the entries in the identified CFP group. In testing for a hit, only the fingerprint values associated with the uncommon names need be examined, since by virtue of being in the correct CFP group, all entries being considered are known to have matching values for the common names.

The performance of this lookup algorithm depends on the distribution of CFPs within a PKFile and on the PKFile's relative number of common and uncommon names. In the case of a compilation, the name of the file being compiled will be one of the common names. Hence, each time a new version of a file is compiled, a new common fingerprint is produced. The expectation is that within a PKFile, there will be many CFPs, but each CFP group will contain relatively few entries. This means that the number of cache entries considered during a lookup is expected to be small.

Moreover, the smaller the number of uncommon names per cache entry, the fewer the fingerprint comparisons that the lookup algorithm must perform. It is easy to see that, in PKFiles corresponding to compilations, the number of common names is large compared to the number of uncommon names, since the set of file names accessed during the compilation of a particular source file does not tend to change much from version to version. In fact, the pattern is borne out for most other PKFiles as well, as the data in Section 11.4.2 shows.

In summary then, the preceding lookup algorithm results in two major cost savings compared to the brute-force algorithm. First, only those entries in the identified

[14] For any name in *AllNames*(*pk*) that is not defined at the call site, the evaluator passes a (unique) null value for the corresponding fingerprint.

CFP group need be considered. Second, for the entries in a CFP group, only the values associated with the uncommon names need be considered. These two effects drastically reduce the number of fingerprint comparisons required to perform a cache lookup.

### 8.6.2 Cache Entry Storage

We can now examine how the data structures described above are physically organized. The function cache is intended to store tens of millions of cache entries. Holding all of the cache entries in main memory is thus impractical, and a two-level memory hierarchy is used instead. Most of the entries are stored in *stable* PKFiles on disk, while the newly created cache entries and those cache entries on which a hit has recently occurred are stored in *volatile* PKFiles in memory. Stable PKFiles are stored using the file system provided by the underlying operating system.

The simplistic approach of creating one disk file for each stable PKFile produces disk fragmentation, so instead the stable PKFiles are aggregated into *MultiPKFiles*. Two PKFiles are stored in the same MultiPKFile if and only if their corresponding primary keys have the same 16-bit prefix.[15] Since the primary keys, being fingerprints, are essentially random numbers, the PKFiles tend to be evenly distributed among the MultiPKFiles.

So, to look up a cache entry, the cache server locates the appropriate volatile PKFile (in main memory), and looks in it for the entry in memory. If no hit results, the server opens the appropriate stable MultiPKFile, and determines the start of the appropriate stable PKFile using a mapping table at the front of the MultiPKFile. The PKFile header, in turn, contains a table that maps common fingerprint values to positions in the PKFile where the entries with each CFP are stored. This table is stored in sorted order by CFP so interpolated binary search can be used for CFP lookup.

The typical cost of a cache lookup on disk is only a few read operations: those needed to open the MultiPKFile and read the index to locate the PKFile, one to read the CFP table from the head of the PKFile, and one to read the cache entry in the event of a hit. (In the case of a miss, a matching CFP is typically absent, so the last of these reads never happens.) The exact number of disk operations varies with the file system's block size, its read-ahead algorithm, its caching strategy for file data and metadata, the number of CFPs in the PKFile, and the size of the CFP table and/or cache entry. What matters, however, is that the overall time required to check the disk-based cache is small compared with the typical time to evaluate a function in the case of a cache miss. Since such an evaluation is typically a compilation, a few disk reads constitute a very acceptable overhead. (For a more quantitative assessment, see Section 11.4.1, which reports the time required to perform cache lookup operations with various outcomes.)

Maintaining the cache organization is complicated by the addition or removal of cache entries. When a new entry is added to or removed from the set *Entries*$(pk)$, the

[15] This prefix size is a compile-time constant, and can be easily changed.

sets *AllNames*$(pk)$ and *CommonNames*$(pk)$ can change. Since a change to the latter requires common fingerprints to be recomputed and cache entries to be reorganized, newly added entries are kept in two in-memory side buffers, one for entries that have all of the common names, and one for those that do not. The lookup algorithm must consult these side buffers in addition to checking for a hit in *Entries*$(pk)$. Once a large enough number of new entries is collected, the entries are merged into *Entries*$(pk)$ together, thereby amortizing the high cost of recomputing all of the common fingerprints and shuffling cache entries among CFP groups. Deletions triggered by the weeder are handled similarly; again, new common names and common fingerprints are not computed for every deletion, but only once for each PKFile as a batch.

### 8.6.3 Synchronization

The function cache uses simple mutual exclusion locks (mutexes) to protect its shared data structures. One centralized mutex protects the main cache variables. To reduce lock contention, a separate mutex protects access to the cache entries and other state of each volatile PKFile. The use of a separate mutex for each volatile PKFile allows lookups on different primary keys to proceed in parallel. When a PKFile is rewritten, its mutex is held only as long as necessary. For example, the mutex is not held while the stable PKFile is read and while its common names and the common fingerprints of its entries are recomputed. This locking strategy allows most of the considerable work required in rewriting a PKFile to occur in parallel with lookups and the addition of new entries, thereby improving the cache's overall performance.

## 8.7 Evaluation and Caching in Action

Having examined the inner workings of the evaluator and function cache, we now turn to some examples of their actual behavior and look at the call graphs that result from the evaluation of several packages.

### 8.7.1 Scratch Build of the Standard Environment

Figure 8.7 shows the call graph that results from evaluating the model for the standard construction environment against an empty cache. In this figure and the two that follow it, the nodes of the graph denote function invocations, and an edge from a node $f$ to a node $g$ indicates that $f$ calls $g$. The edge is solid black if $f$ and $g$ are defined in the same Vesta package, and gray otherwise.

Before we examine these figures, we must consider an aspect of the standard environment model that was not discussed in Section 6.2.1. The standard environment contains the bridges that are used in the construction of libraries and applications in Vesta. How are the programs included in these bridges built? That is, how do the tools (the compilers, linkers, etc.) get built? Many development organizations acquire their tools in binary form, so a simple reference to the tool in a bridge model's

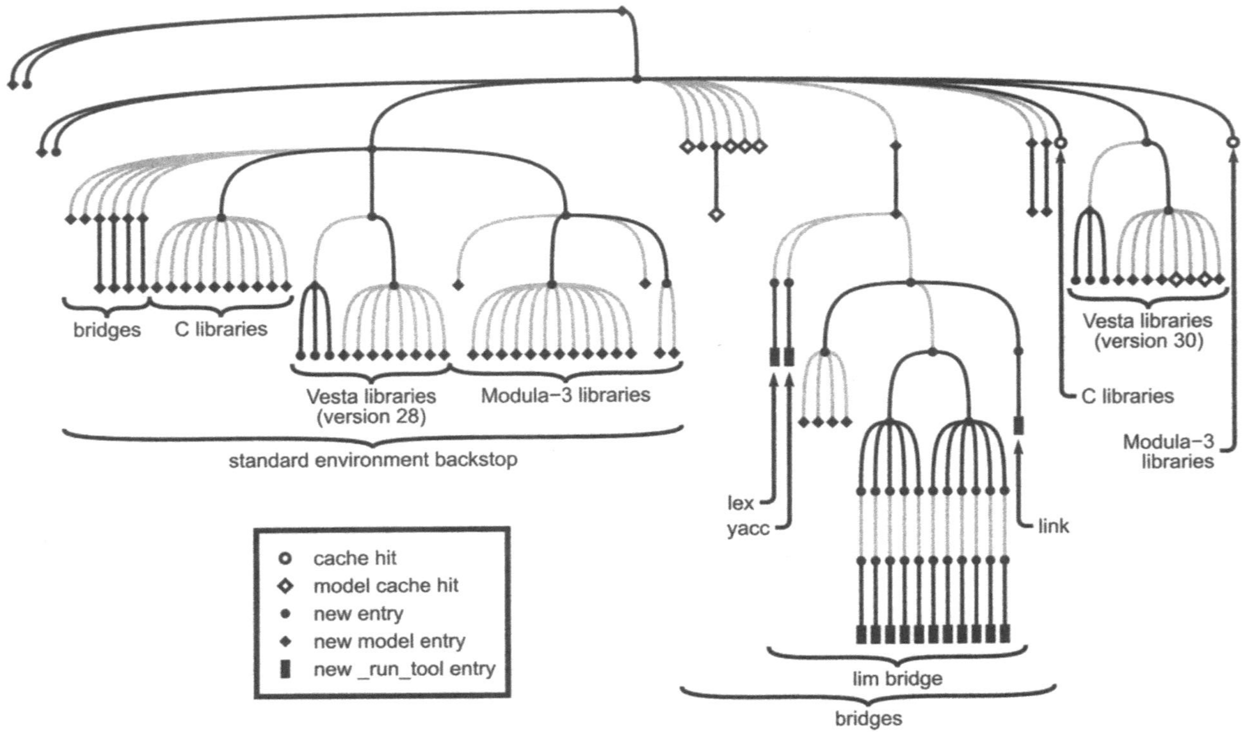


**Fig. 8.7.** The call graph for the construction of the standard environment model. To build the standard environment, a stripped down "backstop" environment is first constructed as shown in the left half of the figure. The environment proper is then built, which includes the construction of three additional bridges. One of these, the lim bridge, requires building the lim tool from source.

`files` clause (see Section 6.2) suffices to incorporate it in the standard environment. However, some organizations have special development tools or custom language processors. Since a Vesta system model must be complete, the bridge packages must describe the construction of these tools. That description must therefore name the tools to be used to build the bridges; that is, it must specify a *previous version of the standard construction environment*. To construct a standard environment, Vesta must first construct the required set of tools, which means building an earlier standard environment.

Obviously, there must be a practical way to terminate this recursion, which would otherwise lead, in principle, back to the dawn of computing. The oldest standard environment consists of pre-built bridges; that is, its system model does not include actual building instructions but instead included the compiler and other tools in their binary, executable form. When Vesta "builds" this initial standard environment, it does not need to invoke any tools, so no recursion occurs. Such an environment is called a *backstop*. The next-oldest standard environment can then reference the backstop to acquire the tools it needs and use them, if appropriate, to build new versions of tools. Similarly, the third standard environment references and uses the second, and so on.

While in principle only one backstop is needed in order to ground this bootstrapping of standard environments, in practice it is useful to make backstops with at other times. A backstop provides the evaluator with a way to get started when the Vesta cache is entirely empty. Having a relatively recent backstop is very handy if, for example, a new repository replica is created and its Vesta cache must be initialized. A backstop is also a convenient way for a vendor to ship binary-only libraries to a customer who uses Vesta. In either case, the backstop is created by taking the essential parts of the result of a build (for example, the standard environment) and writing a new system model in which the key components of the result are captured as sources. Utility programs can automate the creation of this model.

Returning to Figure 8.7, we can see how a build from scratch (that is, a build occurring when the Vesta cache is empty) of the standard environment model uses a backstop. The call graph in the figure can be divided roughly in half. The evaluation of a backstop is on the left, the construction of the full standard environment is on the right. Both portions of the graph involve the evaluation of library models and bridge models. The library models are divided into three groups: C libraries, Vesta libraries, and Modula-3 libraries. The backstop contains six bridge models, while the full standard environment contains the same six plus three additional ones.

Looking at the graph in more detail, we note the following:

- In the backstop portion of the call graph, there are no cache hits and no tool invocations. The former is to be expected because the cache is empty, while the latter results from the definition of a backstop.
- Although this evaluation was performed with an initially empty cache, some cache hits still occurred. In particular, cache hits occurred on five of the six bridges in the full environment because identical versions of those bridges had already been evaluated in the backstop environment.

- The three bridges that appear in the full environment but not the backstop were all built from scratch, as evidenced by the `_run_tool` calls. Those for `lex` and `yacc` involved single tool invocations, while the `lim` bridge was a more elaborate construction, with 11 compilations followed by a link step.
- Cache hits occurred on the complete sub-trees of the C and Modula-3 libraries, again because those libraries had been evaluated in the backstop. In contrast, hits did not occur on all but two of the Vesta libraries because the version of those libraries referenced by the full standard environment model (i.e., version 30) differed significantly from the one referenced by the backstop (version 28). None of the library evaluations resulted in a tool invocation, since in general the actual construction of a library is delayed until a program is built against it (recall Section 6.2).

### 8.7.2 Scratch Build of the Vesta Umbrella Library

Figure 8.8 shows the call graph that results from building a trivial C program (`sample.c`) with the complete Vesta umbrella library, assuming that the construction of the standard environment model shown in Figure 8.7 is already cached. `sample.c` isn't a realistic program, but it enables us to examine the construction of a non-trivial umbrella library, which constitutes the bulk of this figure. The actual construction of the sample program itself consists only of the two rightmost tool invocations.

Although the function cache is relatively empty in this example, the importance of good caching is evident. The cache hit on the standard construction environment in the upper left of the figure is critically important, as it saves the evaluator from having to evaluate the entire call graph of Figure 8.7.

Perhaps the main thing to notice about this call graph is its sheer size. Building the Vesta umbrella library from scratch requires 86 tool invocations. Except for the fingerprint library, each sub-library is constructed by compiling the library's sources one at a time, and then collecting the resulting objects together into a Unix library archive file. These produce the regular-looking "weeping willow" portions of the graph.

The construction of the fingerprint library is more elaborate and has a less regular structure to its call graph. This library provides its client with a C header file that is generated by a specialized program (since it contains a collection of computed fingerprint constants). That program must be built and executed to create the necessary header file, which must be read in the course of compiling the fingerprint library's implementation, which in turn is needed to complete the Vesta library needed by `sample.c`. Accordingly, we see seven tool invocations in this part of the graph: the compilation, linking, and execution of the header-generation program, the compilations of the fingerprint library implementation, and the construction of the library archive for the fingerprint library.[16]

[16] This example provides a nice illustration of the difference between Vesta's source/derived distinction and the C compiler's source/object distinction. Here, a header file, normally

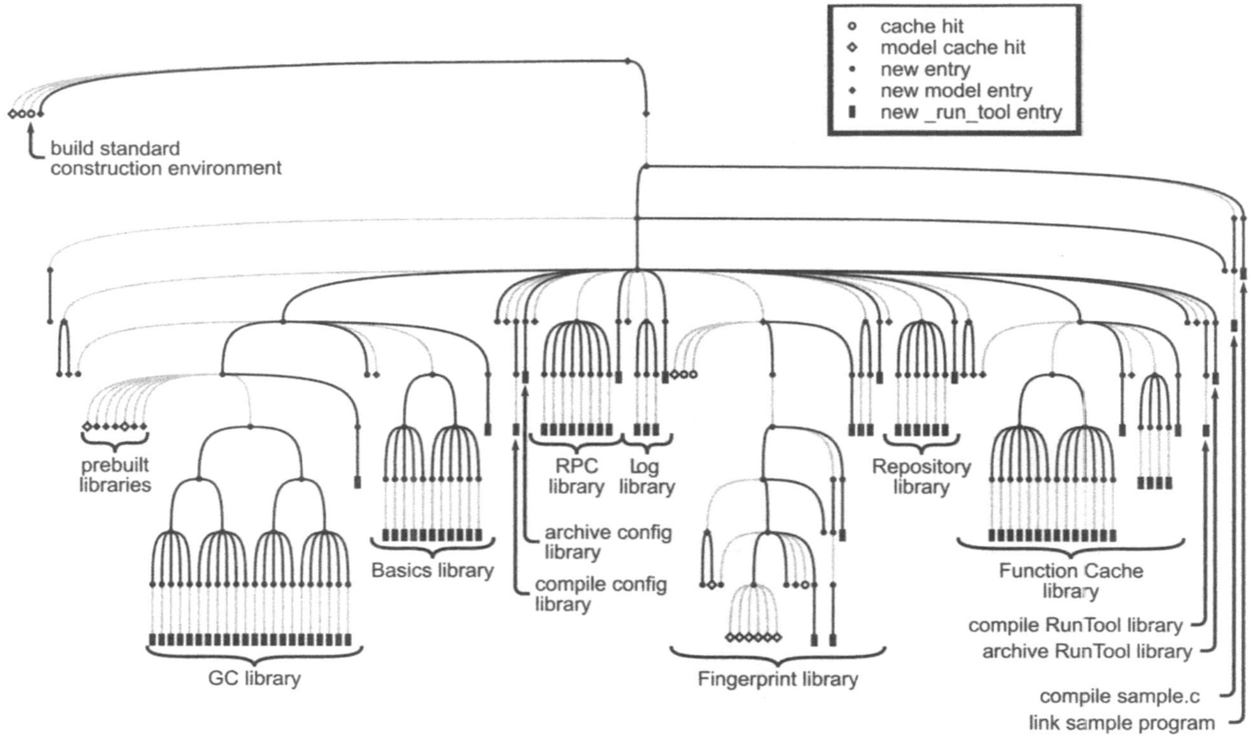


**Fig. 8.8.** The call graph for the construction of a sample program linked against the complete Vesta umbrella library, assuming the evaluation of the standard construction environment is cached. The bulk of this figure depicts the construction of the Vesta umbrella library, which consists of seven prebuilt libraries and nine other libraries built from source.

### 8.7.3 Scratch and Incremental Builds of the Evaluator

We can now look at the cache behavior of the Vesta evaluator as it builds itself. Figure 8.9(a) shows the call graph that results from building the Vesta evaluator package from scratch, assuming that the standard environment and Vesta umbrella library are cached as they would be after the evaluations shown in the two preceding figures. The evaluation builds the Vesta evaluator program, plus a single-module helper program and some derived documentation files.

We see from the figure that the evaluator got a cache hit not only on the evaluation of the standard construction environment, but also on the entire Vesta umbrella library shown in Figure 8.8. By virtue of the latter cache hit, the evaluator avoided the 86 tool invocations shown in the previous figure. The construction of the evaluator itself is then straightforward; its 18 sources are compiled and the results are then linked together with the Vesta umbrella library. The construction of the helper program and documentation files is also straightforward.

Figure 8.9(b) shows the call graph that results from an *incremental* build of the Vesta evaluator. This example illustrates the typical case that occurs during the inner edit-build-test loop of the development cycle that was discussed in Section 4.2.2. After completing the evaluation shown in Figure 8.9(a), one of the evaluator's source files was modified and the evaluator was rebuilt. Figure 8.9(b) shows that there were many cache hits and only two tool invocations: one to recompile the modified source and one to relink the evaluator executable. Because the helper program and documentation sources were not changed, cache hits occur high in the call graph on those parts of the evaluation.

This example also illustrates an interesting feature of the C and C++ bridges. Notice that the 18 source files compiled during the scratch build of the evaluator are arranged in two groups of nine. This is done automatically by the bridge, which is presented with the entire list of files and divides it up. More generally, the bridge produces a balanced subtree when compiling 10 or more files.[17] The purpose of this balancing becomes evident when we examine the incremental build graph more closely. The single altered file is in the right-hand subtree of nine nodes, and as expected the evaluator gets eight cache hits and one miss, which corresponds to the `_run_tool` invocation. However, since none of the nine source files in the left-hand subtree has changed, the evaluator gets a single cache hit on the entire subtree, thereby avoiding nine additional cache lookups. We see that, in the general incremental case, this balanced-tree approach results in a number of cache lookups proportional to the logarithm of the number of sources in the library or application, rather than the linear number that would result had bridge directly compiled the flat list of sources passed to it.

---

considered source code, is mechanically generated by a build, so it is a derived file from Vesta's point of view.

[17] This shows up as a characteristic "weeping willow" in the call graph; we saw a more pronounced one in the construction of the GC library in Figure 8.8.

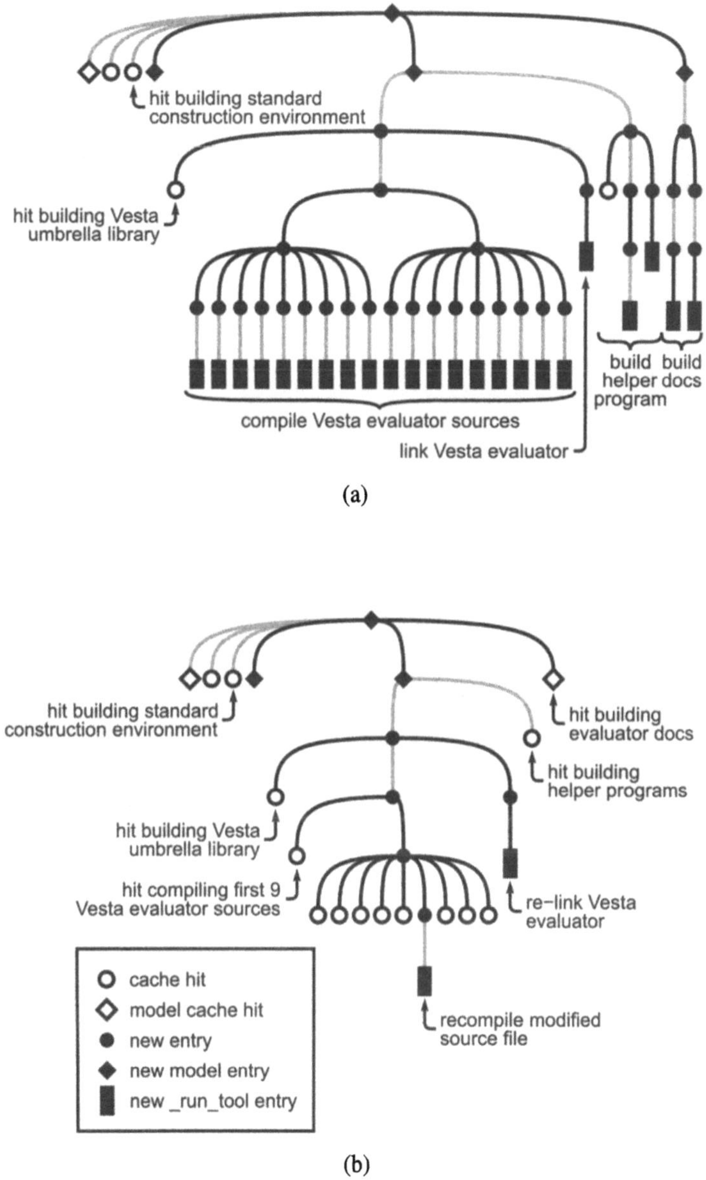


**Fig. 8.9.** The call graphs that result from building the Vesta evaluator package from scratch (a) and again after one of the evaluator's source files has been modified (b). In both cases, hits occur on the standard construction environment and the Vesta umbrella libraries.

## In Summary

In this rather detailed chapter, we have examined how the evaluator and function cache work together to implement the machinery Vesta uses for robust, incremental building. Fine-grained dependency analysis ensures that software components are rebuilt only when necessary, and the function cache server enables developers across a site to benefit from each others' builds, completely automatically. We next turn our attention to the final component of the Vesta system that is required to make incremental building practical, the weeder.

# 9

# Weeder

We have seen that the Vesta evaluation machinery handles the creation and naming of derived files automatically, without user involvement. Vesta also handles the deletion of derived files largely automatically. This is the province of the *weeder*, whose function was briefly examined in Sections 3.1.3 and 8.6. Because derived files and function cache entries are closely related, the weeder also manages the deletion of unwanted cache entries, under the guidance of a system administrator. In this chapter, we look at the operation of the weeder in more detail, considering its design and implementation. Performance measurements appear in Section 11.5.

In the preceding chapter, we saw in detail how cache entries are created. Since all the data contained in a cache entry results from the deterministic evaluation of immutable sources, a Vesta cache entry can never become invalid as caches based on mutable data can. Consequently, deletion of cache entries is never required for correctness; it serves only to recover disk space. It is this characteristic that motivates the weeder's name. In a system that relies on garbage collection to reclaim storage, there is a clear distinction between objects that are reachable from a set of known roots and those that are unreachable and hence are garbage. But because Vesta cache entries never become invalid, they are potentially useful indefinitely, and so are not "garbage" in the strict sense. For this reason, a fully automatic deletion decision is not possible, and a person must decide which cache entries are worth keeping. That decision process is subjective — one person's flower is another's weed.

Even in the absence of true garbage collection, one could imagine a largely automatic weeding process, driven by heuristic rules and triggered when available disk space falls below a specified threshold. The heuristics might instruct the weeder, for example, to delete all cache entries older than some specified age, or to delete all cache entries except those created by evaluations of, say, the most recent three versions of all packages in the repository. Heuristics like these might not do exactly the right thing in all cases, but since cache entries can always be reconstructed by re-evaluation, simplicity of administration might make up for some less-than-optimal deletion decisions.

It is indeed possible to operate the Vesta weeder in this way, although perhaps ill-advised. Experience suggests that it is difficult to devise appropriate heuristics, for the rate of obsolescence of derived files varies dramatically from package to package, making simple rules like "keep the most recent three versions" retain too much for some packages and too little for others. So, the weeder does not have any fixed heuristics. Rather, it provides an easy way to specify the deletion policy and leaves it to a system administrator to determine the circumstances under which the weeder is to be run and that policy carried out.

The weeder operates invisibly to Vesta's users, meaning that while the weeder is running, the users can continue to build packages with no restriction on Vesta's functionality and only minimal degradation of performance. And, while the weeder is not invisible to the Vesta administrator, it does impose only a modest burden. In particular, weeding can occur infrequently, the weeder does not require extensive disk space, memory, or computation resources to do its job, and the instructions specifying the deletion policy are simple to write.

Of course, leaving the deletion policy to a person introduces the possibility of human error. Fortunately, Vesta's semantics make the consequences of sub-optimal deletion rules relatively minor. If the weeder's instructions cause it to delete too few derived files, the administrator will discover that not enough disk space has been freed and can simply run the weeder anew with a less inclusive set of retention instructions. This will be entirely transparent to the developers using Vesta, unless disk space is exhausted in the interim. If the weeder's instructions cause it to delete too much, then the developers may encounter some performance degradation, since some builds will have to be repeated when things that the developers expected to be cached turn out to have been deleted. But because all sources in Vesta are immutable and immortal, and all builds are repeatable, there is never a correctness problem associated with deleting too much. In short, there is a time-space tradeoff inherent in the weeding process. Weeding more derived files frees up more disk space, but it may require time to recreate some of those weeded files (and cache entries) if they are needed later. Experience indicates that finding a comfortable tradeoff, and writing the deletion instructions to the weeder that produce that tradeoff, are not difficult.

## 9.1 How Deletion is Specified

The administrator provides the weeder with a set of instructions that define the cache entries and derived files that are to be retained. To simplify the administrator's task, these instructions describe retention at a coarse grain: package builds. So, if the weeder is instructed to keep the build of a particular package version, it retains all cache entries and derived files generated by that build. The input to the weeder names package builds using a simple but powerful pattern language, similar to that of the replicator (Section 4.3.3). The input specifies the exact versions of control-panel models (Section 6.2.5) whose corresponding builds the administrator deems worth keeping. It is typically short and easy to understand. Here is an example:

```
+ /vesta/vestasys.org/vesta/release/[LAST-1,LAST]/.main.ves
+ /vesta/vestasys.org/vesta/*/LAST/.main.ves
+ /vesta/vestasys.org/vesta/*/checkout/LAST/*/.main.ves
```

The first line causes the two latest versions of releases of the `vesta` packages to be kept. The second line keeps the last checked-in version of every build of the `vesta` packages, and the final line keeps all checkout session builds of the last version of the `vesta` packages. Each pattern ends in "`.main.ves`", meaning that each pattern names a control-panel model on which the evaluator was invoked. Following these instructions, the weeder keeps all derived files and cache entries created by the specified builds.[1]

Note that each line is preceded by a plus sign, indicating that the designated versions are to be kept. The weeder's input language also allows lines beginning with a minus sign, which removes the specified package builds from the set of builds to keep. The input lines are processed in order; plus and minus signs may be alternated to successively include and exclude different sets of package builds.

## 9.2 Implementation of the Weeder

Conceptually, the operation of the weeder is straightforward. Using the input specification of the "roots" to be kept, the weeder walks over the cache data structures performing a mark-and-sweep algorithm, much as a garbage collector would, to identify the cache entries reachable (in the sense of the evaluation call graph) from the roots. For each reachable entry, the weeder also marks the derived files that it references. When the reachability analysis is complete, the weeder then instructs the cache and repository servers to delete all unmarked cache entries as well as any unmarked derived files they reference.

Many practical considerations prevent the actual implementation of the weeder from being this straightforward. These considerations arise chiefly from the requirement that weeding be concurrent with normal operation of the evaluator and that it interfere with the behavior of the evaluator and function cache as little as possible from the perspective of Vesta's users. As in a concurrent garbage collector, the data structures and mutual exclusion regime are quite subtle, with many non-obvious aspects. Moreover, the evaluator(s), cache server, and weeder all operate in a distributed environment with the possibility of independent component failure. Addressing these matters substantially complicates the weeder's implementation. This section examines briefly how the most significant problems are handled.

### 9.2.1 The Function Call Graph

We consider first how the information created by the cache server — the set of extant cache entries — is organized for the weeder. Most of the information logically associated with a cache entry is irrelevant to the weeder, and much of what the weeder

[1] The weeder also accepts a command-line option that permits the administrator to specify that any builds performed recently (for example, in the last 24 hours) should be kept. This is a convenient "safety net" in case the pattern input inadvertently omits something built recently.

requires isn't needed by the cache server or evaluator. In the previous chapter, we examined the organization of the cache from the perspective of the evaluator. To perform the mark-and-sweep algorithm, the weeder requires a data structure that links parent cache entries with their children. This data structure is maintained separately from the cache entry information previously discussed.

To understand this data structure, we ignore the details of the individual cache entries and consider the relationship among them. Conceptually, as Vesta evaluations occur, the function cache builds up a directed acyclic graph (DAG) whose nodes are cache entries and whose arcs correspond to edges in the evaluation call graph (Section 8.7 has some example call graphs). That is, if the evaluation of a function $f$ includes a call on a function $g$, then two cache entries will be produced and the DAG will have an arc from $f$'s entry to $g$'s entry. This graph is a DAG, not a tree, because a node (cache entry) in the graph acquires a new parent (incoming arc) whenever a new cache hit occurs on the entry. The roots of the DAG correspond to the evaluations of the control panel models on which the Vesta evaluator has been invoked.

The cache server maintains the function-call DAG as an explicit data structure in which the nodes are the cache entries stored as described in Section 8.6, while the edges are kept on disk as a separate file called the *graph log*. Each cache entry is uniquely identified by a small integer called its *cache index*, so the graph log edges are represented using cache indices. In particular, each entry in the graph log contains the index of the cache entry to which it corresponds as well as the cache indices of each of its children. The graph log is a "log" in the sense that the cache server creates new edges strictly by appending to the file in which the log is stored. Except during weeding, existing edges are never deleted or altered.

Since the weeder must be able to mark for retention both the desired cache entries and their associated derived files, the shortids (see Section 7.1.1) of all files referenced in a function's result value — that is, the value stored in the cache entry for its invocation — are also stored in the associated graph log entry.[2] This means that all deriveds referenced by an evaluation can be reached by traversing the function call graph corresponding to that evaluation, using the graph log data structure.

With this understanding of the graph log, we can restate in more detail how the weeder operates. The weeder performs a mark-and-sweep algorithm using the graph log, starting with the nodes corresponding to the roots specified in the weeder's input. The marking phase of the algorithm builds up a set of cache entries, each identified by a cache index, and a set of derived files, each identified by a shortid, that are to be retained. In the sweep phase, these sets are passed to the cache server and the repository server, respectively, which then delete all extant cache entries and shortids not included in the retention sets. The weeder also rewrites the graph log with a subset of its original entries corresponding to the cache entries retained by the cache server.

[2] For the most part, these are files created during a build, but it is possible for a function to return a source file as part of its result. Such a file thus becomes both a source and a derived, and it must be protected from weeding like any other derived.

Of course, this description ignores the complexities of concurrent activity by the repository and function cache servers, which we'll consider in a moment. It also doesn't reflect the realities of performing a marking algorithm on a graph log that may be too large to fit in main memory. That is, the marking phase cannot be implemented as a straightforward, depth-first walk of the DAG. Instead, the weeder performs a breadth-first walk by making multiple passes over the graph log. It maintains the "marks" with a bit vector, one bit per cache entry (which does fit in memory). Initially, the weeder sets the mark bits corresponding to the cache indices of the roots to be retained. It also makes a snapshot of the graph log file. It then scans the graph log snapshot serially and writes a subset of its entries to a new temporary file as follows. For each input graph log entry it encounters, the weeder consults the mark bit vector. If the bit corresponding to the entry's cache index is not set, the graph log entry is appended to the temporary file. If, however, the input graph log entry's mark bit is set, the weeder sets the mark bits corresponding to the cache indices of each of its children and does not write out the graph log entry. When the entire graph log snapshot has been read, the weeder repeats this marking process, using the newly written temporary file in place of the snapshot. This process repeats, each time creating a new (smaller) file of entries, until a scan causes no additional mark bits to be set. This concludes the marking phase. During the sweep phase, the graph log is rewritten, retaining from the original file only the entries whose mark bits are set.

This breadth-first algorithm can require up to $d$ iterations, where $d$ is the depth of the call graph. Although $d$ is not expected to be large (perhaps 10-20), the weeder implements an optimization that reduces the number of iterations. Instead of writing out the unmarked graph log entries immediately, it holds as many as possible in a fixed-size memory buffer. Whenever the weeder sets the mark bit for a child of the entry it is processing, it also checks the buffer to see if the graph log entry for the child happens to be there. If so, it recursively processes the child entry and deletes it from the buffer. In effect, the buffer turns a pure breadth-first walk of the DAG into a "best effort" depth-first one, with the weeder descending from parent to child as far as possible based on the contents of the buffer. When the buffer is full, the unmarked entries it contains are written out to the temporary file. It is evident that the performance of this buffer-based algorithm depends on a space-time tradeoff: the larger the buffer, the greater the number of entries processed per iteration, and therefore the smaller the number of iterations required. Experience with this algorithm is reported in Section 11.5.[3]

[3] While this multi-pass algorithm has appealing flexibility, Moore's Law and the passage of time since Vesta was designed have rendered it nearly unnecessary. A system size of 20 million source lines (page 30) and some conservative assumptions about cache maintenance suggest a cache size of about 10 million entries. If a graph log entry averages under 1,000 bytes, then the entire graph log will fit in the memory of a modern server. This suggests that for a system of the size Vesta targeted, the multi-pass mark-and-sweep algorithm is perhaps no longer needed. On the other hand, during the same passage of time, software systems have continued to grow in size, and there are contemporary systems whose size significantly exceeds Vesta's original design target. To accommodate them today, the graph log would again strain memory capacity and necessitate using the multi-pass algorithm.

### 9.2.2 Concurrent Weeding

We turn now to the concurrent interactions of the evaluator, cache server, and weeder. We noted above that the weeder's operation must interfere as little as possible with ongoing evaluations. This means that a simplistic "stop the world" approach, as is used in some garbage collectors, is unacceptable, for it would prevent evaluations from making progress for many minutes or even hours. The weeder does not "lock out" the evaluator and cache server; they continue to operate nearly normally. However, the weeder achieves roughly the same effect as if it had been able to suspend all evaluations, even though it executes concurrently with them. The effect is as if there were a "critical moment" at which the weeder instantaneously examines the state of the cache server and all evaluations, and any cache entry that is not reachable either from a specified root or from a cache entry in use by an evaluation at that moment becomes a candidate for subsequent deletion. Since the weeder cannot do this instantaneous state examination and processing, the challenge in the weeder's implementation is to achieve that effect while coping with complications of the changing cache state. In this section we consider the most significant of these complexities.

Because the cache server and evaluator(s) continue to execute in parallel with the weeder, they continue to create new cache entries and to access existing ones. The weeder must arrange not to delete any of these entries, else chaos will result. This means that, in addition to marking the cache entries reachable from the specified roots, the weeder must also mark for retention any cache entries created or accessed by evaluations in progress while the weeder is running, as well as all their descendants. Obviously, newly created cache entries won't appear in the graph log snapshot that the weeder makes when it begins executing, so an alternate mechanism is required to identify them.[4] Moreover, an ongoing evaluation can get a cache hit on an entry that is not reachable from any of the designated roots, and the weeder needs a way to detect and retain such entries as well (along with all of the entries reachable from them).

Vesta employs a single mechanism for both cases, *leases* [21, 44]. A lease is an agreement between two or more parties that remains valid up to a prearranged time even if the parties are not in active communication. Here, the parties involved are the evaluator, the cache server, and the weeder, and the entities being leased are cache entries. The agreement among the parties is that a lease on a cache entry is quite literally a lease on life; that is, while a lease on a cache entry is in effect, the cache entry may not be deleted. More precisely, the lease protects from deletion the cache entry, the derived files on which its result value depends, and all of its descendants.

[4] At first blush, it might seem that no alternate mechanism is needed, because the cache server could adopt the simple rule that, regardless of the weeder's deletion instructions, it won't delete anything appended to the graph log after the weeder has taken its snapshot. While this would certainly prevent a newly created entry from being deleted, such an entry can have a pre-existing one among its descendants, which might not otherwise be marked by the weeder. The descendant would therefore be identified for deletion, but that would violate the requirement to retain any cache entry needed by an ongoing evaluation.

Intuitively, a cache entry acquires a lease when it is used by the evaluator, indicating that it is of interest to an evaluation in progress. Thus, a newly created cache entry automatically acquires a lease at "birth". Additionally, whenever a cache hit occurs on a cache entry, the entry acquires a lease. If it already had a lease, the lease is renewed, meaning that its expiration time is extended as if it had been newly created. Thus, when a cache entry is created, all of its children are leased, since each one was either newly created or the result of a cache hit. Leases expire after a fixed time, unless they are renewed, either by a cache hit or explicitly by the evaluator. (The latter is rare, but can happen in a long-running evaluation.[5])

In order to respect the leasing agreement, the weeder must discover, at some point before it completes its marking phase, which cache entries have leases. The cache server provides this information to the weeder (as a bit vector, indexed by cache index), and the weeder then repeats the same marking algorithm that it used on the original graph log snapshot, this time using the leased cache entries as the "roots" for the marking. When the marking is completed, the weeder instructs the cache server to delete all unmarked cache entries contained in the original graph log snapshot.

While closer to the truth than the single mark-and-sweep algorithm of the preceding section, the algorithm just outlined still does not deal completely with the asynchronous behavior of the evaluator/cache and the weeder. As we noted above, because the cache server and the weeder are running concurrently, additional cache entries can become leased while the weeder is running. In particular, this can happen after the weeder has begun its second marking pass. The weeder will be unaware of such entries and therefore may fail to mark them for retention, thereby defeating the whole purpose of having leases.

This is a fundamental race, and the interactions between the cache server and the weeder required to address it are complex and subtle. As we examine them, it will help to keep the following invariants in mind, which formulate more precisely the informal statement of the weeder's actions: to preserve all cache entries associated with the specified roots and ongoing evaluations. These invariants are expressed in terms of a particular significant instant during the weeding process, denoted by $t_c$.

- $I_1$ A cache entry identified as a root in the input supplied to the weeder is retained, as are all its descendants.
- $I_2$ A cache entry created after $t_c$ is retained.
- $I_3$ A cache entry leased at $t_c$ is retained, as are all its descendants.
- $I_4$ A cache entry created before $t_c$ that becomes leased between $t_c$ and the completion of weeding must have been identified for retention before $t_c$.

The first three invariants follow intuitively from the description of the intended effect of the weeder. The final one is less evident, but fundamental. It establishes a

[5] The evaluator must ensure that leases on cache entries don't expire while it is using them. This suggests that the lease duration should equal or exceed that of the longest conceivable evaluation. Parameters of this sort are notoriously fragile; instead, the Vesta evaluator includes the necessary machinery to renew leases when necessary, permitting an evaluation to run indefinitely.

window of time during which a certain set of pre-existing unleased cache entries cannot become leased. These cache entries are then candidates for deletion.

With this background, we can now look at the actual weeder algorithm.

1. The weeder tells the cache server to suspend lease expiration until further notice.
2. The weeder snapshots the graph log and records the set of all cache indices in use, $C_u$.
3. The weeder carries out the marking algorithm of Section 9.2.1, using the roots supplied as input to the weeder. This algorithm produces $C_r$, the set of cache indices for entries reachable from the specified roots.
4. The weeder computes $H = C_u - C_r$, the set of unmarked cache indices, and passes it to the cache server. The cache server establishes $H$ as a *hit filter*, meaning that, until otherwise instructed, the cache server forces a cache miss on an unleased cache entry whose index is in the hit filter. (The moment at which the hit filter takes effect is $t_c$, which we demonstrate below.)
5. The weeder obtains from the cache server the set of cache indices for leased cache entries.
6. The weeder tells the cache server to resume lease expiration.
7. The weeder performs the marking algorithm on the graph log snapshot, using the leased entries obtained in step 5 as the roots. This algorithm produces $C_l$, the set of cache indices for entries reachable from the leased cache entries.
8. The weeder computes $D = H - C_l$, the set of unmarked cache indices remaining after the preceding step, and passes it to the cache server, instructing it to delete them and then discard its hit filter.
9. The weeder writes a new graph log consisting of the subset of the snapshot entries whose indices are in $C_r \cup C_l$, plus any entries that were added to the graph log since the snapshot was taken at step 2.

We now sketch how this algorithm maintains the four invariants. The notation $t_i$ refers to the time at which the $i^{th}$ step in the algorithm begins. It is easy to see that $C_r$ is the set of all cache entries specified as roots to the weeder, plus all of their descendants. Since $D$, the set of entries that is deleted, excludes $C_r$, invariant $I_1$ is established. Establishing $I_2$ is equally straightforward, since $D$ is a subset of $C_u$, the entries in the graph log snapshot, so an entry created after the snapshot is made will not be deleted. To see how $I_3$ is established, consider the set of cache entries obtained by the weeder at step 5. Since lease expiration is disabled between $t_2$ and $t_6$, this set contains the set of leased entries at $t_c$. Hence the set $C_l$ computed at step 7 includes the set of cache entries leased at $t_c$ and all their descendants, as required by invariant $I_3$.

Establishing $I_4$ is more involved. Consider a cache entry created before $t_c$ that becomes leased between $t_c$ and the completion of weeding after step 8. If it had been created after $t_2$, its cache index would not be in $C_u$, and hence the entry would implicitly have been identified for retention at $t_c$, since only the entries corresponding to a subset of $C_u$ (namely, $D$) will be deleted. Therefore, the entry was created before $t_2$ and its cache index is then in $C_u$. Now suppose the cache index is also in $H$, the hit filter. Then, the entry cannot have become leased between $t_c$ and the end of weeding, since during this interval the cache server would force a miss on the entry. Therefore, the entry's index is in $C_u - H$, or $C_r$, which is precisely the set of cache entries marked for retention before $t_c$. This establishes $I_4$.

This informal proof sketch shows that the weeder algorithm maintains the invariants, but the invariants do not actually specify what is to be deleted. That is, although they specify what is to be retained, they do not prohibit additional entries from being retained. The weeder is permitted to do this, but it must maintain another invariant: everything referenced by a retained cache entry must be retained. More formally, we must show that after weeding is complete and the set $D$ of cache entries has been removed, no retained cache entry has a descendant in $D$.

Let $C$ be the set of cache entries at the moment that deletion begins, and let $D$ be the set of cache entries to be deleted, as defined in step 8 of the algorithm. For a cache entry $e$, let children($e$) denote the set of cache entries that are immediate descendants of $e$. We want to show that $\forall e \in C - D : children(e) \cap D = \emptyset$.

Assume $e \in C - D$, so $e \notin D$. Since $D = H - C_l = C_u - C_r - C_l = C_u - (C_r \cup C_l)$, either $e \in C_r \cup C_l$ or $e \notin C_u$.

1. $e \in C_r \cup C_l$. Suppose $e \in C_r$. By the definition of $C_r$, $children(e) \subset C_r$ and hence by the definition of $D$, $children(e) \cap D = \emptyset$. The reasoning for $e \in C_l$ is similar.
2. $e \notin C_u$. Since $C_u$ is the graph log snapshot, $e$ must have been created after $t_2$. There are two cases.
   a) If $e$ was created at or before $t_c$, then since lease expiration was disabled between $t_2$ and $t_c$, $e$ must be leased. Therefore, $children(e) \subset C_l$ and by the definition of $D$, $children(e) \cap D = \emptyset$.
   b) If $e$ was created between $t_c$ and $t_8$, then for each $e' \in children(e)$ there are three cases.
      i. If $e'$ was created after $t_5$, then $e' \notin C_u$, so $e' \notin H$, the hit filter. Since $D \subseteq H$, $e' \notin D$.
      ii. If $e'$ was created between $t_2$ and $t_5$, its lease cannot have expired by $t_5$ and it therefore must be in $C_l$. By the definition of $D$, $e' \notin D$.
      iii. If $e'$ was created before $t_2$, then $e' \in C_u$. If $e' \in C_r$, then by the definition of $D$, $e' \notin D$. Since $e' \notin C_r$, then by the definition of the hit filter, $e' \in H$. Now, $e'$ must be leased no later than the time $e$ was created, which by assumption is after $t_c$. This is because the evaluator ensures that when a cache entry is created, all its children are leased. If $e'$ was leased before $t_c$, then its lease cannot have expired by $t_5$, so $e' \in C_l$ and therefore $e' \notin D$. If $e'$ did not become leased until after $t_c$ (but before $e$ becomes leased), then it must be the result of a cache hit at that moment. But this is impossible, since $e' \in H$ and the hit filter prevents cache hits on unleased entries it includes.

The forgoing presentation of the weeder's algorithm focuses on the retention and deletion of cache entries, but the weeder must arrange for deletion of derived files as well. This essential detail is easily added. As the weeder marks cache entries for retention in steps 3 and 7, it accumulates the shortids of their associated derived files. Following step 8, the weeder instructs the repository server to delete any derived files created before weeding commenced that are not included in the set of shortids it has built up. It is easy to see that these actions retain all the derived files associated with cache entries in $C - D$.

A number of additional complexities of the weeder's implementation have been omitted from this brief discussion. Naturally, the weeder must be able to recover gracefully from failure of itself or of the cache server at any point in the course of its execution. In some cases this is handled by restarting, in other cases by forward error recovery. The latter is necessary once the deletion phase has begun. These details are essential for a robust system, but they use well-known techniques and so are not further elaborated here.

## In Summary

The Vesta weeder, while essentially invisible to the users of the system, performs an essential role in implementing the automatic management of derived files. This feature of Vesta greatly simplifies the use and administration of the system, since users never need to know or manage the name space of derived files, and administrators can, with a few simple lines of input to the weeder, arrange for coherent reductions in storage consumption.

# Part IV

# Assessing Vesta

Parts I–III presented the overall design of the Vesta configuration management system, its functionality as seen by a user, and many aspects of its implementation. This final series of chapters assesses Vesta in several ways. Chapter 10 surveys competing configuration management systems and qualitatively examines their relative strengths and weaknesses. Chapter 11 quantitatively evaluates Vesta's performance and how it compares to the most widely used system-building tool, Make. Finally, Chapter 12 concludes with a reflection on Vesta's goals and the extent to which they were achieved, as well as the practical impact of the system to date and its potential future.

# 10

# Competing Systems

Virtually every organization with a large code base uses a collection of software tools to build and manage it. Sometimes an organization develops its own custom set of tools, but more often it satisfies its software configuration needs by acquiring software externally. In the latter case, the configuration management solutions fall into two broad categories: loosely connected individual tools and tightly integrated suites. In this chapter we will look at representatives of both types. Our purpose in examining these tools is to understand how they differ from Vesta and to identify ways in which their functionality is lacking.

## 10.1 Loosely Connected Configuration Management Tools

Probably the majority of development organizations use a loose combination of tools to address their software configuration management needs. In general, each of these tools is designed to work to a considerable extent in isolation, solving a particular part of the "SCM problem" (see Chapter 1). While they may be cognizant of other tools and include functionality intended to facilitate interconnection with them, these tools cannot be considered integrated to the extent that Vesta or the other systems designed to address the overall SCM problem are. Most of these tools were originally developed for small-scale systems of perhaps a few hundred thousand source lines.

Representative of the most common SCM tools in use today are RCS (the Revision Control System) [59, 60], CVS (the Concurrent Versions System) [23], and Make [18]. They are often used together, with RCS or CVS handling version management and source control, and Make handling system description and building. We have briefly touched on these systems, especially Make, in the preceding chapters; we now look at them in more detail. All are widely available on both Unix and Windows platforms.

### 10.1.1 RCS

RCS is a tool for storing and managing multiple versions of individual source files. A file's version history can branch into an arbitrarily complex tree. RCS provides locking to enforce source control, and includes tools for merging changes made by different developers.

RCS stores multiple versions of a source file in a single disk file, in a way that avoids duplicating material that is common to more than one version. This technique saves disk space, but makes the individual versions inconvenient to access, since a particular version cannot be read directly and must first be extracted into a separate file. In a modern computing system, the benefits of storing multiple versions of a source file compactly are slight, since the disk requirements of most development environments are dominated by the space consumed by derived files. (Data in support of this observation appears in Section 11.3.2.) Moreover, the price of disk space has been dropping exponentially for years and continues to do so, while the growth in the rate of source file production is much more gradual.

In place of RCS, some organizations use SCCS (the Source Code Control System) [53], an older but essentially similar system.

### 10.1.2 CVS

One disadvantage of both RCS and SCCS is that source files are versioned individually; these systems provide no coordinated versioning across related files. Although RCS provides mechanisms for *tagging* a group of versioned files, those mechanisms are manual and error-prone. CVS attempts to remedy this problem. CVS is a front-end to RCS that extends the notion of version control from individual files to arbitrary directory trees called *modules*. In CVS, the unit of check-out is an entire module. Hence, it is easier to work on a group of related files with CVS. A drawback is that whenever a user checks out a module for the first time, all the files are copied from shared storage to a private workspace, which can be slow.

Another important difference between CVS and the other systems is that CVS does not use locking to enforce source control. Instead, it uses an optimistic concurrency control model in which each developer is free to modify a copy of any source in the central repository at any time. CVS includes a facility for mechanically merging changes made by other developers into one's own source tree. Developers typically apply this facility just before checking in their own changes, without giving much thought to whether the two sets of changes are compatible. The assumption is that if the changes do not both affect the same region of the same file, there is no problem. Changes in the same region are reported as conflicts, and the developer is required to fix them before checking in. But if two developers make semantically conflicting edits to different files, or even to distinct portions of the same file, these conflicting changes are not reported. Despite these dangers, some organizations prefer the CVS approach to concurrency control, which permits looser coordination than the check-out, check-in approach used in Vesta.

A related problem with CVS's concurrency control is the lack of atomic operations on the CVS repository. If user *A* is checking in a module while user *B* is checking it out, *B* may get some but not all of *A*'s changes. Hence, there are time windows in which users can see inconsistent versions of files in a CVS module.[1]

### 10.1.3 Make

The functionality and behavior of Make was discussed in Section 2.5. In its myriad variants, Make is perhaps the most widely used system description and building tool and, as such, the natural point of comparison for any other software configuration management system that includes building functionality.

Recall that the input to Make consists of *Makefiles*, which specify the dependencies between the components of a software system and provide instructions for building them. When it is run, Make examines the dependencies and rebuilds any components that are out of date. Developers like Make because the Makefile syntax is simple (if a little cryptic), the tool is fairly easy to use, and, as a fairly general-purpose engine, it can be adapted to other tasks besides building software in which programmable actions must be carried out on the basis of dependency relationships.

The most serious problems with Make are that (1) it does not maintain dependencies automatically, and (2) many dependencies are simply inexpressible or too costly to express in practice [19]. Because the dependency relation for a large software system is complicated and changes frequently over time, one can easily specify too few or too many dependencies. Excess dependencies can lead to unnecessary work being done during a build, while insufficient dependencies can lead to inconsistent builds.

To alleviate the first problem, many organizations employ tools that compute dependencies automatically from source files and alter the dependency relation encoded in the Makefile. A widely used tool in this category is Makedepend. However, Makedepend suffers from at least two deficiencies. First, it detects only certain kinds of dependencies, namely, dependencies between C/C++ source files and any files directly or indirectly included by them. Second, there is no mechanism to run Makedepend automatically when dependencies change. Since Makedepend can take a substantial amount of time to run, developers tend not to use it routinely, relying instead on their intuition about whether dependency relationships have changed. Of course, this is risky and error-prone, since the failure to run Makedepend can result in an inconsistent build, which is precisely the problem it was created to solve.

The second problem — the impossibility or cost of expressing dependencies in a Makefile — has not been addressed by auxiliary tools in the Make marketplace. As a result, even if a development organization religiously uses Makedepend, its Makefiles rarely if ever capture all the dependencies on the environment. For example, every derived file produced by a Makefile depends on the building instructions in the Makefile itself, but developers typically omit this dependency. Were they to

[1] Some vendors of CVS-based systems have made check-ins atomic, but not all. In particular, non-atomic check-in is a documented property in the release of CVS current as of this writing, which is version 1.12.11.

include it, they would find every derived file being rebuilt every time the Makefile changed, which is of course excessively conservative and a big time-waster. However, by omitting the dependency, developers must instead manually invalidate or delete those derived files that are affected by a Makefile change, an error-prone process in itself. There are many other dependencies that are cumbersome or impossible to specify in Make, including dependencies on the particular versions of tools (compilers and linkers) that a software system requires, on command-line switches, and on environment variables.

Make is a stand-alone tool, meaning that it is not integrated with version management tools such as those discussed above. The lack of integration manifests itself in two important respects. First and most obviously, the sources to be built must be explicitly extracted (checked out) from the version management software's repository before they can be built, since they cannot otherwise be named as ordinary files in the underlying file system. In an attempt to provide some integration along these lines, some variants of Make have machinery to perform RCS check-outs on missing source files, but this facility is quite limited and clearly not a general solution to the problem. Second, explicit source versions are not specified in Makefiles, since Make and the underlying file system on which it depends have no concept of a file version. This means that Make provides no configuration management support; it does not enable developers to specify which source versions go together. Instead, it becomes the developer's responsibility and burden to check out the correct versions of all components before performing a build, a laborious and error-prone process if one is not building the latest version.

Make also fails to scale well. A large software system can be specified by a hierarchy of Makefiles, in which one Makefile invokes Make recursively on other Makefiles. However, there are some substantial problems with such an arrangement. The complete tree of system components must be checked out before building, for the reasons described in the preceding paragraph. More seriously, the recursion always has to be completely carried out; that is, when Make is invoked on the root Makefile, it must run all the way down to the leaves of the dependency tree to check for stale dependencies. Because Make uses file timestamps to test whether a derived file is up to date, the test for stale dependencies requires Make to determine the last-modified time of *every source and derived file* comprising a system. Although some of these timestamps may be cached by the file system, they often require network round-trips to file servers and/or disk reads. Thus, Make's dependency checking can be an extremely time-consuming process for multi-million line software systems. All the dependency checks are required even if the entire system to be built is up to date. By contrast, Vesta can determine, with a single cache hit, that a subtree of a large system need not be built. Make's inability to do so cripples its performance for large systems, and the larger the system, the worse the problem becomes.

Finally, Make's reliance on last-modified times can lead to inconsistent builds in several ways. A common instance of this problem arises when building an older version (not the latest one) of a system. When the old source versions are checked out (that is, extracted from the version control system), they frequently have timestamps that precede the timestamps of the latest ones and therefore also tend to precede the timestamps of the derived files from the most recent build. Hence, Make's simplistic comparison strategy causes it to conclude that the derived files are up to date. The developer's only safe recourse is to delete all of the derived files, thereby forcing Make to build the system from scratch. This is more drastic than is typically needed, and wasteful of the developer's time. Yet the use of last-modified times affords no other options.

Bell Laboratories' Nmake [19] addresses most of the problems with Make that we have just discussed, along with others, though it does not fully solve them. For example, Nmake includes a built-in static dependency generator that does its own parsing of source files looking for `#include` statements in C code. This greatly reduces the likelihood of omitted dependencies, but the dependencies generated can be overly conservative, increasing the amount of rebuilding work needed. Moreover, new parsing support has to be written whenever Nmake is used on code written in a new language. Nmake includes an improved timestamp-checking algorithm that fails only when an erroneous system clock gives two different versions of a file the same timestamp, and it caches timestamps and other state information in order to speed up its dependency analysis somewhat. These improvements eliminate the most common pitfalls in applying Make to large system builds, but they do not help with the fundamental scalability problems.

## 10.2 Integrated Configuration Management Systems

Integrated configuration management, in contrast to the systems we have just examined, tightly couples the functions of version management and system building. This integration sometimes extends further, perhaps even encompassing the entire development environment. For example, a language-specific editor and incremental compiler may be tightly connected with each other and with the versioning and building tools. Many such language-specific systems have been built. For the present discussion, however, we consider only systems that support, at least in principle, language-independent development while replacing individual software configuration tools with integrated management functions.

### 10.2.1 DSEE

Perhaps the first widely known system to integrate versioning and building outside of a specific language context was the DOMAIN Software Engineering Environment (DSEE), which effectively addressed many of the problems with Make and loosely connected version management systems [37, 38].[2] For source control, DSEE used a custom file system that allowed individual versions of source files to be named directly; no separate check-out step was required. However, the tools (including the builder) did not generally traffic in explicitly version-numbered files. Instead, files

[2] Although DSEE was widely known in academic circles, its availability was limited to Apollo platforms.

were named without version numbers, and each developer could control the binding of these names to specific versions of files in the file system. The means of controlling this binding was called a *configuration thread* and was effectively a list of rules for translating unversioned names into versioned ones. The rules were quite flexible and permitted various styles of development. Indeed, DSEE's designers characterized development styles as "cautious" and "dynamic" [37], the former being one in which the configuration thread isolates the developer from changes made by others by using binding rules that specify only files under the developer's direct control. A more "dynamic" rule might be "use the checked-out version of file $F$ if one exists, otherwise use the latest version on the main branch of the development tree." Obviously, such a rule could cause the binding of a name to change if another developer checks in a file on the main branch. Dynamic rules like this can become problematic as the number of developers working simultaneously on a system increases, since the potential for unexpected "rebinding" increases as well, causing one developer's build to break as a side-effect of another's check-in action.[3]

For building, DSEE read *system models* that enumerated the sources to be built, their dependencies (e.g., header files), and the build rules for constructing the software. DSEE provided automatic derived file management and the capability for the derived files produced by one build to be reused in another. Unfortunately, the DSEE papers do not describe the system modeling language in any detail, nor do they discuss either the consistency guarantees or the performance characteristics of building with derived reuse. Nevertheless, these overall characteristics significantly influenced Vesta's designers, and the inclusion of related concepts and mechanisms in Vesta reflect their use in DSEE.

In addition to version management and software construction facilities, DSEE also included work-flow facilities required by the broader software engineering process. For the most part, these facilities were independent of the configuration management facilities described above, but there was a small degree of integration between them. For example, checking in a source module might cause a task on a task list to be recorded as being completed. DSEE also included a facility for specifying human-sensible semantic dependencies between sources. For example, the dependence between a program's interface code and its documentation might be recorded as a semantic dependency. Whenever the program's interface was modified, a technical writer would be informed of the need to update the documentation.

[3] DSEE also incorporated the notion of a *bound configuration thread*, essentially a snapshot of the binding computed by a configuration thread at a given instant. A bound configuration thread provides the ultimate in cautious development, as it binds all unversioned names to explicitly versioned ones, but it does not appear to have been used for this purpose in DSEE. Rather, it seems to have been used chiefly for keeping an archival record of the versions used in a particular build. The `files` and `import` clauses of Vesta system models are quite similar to DSEE's bound configuration thread or, more precisely, to configuration threads that restrict themselves to rules that include explicit version numbers. In fact, these Vesta notions were originally inspired by DSEE, though they found their way into Vesta via at least two intermediate systems, including Cedar [35].

### 10.2.2 ClearCASE

In the early 1990s, the DSEE developers started a company to build ClearCASE [4], a commercial SCM system based on the DSEE philosophy but not tied to the Apollo platform. The company was subsequently acquired by Rational Software Corporation and, more recently, by IBM. ClearCASE is probably the best known integrated software configuration management system.

ClearCASE's source control mechanism is quite similar to DSEE's. In ClearCASE, the configuration threads are called *views*, but the idea is exactly the same; rules are used to map unversioned file names to particular source versions. ClearCASE views are implemented by a custom *multiversioned* file system that plugs into the operating system's file system switch. As in DSEE, looking up a file in a ClearCASE view requires some form of database access to translate the unversioned name to a versioned one, which introduces some overhead on file opening operations.

ClearCASE differs from DSEE in two important respects. First, ClearCASE is more portable; it runs on both Windows and Unix systems. Second, ClearCASE is Make-based. That is, ClearCASE system models retain the syntax and semantics of Make. However, ClearCASE includes an alternative builder, ClearMake, that corrects many of Make's problems. In particular, ClearMake includes a mechanism that, during a build, automatically records the file dependencies and results of each external tool invocation (e.g., compilers and linkers). These cached dependencies and results are then used during subsequent builds to bypass tool invocations if the specified files are unchanged. ClearMake can therefore perform more reliable incremental builds than standard Make since it does not depend for correctness on manually created dependency information. However, build-order dependencies and dependencies on files outside of ClearCASE's control must still be listed explicitly.

Although the quality of dependency checking has improved in ClearMake, it is no faster than in standard Make. Only invocations of external tools are cached so, just like Make, ClearMake builds programs upwards from the leaves, rather than downwards from the root. As we noted above in the discussion of Make, this approach has serious performance problems in building large systems.[4]

One advantage provided by ClearMake over standard Make is that derived files are managed by the system and can be shared, enabling developers to benefit from each other's builds. However, ClearCASE uses heuristics to select the candidate derived files for sharing, so the specific cases in which such sharing is possible are not evident. It is possible for the heuristics to fail to select a valid candidate for sharing, in which case an unnecessary tool invocation will occur. In Vesta, these events correspond to false cache misses and, because of the considerable pains Vesta takes in its fine-grained dependency analysis (Section 8.4), they are quite rare. More seriously, ClearMake does not automatically capture all dependencies that affect building, so it can occasionally produce an inconsistent result. In Vesta, dependency detection is automatic and complete, so inconsistent builds cannot occur.

[4] In Vesta parlance, the approach used by Make and ClearMake is analogous to caching only `_run_tool` calls. Section 11.2.3 shows that much better performance is achieved by caching larger units of work.

The ClearCASE MultiSite product supports replication of ClearCASE source repositories across multiple, geographically distributed sites [3]. Vesta's approach to replication (Section 4.3) differs sharply from that of ClearCASE. In ClearCASE, the choice of what to replicate is made at a coarse grain — an entire Versioned Object Base, of which there are typically only one or a few per site. In Vesta, one can choose what to replicate down to the level of individual versions of software packages, if desired. ClearCASE replicas exhibit eventual consistency — that is, an update algorithm is used that would eventually make the replicas identical if they all were to stop changing for sufficiently long — but there are no clear guarantees on what differences can exist between replicas when changes have been made recently. Vesta defines a simple, flexible notion of consistency for its replicas that takes advantage of the fact that sources are immutable once they have been added to the repository. ClearCASE's replica update algorithm is operation-based and requires knowledge of the full set of replicas. That is, each ClearCase replica must keep a history of recent operations that have changed it and for each other replica keep track of which changes have not yet been propagated. Vesta's algorithm is state-based and works when the set of replicas is unknown and changing; the replication tool simply compares the states of two replicas, copying any data from the first that is missing and desired in the second. The ClearCASE approach has some advantages; in particular, fewer administrative decisions are required as to what to replicate, and the operation-based approach to updates should scale better when replicas share a great deal of data but very little is changing. However, the Vesta approach is much simpler, provides a clearly defined level of consistency, and supports usage patterns where the replicas are more loosely coupled.

## 10.3 Other Systems

In this chapter, we have surveyed only a few representative (and, generally, widely known) software configuration management tools and systems. Numerous others are described in the research literature, or are distributed commercially, or are available as open source [2, 5, 8, 14, 41, 42, 45, 46, 51, 58, 61]. Many of these systems do their version management and source control using paradigms very similar to those of RCS or CVS, and a great many handle system modeling and building using versions of Make with various improvements. Thus, although RCS, CVS, and Make are now very old tools, they still represent of the state of the industry. This is not to imply that other aspects of software configuration management have not advanced. Indeed, commercial systems often have sophisticated features for bug tracking, workflow management, high-level project dependencies, and graphical user interfaces that go beyond the scope of what is included in Vesta, while the research and open source systems explore a wide variety of ideas in these and other domains.

Although the RCS/CVS/Make paradigm is dominant, there are some notable exceptions, especially in version management. Several systems name and manage the sets of *changes* in a software system rather than complete versions of the system itself [8, 45, 46]. A motivating idea behind change sets is that users can synthesize many different versions of a system by mixing and matching various change sets. It is hard to see the practicality of this idea, since changes from different sets seem quite likely to conflict with one another. Another notable difference in version management appears in systems that assign a version identifier to every object in a hierarchical directory tree, including the directories themselves [41,42,61] (and there are even more complex models for version management [17]). While these approaches have some intellectual interest, they impose a cognitive burden on the user that Vesta avoids and whose necessity is doubtful.

Finally, there is the SCM approach taken in integrated development environments, such as Microsoft's Visual Studio. These environments attempt to bring all phases of the development process beginning with the creation of code under one roof, with tight integration of editor, compiler, debugger, performance analysis tools, versioning, building, and configuration management. These systems provide a productive environment for small-to-medium sized programming projects, whose configuration management needs are generally modest. The philosophy of these environments emphasizes an "edit, then run" approach, with the machinery for compilation and linking being hidden from the user. While obviously attractive when it works, this approach does not scale well. It breaks down when simple heuristics fail to address the realities of version selection (say, in an organization with parallel threads of development), multi-platform deployment, control over compilation options (such as optimization levels) or library selection (for example, performance-based alternatives), distributed development (and the requisite replication of the code base), etc. In short, these systems address an important class of software development, but they do not address the problems that Vesta specifically targets.

# 11

# Vesta System Performance

Throughout the preceding chapters, we have focused on the "what" and the "how" of Vesta in order to show that, as a tool, Vesta provides the developer with essential functionality for large-scale software construction. In this chapter, we look at Vesta's performance. We will see that Vesta's functionality comes at no loss (and sometimes a gain) in performance when compared to Make, the most widely used alternative, and that it is practical to deploy Vesta's server-based facilities in support of a large development organization. The measurements presented here therefore assess resource usage on client machines (the evaluator and runtool server), on server machines (the repository and cache servers and the weeder), and on the network (the remote procedure call library used for client/server communication).

First, however, an important caveat. Vesta was designed to scale to handle the construction of very large software systems (see page 30), but at the time the measurements in this chapter were taken, no software system approaching the design target was under development in the Vesta environment. Thus, the measurements presented here do not directly validate the implementation within its design center. Instead, we must settle for measurements on smaller systems and extrapolate.

On the one hand, this is obviously less convincing than measurements on a production-scale system would be. Measuring the cache server on a cache of 10,000 entries doesn't directly provide any intuition about performance of the server on its design target of 1,000,000 entries. On the other hand, since these measurements were taken, Vesta's user community has grown substantially. At one installation, over 300 developers are using it to manage a multi-million line code base. This is much closer to the design target established for Vesta. Anecdotal evidence indicates that the system has performed well, and that the bottlenecks that have arisen have not resulted from fundamental limitations but rather from implementation shortcuts that made sense in a prototype system. There is reason to hope that, with an open-source community now supporting Vesta, some of these deficiencies will eventually be corrected.[1]

---

[1] For example, the repository server is implemented entirely as a user-level process. This creates inefficiencies for the NFS server that could be eliminated if it were included in

In this context, we examine measurements of Vesta's behavior on small to medium-sized systems and project, qualitatively, how they would change for larger systems.

## 11.1 Platform Configuration

The measurements described in this chapter were performed with a typical Vesta system configuration, in which the evaluator and runtool server run on a single client machine, and the repository and function cache run on a single server machine. For the experiments involving Make, execution of Make occurred on the client machine, accessing a file server running a standard in-kernel NFS version 3 implementation. In both sets of experiments, the underlying files being served by the repository and NFS3 servers were mounted on a local Digital AdvFS file system using two directly attached Digital RZ28 SCSI disks.

The client machine used in these tests was a Digital AlphaStation 500 5/333, with a 333 MHz CPU and 192MB of memory. The server machine was a Digital AlphaStation 400 4/233, with a 233 MHz CPU and 192MB of memory. Both machines ran versions of Digital's Tru64 Unix. The two machines were connected by AN2, a custom, switched local-area network with 155 Mbps links. AN2 was a prototype of Digital's GIGAswitch/ATM high-bandwidth ATM network.

Obviously, these machines are several generations old and not representative of current hardware. They were the current technology in the late 1990's when the measurements reported in this chapter were taken. One would naturally expect the absolute performance for both Vesta and Make to be substantially better on modern hardware (and this is borne out anecdotally).

## 11.2 Overall System Performance

This section presents measurements of the overall performance of the Vesta system, as seen by a user. Here's a summary of the results:

- We compare the performance of Vesta against that of Make [18]. The measurements show that Vesta outperforms Make on both scratch and incremental builds. Moreover, in the most common case — an incremental build in which a small number of files are recompiled — Vesta substantially outperforms Make. This improved performance comes despite the fact that Vesta provides considerably stronger consistency guarantees than Make does.
- We present more detailed measurements of Vesta's client performance. The measurements show that the Vesta caching machinery performs quite well. The cost of incremental builds is indeed proportional to the magnitude of the change, not

the kernel. The implementers knew this when they initially developed Vesta, but at that time the convenience of development outside the kernel easily outweighed the inevitable performance hit.

to the total size of the software being built. The measurements also confirm that Vesta spends most of its time in `_run_tool` calls, indicating that the overhead induced by the evaluator and function cache is low.

- We characterize the memory usage of the evaluator and the runtool server — the two Vesta processes that generally run on client machines. The measurements show that the run-time memory consumption of these processes is reasonable and that Vesta does not compromise the performance of the other applications on the client machine because of its memory consumption.

The first two sets of measurements, which compare Make and Vesta, consist of three tests. The *Hello* test requires compiling and linking a toy "hello world" program. The *Evaluator* test requires building the Vesta evaluator, which in turn requires building all of the Vesta libraries used by the evaluator. The *Release* test entails building the entire Vesta release, which includes building all of the Vesta libraries, server programs, utilities, and test programs.

Table 11.1 summarizes various attributes of these three tests. The figure for total source lines includes all the C, C++, and header files in the Vesta implementation. The figure for the number of modules counts only the C files, not the header files. The number of `_run_tool` calls reported in the table is the number of times an external tool invocation is required during the test; it includes invocations of compilers, linkers, and archivers.[2] Finally, the number of packages reported is the number of separate packages comprised by the sources.

| Test | Total Source Lines | Number of Modules | Number of Runtools | Number of Packages |
|---|---|---|---|---|
| Hello | 10 | 1 | 2 | 1 |
| Evaluator | 53,304 | 103 | 117 | 11 |
| Release | 119,602 | 255 | 333 | 16 |

**Table 11.1.** Sizes of the Three Build Tests

To reiterate, even the largest test's size is well below that of the software systems for which Vesta was designed. In interpreting the results of these measurements later in this chapter, we consider how to extrapolate from this data to assess Vesta's scalability.

### 11.2.1 Performance Comparison with Make

As we examine the performance of Vesta and Make for both scratch and incremental builds, it is important to keep in mind exactly what we are comparing. Section 10.1.3 noted that Make does not always build consistent software systems, as Vesta does. Figures 11.1 and 11.2 show that Vesta's performance is competitive with

[2] Recall that the archiver is the Unix program that assembles a collection of object files into a library; see Section 2.4.

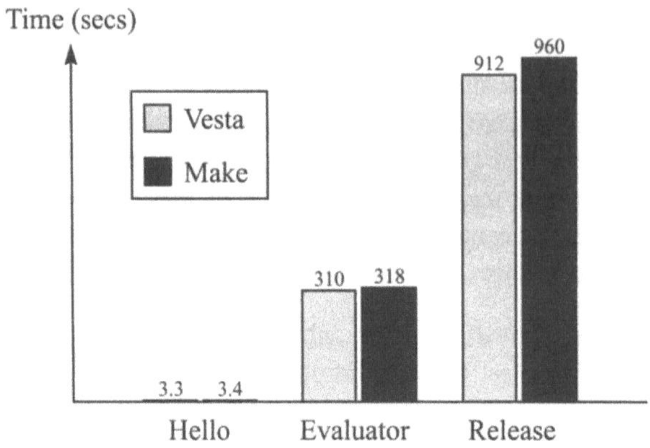


**Fig. 11.1.** Elapsed time in seconds for scratch builds of the three tests using Vesta and Make.

Make's even though Vesta is additionally providing a consistency guarantee. We previously noted that many organizations reduce inconsistencies in their builds by using Makedepend with Make. The times in these figures do not include the time to run Makedepend, for to do so would obviously tip the performance balance in Vesta's favor and Vesta would still provide a stronger consistency guarantee.

Figure 11.1 shows that Vesta is slightly faster than Make on scratch builds of all three build tests. Even though Vesta outperforms Make on scratch builds, it is worth noting that scratch builds occur less often under Vesta. Users of Make often initiate scratch builds in order to achieve consistency, as this is the only way to ensure it under Make. Vesta eliminates the need for scratch builds because Vesta always produces consistent incremental builds. However, if a user changes a low-level header file that is used in many places, a near-scratch build will result in which many files are recompiled. Figure 11.1 indicates that Vesta performs quite well on such builds.

Figure 11.2 shows that Vesta outperforms Make on incremental builds. The scenario it reports is an alteration to a single source file in each of the three tests followed by a run of the evaluator. The figure shows the elapsed incremental build times. In each test, the incremental build included one invocation of the compiler and one invocation of the linker. The time to run these tools is included in the elapsed times shown, and while it is different for each test, it is roughly the same for the three cases within a test.

What is the difference between the "Make One" and "Make All" columns? When a program is composed of sources spanning multiple packages (as occurs in the *Evaluator* and *Release* tests), developers using Make typically run Make only in the package (directory) on which they are working; these are the times reported under the "Make One" column. However, such incremental builds can lead to inconsistent results if files in any of the other packages of the program have changed. To get a more consistent build, developers can run Make in all of the contributing packages; these are the times reported under the "Make All" column. In this incremental test, however, no other packages were modified, so the difference between the "Make One"

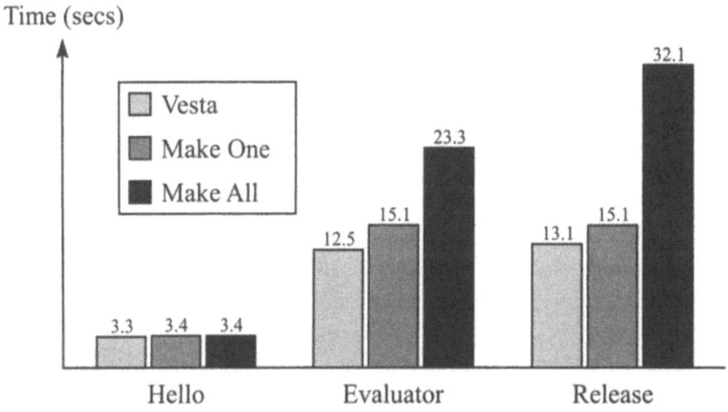


**Fig. 11.2.** Elapsed times in seconds for one-module, incremental builds under Vesta and Make. The "Make One" column is the time required to run Make in the single package in which the change was made, while the "Make All" column also includes the time required to run Make in each of the program's other packages.

and "Make All" columns is simply the time required by Make to determine that all the other packages were up-to-date.

The "Make All" scenario is much more of an apples-to-apples comparison with Vesta than the "Make One" scenario. However, neither Make scenario comes close to matching Vesta's consistency guarantees, particularly because they do *not* include the time required to run Makedepend in each of the relevant packages. Adding the time to run Makedepend would significantly heighten the "Make One" and "Make All" bars.

This figure shows that, except for the trivial Hello program, Vesta ran substantially faster than Make alone. One expects that Vesta's performance advantage would increase when building larger software, since incremental builds under Make and Makedepend require time proportional to the size of the software being built, while incremental builds under Vesta require time proportional to the magnitude of the change. This claim is confirmed by the fact that Vesta ran 86% faster than Make alone on the Evaluator test, but 145% faster on the larger Release test.

### 11.2.2 Performance Breakdown

Let's look in more detail where the time goes in Vesta in the scratch and incremental builds of Figures 11.1 and 11.2. The total elapsed time can be divided into three parts: the time spent in the Vesta evaluator itself, the time spent by the evaluator in remote procedure calls on the Vesta function cache, and the time spent in external `_run_tool` invocations. (The overheads due to the repository and the tool encapsulation machinery are included in the `_run_tool` time; as part of the tests, these overheads were not analyzed in any greater detail.)

For scratch builds, Figure 11.3 shows that the time spent doing evaluation and caching for non-trivial builds is no more than 8% of the total running time. Moreover,

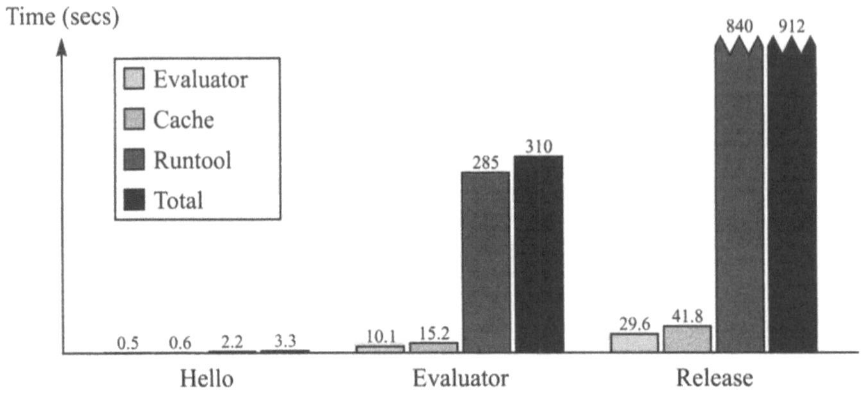


**Fig. 11.3.** Breakdown of scratch build elapsed times in seconds for each of Vesta's major components.

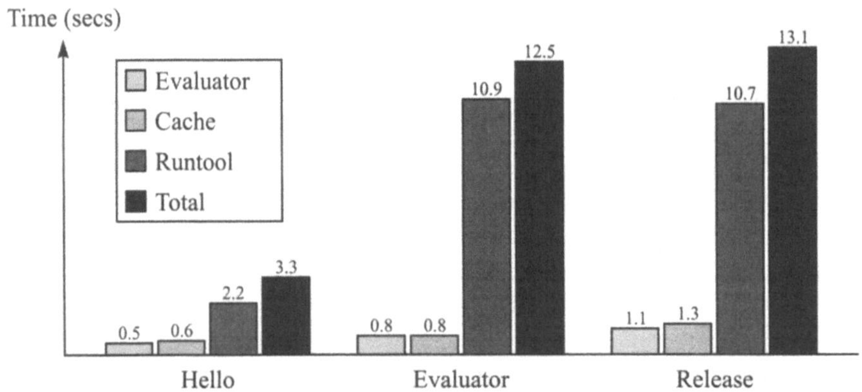


**Fig. 11.4.** Breakdown of one-module, incremental build elapsed times in seconds for each of Vesta's major components.

the larger the software being built, the smaller the fraction of total elapsed time spent running the evaluator and cache. As larger software is built with Vesta, this fraction should continue to decline somewhat and certainly should not increase.

The breakdown of the elapsed time for incremental builds is shown in Figure 11.4. It demonstrates that Vesta's performance scales well, at least for medium-sized programs. Even though the sources for the *Release* test are more than twice the size of those for the *Evaluator* test, the absolute times spent in the Vesta evaluator and function cache are small and nearly identical across the two builds. This result supports the claim that the time spent in the Vesta system proper is proportional to the magnitude of the change, not to the total size of the software being built.

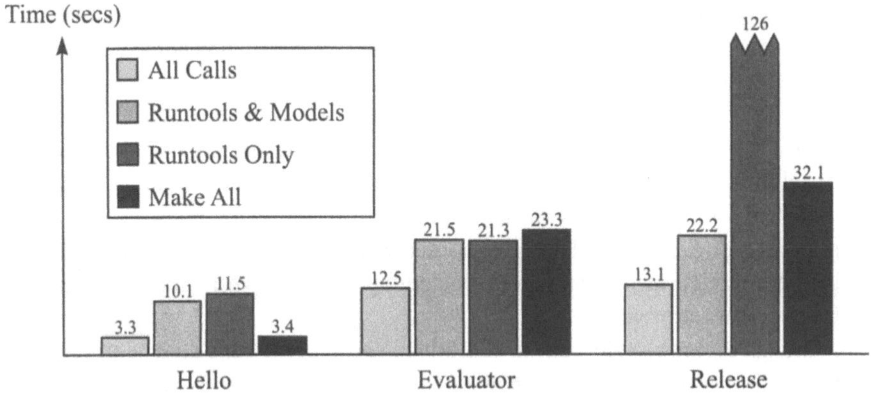


**Fig. 11.5.** Elapsed times of one-module, incremental builds in seconds with different Vesta caching levels. For comparison, the final column shows the incremental build time under Make.

### 11.2.3 Caching Analysis

Having seen that Vesta's overall performance, from a user's perspective, dominates Make's, let's look at some aspects of Vesta's behavior in more detail in order to project its scalability. In Chapter 8, we examined Vesta's caching machinery and emphasized that caching of user-defined function calls is necessary to achieve good overall system performance. This caching has its costs, most notably, the cost of computing each function's fine-grained dependencies. In this section we will see that, in practice, the benefits outweigh the costs.

To measure the effectiveness of caching user-defined functions, the same three tests were performed with three different levels of caching:

- calls of `_run_tool` only,
- calls of `_run_tool` and models,[3] and
- calls of `_run_tool`, models, and user-defined functions.

The first of these corresponds closely to what Make provides — the ability to avoid invocations of individual tools — but with Vesta's strong consistency guarantee. The second level, in caching model calls, incorporates a natural caching boundary because every package build is performed by evaluating the package's root model. The third level is Vesta's normal caching behavior. Figure 11.5 shows the results of doing incremental builds of the three tests with these three caching levels (in reverse order); the final column shows the "Make All" elapsed time from Figure 11.2 for comparison.

We can draw three main conclusions from this data:

[3] Recall that a Vesta model represents a one-argument closure that can be called from other functions and models.

- Caching all function calls produces substantial performance gains over the two lower levels of caching. This performance difference should become even bigger for larger software.
- Caching only `_run_tool` invocations is clearly *not* sufficient. When only these invocations are cached, the cost of doing incremental builds becomes proportional to the size of the software being built, not to the number of tool executions required. This is especially evident in the case of the *Release* test, where caching only `_run_tool` calls creates so many requests on the function cache that the build time grows by an order of magnitude over the Vesta norm in which all function calls are cached.
- Although caching model calls in addition to `_run_tool` calls does help, substantial additional performance benefits result when calls to user-defined functions are also cached. Again, the *Release* test demonstrates this point well; caching models in addition to `_run_tool` calls gives a 5.5x speedup, but caching user-defined function calls as well yields almost a 2x additional speedup factor.

We can therefore conclude that the benefits of performing fine-grained dependency analysis clearly outweigh its cost.

Recall from Section 8.4.4 that in addition to the normal cache entry created for each model evaluation, the evaluator also creates a special cache entry. These special cache entries yield faster cache hits, and the overhead required to create them is quite small. In the tests above, such special cache entries accounted for all the cache hits for model evaluations. This result clearly indicates the usefulness of these special cache entries.

### 11.2.4 Resource Usage

Let's now examine the CPU usage of the main components of the Vesta system, as well as the memory usage of client processes. More detailed measurements about the server components, the function cache and repository, appear in Sections 11.3 and 11.4 below.

#### CPU Usage

To measure the CPU usage, a simple script was used to monitor the evaluator, the runtool server, the function cache, and the repository during both scratch and incremental builds. This script invoked the Unix **ps** utility once every second.[4] During the builds, there was no other build in progress that was using the same function cache or repository, that is, the Vesta system was being used by a single client.

The evaluator and the runtool server execute on the client machine. As the data in Figure 11.6 show, the average CPU load on the client machine is below 5%. The CPU load caused by these two programs should remain about the same when building larger software.

[4] **ps** is a program that displays resource usage data about currently executing programs.

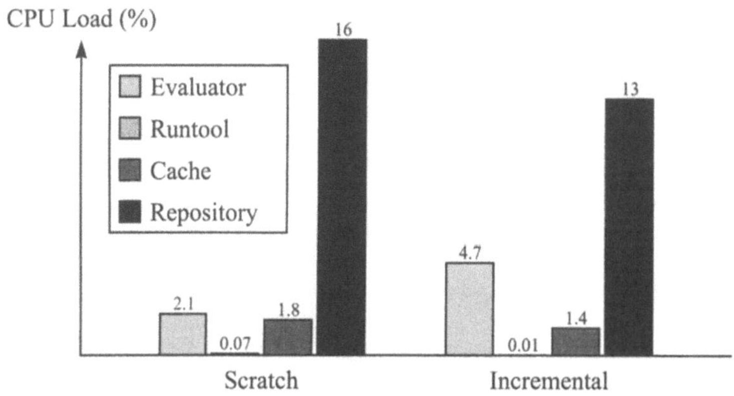


**Fig. 11.6.** The mean CPU loads of the Vesta evaluator, runtool server, function cache server, and repository server during scratch and incremental builds.

As Figure 11.6 shows, the server load is dominated by the repository, which, for a single build, consumed between 13% and 16% of the server's CPU.[5] This suggests that a dedicated repository server could accommodate about 7 simultaneous builds. Assuming that developers spend significantly more time thinking and editing than building (say, a factor of 5 to 10), a single server could plausibly accommodate around 50 developers. This is, of course, only a rough estimate, for it does not account for interactions between builds (e.g., files in common) that might affect CPU load. It also doesn't account for the relatively underpowered server machine used in these tests and the substantial improvements that could be achieved with modern hardware. Nevertheless, the rough estimate is supported by anecdotal experience, since a team of 130 engineers successfully developed a substantial code base (700,000 source lines) in Vesta and the server (a somewhat more powerful machine) held up well under that load. (See Section 12.1.)

### Client Process Memory Usage

In the typical Vesta system configuration, the evaluator and the `_run_tool` server are both run on the client machine. The memory usage of the `_run_tool` server is always well below 2MB. The evaluator, on the other hand, can consume somewhat more memory during a large scratch build. Figure 11.7 shows the memory consumption of the evaluator for both scratch and incremental builds of the test programs.[6]

How would these memory requirements scale for larger builds? Incremental builds should consume memory similarly, even for much larger software, since (see Section 11.2.2) the cost of an incremental build is determined by the magnitude of the change. Since the evaluator's memory consumption is roughly proportional to

[5] In these tests, the function cache and repository servers executed on a single dedicated server machine.

[6] These are the memory usages reported by **ps** just before the evaluator exits.

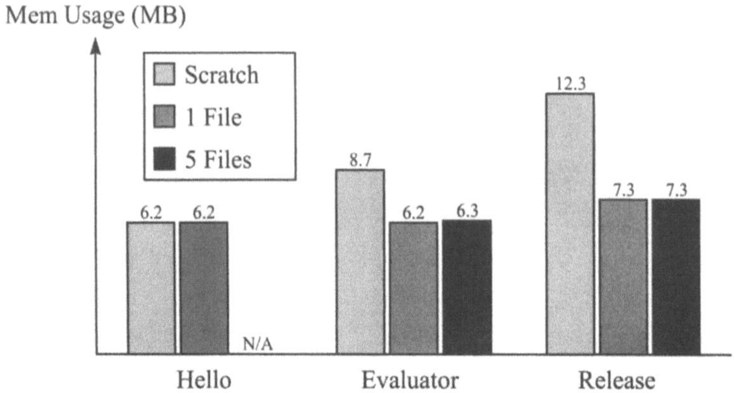


**Fig. 11.7.** The run-time memory usage in megabytes of the Vesta evaluator on scratch and incremental builds. The last two columns in each case show the incremental results in which 1 file and 5 files were changed, respectively. (The 5-file change test is not applicable in the Hello case because that program consists of only a single file.)

the size of the call graph it must evaluate, the memory required by the evaluator to do an incremental build is almost completely independent of the size of the software being constructed. For scratch builds, however, it is harder to judge how well the evaluator's memory usage will scale when Vesta is used to build multi-million line software systems. It should be remembered that scratch builds are rare when using Vesta, so their performance is of less importance.

The memory requirements reported above may be artificially high because the evaluator uses a garbage collector for its memory management. The collector uses heuristics to decide when it should grow its heap and has been observed doing so unnecessarily. The evaluator's memory usage for large scratch builds could be decreased by tuning the collector's heuristics. However, that might also increase the frequency of collections, thereby slowing down evaluations. Also, the typical memory configurations of modern hardware would likely make these concerns irrelevant.

## 11.3 Repository Performance

The preceding section focused on macroscopic measurements of Vesta system performance as seen by a user. We now look at a collection of measurements of the repository's performance, which can be briefly summarized.

- We consider the speed of basic file operations through the repository's NFS server interface. This aspect of repository performance is most important during builds when encapsulated tools make intensive use of the repository to provide file service. If the repository is fast enough to service builds adequately, it will easily meet the lighter demands placed on it by users browsing through the append-only source tree or editing files in mutable source directories. The measurements show that repository performance is indeed adequate. In comparisons on the same hardware, the repository shows a write data rate of about 96% of a standard NFS server, a read data rate of about 55%, and comparable performance on other operations.

- We quantify the repository's memory and disk space consumption with measurements of the amount of source code stored in the repository (number of packages, versions, files, etc.), together with a breakdown of the actual memory and disk space used by the server for various purposes. The repository's technique of keeping directory structures in memory appears successful; a significant but reasonable amount of memory is used, and memory does not grow unreasonably as the amount of source code increases. The repository's approach to file versioning appears successful too, for even though it does not use any form of source compression, deriveds still take up considerably more disk space than sources, and the space consumed by old versions of sources is inconsequential at today's disk capacities and prices.
- We examine the speed of the repository's development cycle tools: **vcheckout**, **vadvance**, **vcheckin**, etc. These tools all run very fast (roughly 0.5 to 1.5 elapsed seconds for the cases tested), making the system pleasant to use.

### 11.3.1 Speed of File Operations

The performance of the repository as a file server is assessed on two commonly used file system benchmarks: the Connectathon '97 Basic Benchmark (CBB) [15] and the Modified Andrew Benchmark (MAB) [30, 50]. CBB is a microbenchmark that tests small groups of related operations. MAB is a higher-level benchmark that measures performance on a software development task. Neither benchmark provides a measurement of file server performance in isolation; both measure overall file system performance, including the buffer cache of the client operating system. Both (especially MAB) can at times be CPU-bound, not I/O-bound. Nonetheless, the benchmarks provide a rough basis for comparison between the repository and an ordinary NFS file server.

These measurements used the Vesta configuration and hardware described in Section 11.1. The benchmarks either accessed a mutable directory in the user-space repository server via NFS version 2, or (for comparison) accessed a directory in the underlying AdvFS file system through the standard kernel-space NFS version 3 server. In both cases, accesses were over the ATM network described in Section 11.1.

On the Connectathon Basic Benchmark (Table 11.2), the repository is slightly slower than the kernel NFS server on most operations, but there are substantial differences on a few. Data writes and reads (tests 5a and 5b) are the most interesting. Converting the elapsed times to bytes per second and comparing, we see that the repository's write data rate is 96% of kernel NFS, while its read data rate is 55%.

These differences probably arise from the fact that writes appear artificially fast under Vesta because the repository cheats, as explained in Section 7.2.5. The repository server violates the expected NFS2 semantics by not forcing writes all the way through to disk before returning to the client, so the benchmark does not get the expected "write-through on close" semantics at user level. The kernel NFS server,

| Test | Description | AdvFS+NFS3 | Vesta+NFS2 |
|---|---|---|---|
| 1 | file and directory creation:<br>creates 155 files and 62 directories. | 6.13 (0.19) | 7.32 (0.38) |
| 2 | file and directory removal:<br>removes 155 files and 62 directories. | 5.56 (0.19) | 6.53 (0.36) |
| 3 | lookup across mount point:<br>500 getwd and stat calls. | 1.35 (0.07) | 1.37 (0.04) |
| 4 | setattr, getattr, and lookup:<br>1000 chmods and stats on 10 files. | 11.38 (0.17) | 3.04 (0.42) |
| 4a | getattr and lookup:<br>1000 stats on 10 files. | 0.11 (0.02) | 0.01 (0.03) |
| 5a | write:<br>writes a 1048576-byte file 10 times. | 5.88 (0.57) | 6.26 (0.82) |
| 5b | read:<br>reads a 1048576-byte file 10 times. | 1.40 (0.02) | 2.54 (0.08) |
| 6 | readdir:<br>reads 20500 directory entries, 200 files. | 5.28 (0.18) | 7.27 (0.24) |
| 7a | rename: 200 renames on 10 files. | 3.51 (0.13) | 6.75 (0.34) |
| 9 | statfs: 1500 statfs calls. | 1.16 (0.04) | 1.18 (0.17) |

**Table 11.2.** Connectathon Basic Benchmark, run on a standard file system through NFS version 3, and on the Vesta repository through NFS version 2. Each table entry is an average elapsed time in seconds; smaller numbers are better. All values are averaged over 20 runs of the benchmark. Standard deviations are included in parentheses.

on the other hand, implements the NFS3 protocol correctly and thus does provide write-through on close.

Read operations are slow because the data is really being read from disk, so the extra overhead of going through the user-space repository server is fully visible. The Connectathon read test flushes the client machine's buffer cache before each read.

Curiously, the repository is a great deal faster than kernel NFS on tests 4 and 4a. This may be due to the repository's in-memory directory structure, but in any case the difference is probably unimportant for overall system performance.

Tests 7b and 8 of the benchmark were omitted because they test hard links and symbolic links, neither of which are supported in repository mutable directories.

The first phase of the Modified Andrew Benchmark (Table 11.3) creates a tree of directories. The second phase copies a 350 KB collection of C source files into the tree. The third phase traverses the new tree and acquires basic file information for each file and directory.[7] The fourth phase reads every file in the new tree. The fifth phase compiles and links the files. This benchmark does not use the Vesta evaluator or tool encapsulation; it assesses the performance of the repository as a file server only, not the overall Vesta system performance on software building.

On this benchmark, surprisingly, the repository is actually somewhat faster than the kernel NFS server in some phases and in the overall time. It is likely that some of

[7] That is, it executes the Unix "stat" system call.

| Phase | Description | AdvFS+NFS3 | | Vesta+NFS2 | |
|---|---|---|---|---|---|
| 1 | Create Directories | 947 | (175) | 756 | (116) |
| 2 | Copy Files | 9286 | (366) | 5776 | (280) |
| 3 | Directory Status | 3609 | (56) | 3750 | (90) |
| 4 | Scan Files | 4393 | (189) | 4414 | (112) |
| 5 | Compile | 22627 | (536) | 18913 | (630) |
| | Total | 40862 | (654) | 33609 | (840) |

**Table 11.3.** Modified Andrew Benchmark, run on a standard file system through NFS version 3, and on the Vesta repository through NFS version 2. Each table entry is an average elapsed time in seconds; smaller numbers are better. All values are averaged over 20 runs of the benchmark. Standard deviations are included in parentheses.

the difference (especially in Phase 1) is due to the repository's in-memory directory structure, and some (especially in Phases 2 and 5) is due to the lack of write-through on close, previously discussed.

Although these measurements do not fully illuminate the details of the repository's NFS performance, they do to establish that the performance of the repository is adequate for Vesta's purposes. Even though reading from the repository server takes almost twice as long as reading from an in-kernel NFS server, the actual elapsed time required for builds is slightly less. Both the small, non-encapsulated build measured in the Andrew benchmark and the Vesta builds measured in Section 11.2.1 show this effect.

Although the repository performance is adequate, improving it would certainly be beneficial. One obvious possibility would be to move repository NFS reads and writes from the user-space server into the kernel (where "real" NFS servers reside). The repository server does no useful work on these operations other than mapping from its file handles (longids) to the corresponding files in the underlying file system. It would be straightforward to move this functionality into the kernel, thereby eliminating the user-space server from the path of these time-critical operations. All other repository NFS operations would continue to be handled in user space, minimizing the amount of code added to the kernel. Of course, moving code into the kernel compromises portability, which is more easily achieved with a pure, user-space server.

### 11.3.2 Disk and Memory Consumption

The results presented in this section are based on a snapshot of the working repository on October 27, 1997. This is the repository that was being used to develop the Vesta system itself. It also contained a few other software packages that served as test cases for the repository and evaluator. In particular, it included the Juno-2 constraint-based drawing editor [29,32] and the many Modula-3 [47,48] libraries required by Juno-2.

The snapshot contains 69 top-level packages and 26 branches comprising 648 checked-in versions and 10 reservation stubs for versions under development. There are 631 checkout sessions; this includes both active sessions associated with the reservation stubs (10), and old sessions associated with checked-in versions (621).

These checkout sessions comprise 4,981 package versions, for a grand total of 5,629 versions.

### Disk Space Usage

Summing over the entire snapshot, including both checked-in versions and check-out sessions, there are 24,556 directories and 407,662 files. These numbers represent distinctly named directories and files in the externally visible hierarchical name space. In the repository's internal DAG structure, many of these directories and files share storage. If all 407,662 files were stored without sharing, they would occupy about 11.7 GB (more precisely, 12,018,130 1-KB blocks). Performing a similar count for the mutable portion of the repository (which was also included in the above count), we find it contains 29 directories and 449 files. Again, some of these files may share storage with each other or with immutable files. If stored without sharing, the files would occupy about 2.9 MB (2,986 1-KB blocks). But, because of the repository's internal sharing of storage between identical files, the actual storage consumption is far less. In reality, only 10,856 distinct source files exist in the snapshot's shortid pool, occupying only about 263 MB (269,030 1-KB blocks).

How much disk space is spent on old versions and branches? To get an approximate answer to this question, we look at only the latest version of each package and each branch. There are 66 latest top-level versions (not 69, because a few packages have no versions), comprising 445 directories and 4,367 immutable files. If they were stored without sharing, these files would occupy about 93 MB (93,391 1-KB blocks). Since only one version from each package is counted here, there is little or no sharing, so we can take these figures as a good estimate of the actual amount of space consumed. This represents about 35% of the source disk space, so about 65% (about 172 MB or 175,639 1-KB blocks) is spent on old versions and branches.

The snapshot was taken immediately after running the weeder and keeping only the deriveds produced by evaluating the latest version of each package, branch, and check-out session; all other deriveds were deleted. This left the snapshot with 2,958 derived files. (The few files that are both sources and deriveds are counted only as sources.) These deriveds occupy about 282 MB (288,367 1-KB blocks). Thus, the entire pool of sources and deriveds occupies about 545 MB, 17% of which is consumed by latest source versions, 31% by old versions and branches, and 52% by deriveds.

Of course, if the snapshot had not been taken just after weeding, the proportion of deriveds would be much higher. Weeding usually occurs when the disk (whose capacity was about 4 GB) is nearly full. At this point over 93% of the disk would be occupied by deriveds.

### Main Memory Usage

Main memory also represents a potentially limiting resource because the repository keeps all of its directories in main memory (see Section 7.2.1). For the snapshot, the repository's packed, garbage-collected memory pool used 3.0 MB to store immutable directories, 0.34 MB to store appendable and mutable directories, 0.44 MB to store mutable attributes, and a few tens of kilobytes for other structures. A checkpoint taken just before the snapshot was 3.77 MB; this checkpoint holds an exact image of the repository's runtime memory pool and encodes its complete state. In addition, 0.24 MB of the repository's general-purpose heap (that is, memory allocated by the `new` construct in C++) were consumed by an inverted index that maps from immutable directory shortids to the in-memory directory data structures (see Section 7.2.2). This index was not included in the checkpoint because it can be reconstructed at recovery time. Thus, 4.0 MB were used to store 24,585 directories and related structures such as attributes, giving an average cost of about 171 bytes per directory.

The repository saves memory as well as disk space by storing the hierarchical name space internally as a DAG. Although there are 24,585 directories with distinct hierarchical names, internally the snapshot contains only 8,411 directory data structures (7,560 immutable and 851 appendable or mutable). Within those directories, the repository's technique of recording directories internally as lists of changes relative to other directories saves additional space. Although there are 432,696 files and directories with distinct hierarchical names, and hence an average of 17.60 entries in each external directory, the internal directory data structure used to represent those directories contains only 85,650 entries, for an average of 10.18 entries per internal directory. Internal directories can also contain placeholder entries for objects that have been deleted; the snapshot contained 1,866 of these, an average of about 0.22 per internal directory.

An internal directory consists of one or more blocks (usually just one), each containing a fixed-sized header, a packed list of entries, and (for appendable and mutable directories) some optional space for expansion. The snapshot used 8,502 blocks to store the 8,411 directories, for a total of 0.28 MB of header (34 bytes each), and a total of 0.21 MB of expansion space in the 851 appendable and mutable directories (an average of about 258 bytes each). An entry contains a pathname arc plus either 10 or 26 bytes of overhead depending on whether it points to a directory or file, respectively. The snapshot used a total of 2.8 MB to store active directory entries and an additional 29.0 KB to store placeholder entries for deleted objects. The average space required was thus 33.78 bytes per entry.

### Scaling Projections

Stepping back from these details, what do we learn about the repository's overall memory and disk consumption, and how would we expect it to grow as more sources are stored?

Disk consumption for sources is proportional to the number and size of distinct source file versions. After about a year of development of Vesta under Vesta, the data above shows about a threefold expansion in disk storage to store all package versions instead of keeping only the most recent version of each package. Of course, the factor of three would grow a bit larger on a source pool that evolved over a longer time and had more active branches. Nevertheless, considering the exponential growth in disk space for constant cost and the fact that humans are not learning to type in new source code at correspondingly higher rates, one can reasonably conclude that the disk space required to store old source versions is not a limiting factor in Vesta.[8] As the numbers on page 184 show, deriveds, not source, dominate the disk space usage. Disk space for sources is not a barrier to scaling.

Main memory consumption is potentially a greater concern, but as with disk space, it is roughly proportional to the number of distinct source file versions. Each new source file version added to the repository requires at most a small number of directories and directory entries to be added to the data structure. A conservative estimate, roughly valid if a separate **vadvance** is used to insert each new file version, is one new directory and two new directory entries per new file version, for a total of about 100 bytes. Thus, a repository server machine with 200 MB of physical memory could hold the directory structure for about two million source file versions. Moreover, the repository will still run correctly with less physical memory; it will simply run more slowly due to paging. Larger repositories will become feasible as affordable memory capacities continue to increase. Finally, a few opportunities remain to shrink the present data structures: eliminating the per-directory expansion space would save almost 10% with essentially no loss in performance,[9] and trading time for space would achieve further savings.

### 11.3.3 Speed of Repository Tools

We now turn to the final set of repository measurements, the performance of the development tools that manipulate files and directories. We look first at the case of a local repository; the next section considers the remote case.

The benchmark is a simple one consisting of a series of repository actions:

1. Run **vcreate** to create a new package.
2. Run **vcheckout** to create a check-out session for the empty package.
3. Copy the repository's own source code from an ordinary (NFS-mounted) file system into the new working directory for the package. The source code consists of 92 files, containing 835,120 bytes or 876 1-KB blocks.
4. Run **vadvance** to install the source as the first version of the check-out session.
5. Run **vadvance** again. In this case **vadvance** detects that the working directory has not changed and does not create a new version.
6. Touch (modify) one file in the package, triggering a copy-on-write. The chosen file was 79,357 bytes long.

---

[8] The earlier Vesta-1 repository implemented an optional feature that could compress old source versions by encoding them as deltas, similar to the representation used by RCS. When the system entered daily use, however, it transpired that 80% of the disk space was typically occupied by derived files [13]. Thus, delta-compressing the source files would have saved only a small percentage of the available disk space, so there was no motivation to turn on the feature, and it was eliminated from Vesta-2 entirely.

[9] In fact, this improvement appears in a later version of Vesta than the one measured here.

7. Run **vadvance**.
8. Touch (modify) all the files in the package, triggering a copy-on-write for every one.
9. Run **vadvance**.
10. Run **vcheckin**, installing the final version from the check-out session as version 1 of the package and deleting the working directory.
11. Run **vcheckout** on the package, creating a new check-out session initialized from version 1.
12. Again touch one file, same as step 6.
13. Run **vadvance**.
14. Yet again touch one file, same as step 6.
15. Run **vadvance**.
16. Run **vcheckin**, installing the final version from the check-out session as version 2 of the package and deleting the working directory.

The entire benchmark was run 5 times, each time on 10 packages. The results are shown in Table 11.4, and we see that every step (repository tool invocation) took well under 1.5 seconds to run, with most taking 0.5 seconds or less. Steps that copied new source code into the repository, or modified an existing source file for the first time (triggering a copy-on-write), took longer but were consistent with the performance measurements of Section 11.3.1 above.

| Step | Description | Time per package |
|---|---|---|
| 1 | create an empty package | 260 ms |
| 2 | check out the new package | 560 ms |
| 3 | copy in 835 KB of source code | 12000 ms |
| 4 | advance the package | 1400 ms |
| 5 | advance again (no changes) | 120 ms |
| 6 | touch a 79 KB file | 110 ms |
| 7 | advance the package | 200 ms |
| 8 | touch all 92 files in the package | 7600 ms |
| 9 | advance the package | 1300 ms |
| 10 | check in the package | 470 ms |
| 11 | check out the package | 660 ms |
| 12 | touch a 79 KB file | 140 ms |
| 13 | advance the package | 180 ms |
| 14 | touch a 79 KB file | 120 ms |
| 15 | advance the package | 190 ms |
| 16 | check in the package | 460 ms |

**Table 11.4.** Vesta repository tool performance. The entire benchmark was run 5 times, each time on 10 packages. The average time taken per package is given for each step, in milliseconds rounded to two significant digits.

As these are interactive tools, their performance needs to be comparable with human reaction/perception times. The table indicates that they clearly are; that is, they are fast enough to make the system pleasant to use.

### 11.3.4 Speed of Cross-Repository Tools

The benchmark was used to compare the performance of the tools on the single-repository and cross-repository (Section 4.3.4) cases. However, these measurements occurred several years after those reported above, by which time both the computers and the networks used for the earlier measurements had been replaced with faster hardware. Steps 14 and 15 of the earlier benchmark are omitted here, since they are purely local and duplicate earlier steps in the benchmark.

Table 11.5 shows the results of the cross-repository performance benchmark. In this test, the steps listed were run in order, 50 times each on 50 separate packages. The table gives the average time for each step, rounded to two significant figures. The *Local* column is the single repository case, *Nearby* is the cross-repository case where the local and remote repositories are connected by a single hop of gigabit Ethernet, and *Distant* is the cross-repository case where the repositories are separated by 3000 miles and ten hops through a corporate intranet. Each repository was running on a 500 to 600 MHz Alpha 21164A processor. In each case, the tools were run on a client workstation with a 667 MHz Alpha 21264A processor, connected to the local server by a 100 Mb ethernet. As the table shows, the tools are very fast in the local and nearby cases, and fast enough to be usable even in the distant case.[10]

Comparing the figures from the older tests of Table 11.4 done on slower hardware with the newer ones in Table 11.5, we see that the tools have sped up on most

| Step | Description | Local | Nearby | Distant |
|---|---|---|---|---|
| 1 | create an empty package | 50 ms | 250 ms | 6400 ms |
| 2 | check out the new package | 64 ms | 590 ms | 5700 ms |
| 3 | copy in 1204 KB of source code | 5300 ms | 5400 ms | 5200 ms |
| 4 | advance the package | 2500 ms | 2600 ms | 2500 ms |
| 5 | advance again (no changes) | 170 ms | 170 ms | 180 ms |
| 6 | touch a 108 KB file | 34 ms | 32 ms | 30 ms |
| 7 | advance the package | 160 ms | 180 ms | 180 ms |
| 8 | touch all 92 files in the package | 3200 ms | 3300 ms | 3200 ms |
| 9 | advance the package | 2500 ms | 2500 ms | 2600 ms |
| 10 | check in the package | 110 ms | 780 ms | 18000 ms |
| 11 | check out the package | 49 ms | 730 ms | 5800 ms |
| 12 | touch a 108 KB file | 49 ms | 73 ms | 59 ms |
| 13 | advance the package | 150 ms | 160 ms | 160 ms |
| 16 | check in the package | 64 ms | 170 ms | 4700 ms |

**Table 11.5.** Vesta repository tool performance, comparing the local (single-repository) case with two cross-repository cases, one where the remote repository is nearby and the other where it is distant. Times are in milliseconds.

[10] Note that copy, touch, and advance are always local operations.

tests, but appear notably slower on tests 4 and 9 (advance). There are two reasons for the difference: first, the tests were done on a larger package (835 KB vs. 1204 KB), and second, the measurements in Table 11.4 were taken before the repository implementation fingerprinted files by content (Section 7.1.3), so they do not include fingerprinting costs.

### 11.3.5 Speed of the Replicator

We conclude our examination of the Vesta repository's performance with a few simple measurements of the replicator **vrepl** (see Section 4.3.3). These measurements were taken at the same time as the cross-repository measurements reported in the preceding section, using the same hardware and networking configurations. The replicator itself ran on the same class of machine as the repository servers (500 to 600 MHz Alpha 21164A processor).

Table 11.6 compares **vrepl** copying files between repositories with **rcp** (the Unix inter-machine copy utility) copying the same files directly out of the native file system on which the repository is built. The first column identifies the type of copying operation, where "+" means "copy the *directory* and everything it contains" (that is, follow the repository name hierarchy) and "@" means copy the *package* and everything it imports" (that is, follow the SDL import hierarchy). The second column is the amount of data transferred. The remaining columns give the data transfer rates in KB/s. These values were averaged over three trials and rounded to two significant figures.

| | | vrepl | | rcp | |
|---|---|---|---|---|---|
| Replicate | Size | Nearby | Distant | Nearby | Distant |
| +repos/124 to empty repository | 1.2 MB | 710 | 27 | 71 | 21 |
| +repos/125 with 124 present | 582 KB | 970 | 42 | 360 | 42 |
| @repos/124 to empty repository | 127 MB | 910 | 40 | – | – |
| @repos/125 with 124 present | 640 KB | 67 | 5.3 | – | – |

**Table 11.6.** Vesta replicator performance. Values in **vrepl** and **rcp** columns are inter-repository transfer rates in KB/sec.

Comparing the *Distant* columns for the first two rows, we see that **vrepl** and **rcp** have comparable performance over a slow network. This is the expected common case for repository replication. We also see that **vrepl** significantly out-performs **rcp** for the *Nearby* case, in which the network performance is not the limiting factor, probably because of the repository's in-memory directory representation. The last two rows present numbers for **vrepl** only, since **rcp** doesn't implement anything comparable to the "@" functionality. The amount of data transferred in these two cases differs by a factor of 500. Comparing row 4 with row 2, we see that the "@" functionality induces significant overhead for small transfers. However, comparing row 3 with row 1 shows that the overhead can be fully amortized over large transfers.

## 11.4 Function Cache Performance

We turn now to some measurements of the performance of the function cache and their implications for scaling.

### 11.4.1 Server Performance

Recall from Section 8.3 that looking up an entry in the function cache is a two-step process. In the first step, the evaluator invokes the cache's SecondaryNames function to learn the set of all secondary dependency names associated with a given primary key (PK). In the second step, it invokes the cache's Lookup function. In the event that there are no entries associated with the primary key passed to the SecondaryNames function, the Lookup call is skipped. If there is a cache miss, the evaluator invokes the cache's AddEntry function to create a new entry and add it to the cache.

An experiment measured the elapsed time spent in the function cache server process while it was handling various requests (via RPC) from the client. Each run of the experiment performed a scratch build of the Vesta evaluator (starting from a nearly empty function cache in which only the standard environment had been built), followed by five incremental builds of the evaluator triggered by a trivial modification to a single evaluator source file. The mean times for each operation were calculated for each run of the experiment; the means and standard deviations of those mean times are reported in Table 11.7.

| Operation | Number of Calls | Mean Time (ms) | Std. Dev. (% of Mean) |
|---|---|---|---|
| SecondaryNames | 518 | 16.8 | 0.63% |
| Lookup | 112 | 11.7 | 0.44% |
| AddEntry | 438 | 8.1 | 0.24% |

**Table 11.7.** Elapsed times in milliseconds of key function cache server operations.

A more detailed analysis reveals that misses account for 34% of the Lookup calls and take 17.8 ms on average. In this experiment, 90% of the hits were to cache entries in memory, taking only 6.3 ms each, while the remaining hits to cache entries on disk took 30.3 ms on average. The limiting factor in cache operations appears to be disk latency, probably because the function cache and repository server, which run on the same machine during this experiment, are competing for CPU and disk. Such contention could be eliminated by running the processes on separate server machines and by storing their files on separate file systems.

These results are for a relatively small build. A second experiment performed a scratch build of the entire Vesta release followed by incremental builds of newer and older versions of the entire Vesta release. The number of cache operations in this experiment was significantly larger, as was the number of new entries added to the cache. Table 11.8 shows the results.[11]

[11] This table lacks standard deviations because the experiment was performed only once.

| Operation | Number of Calls | Mean Time (ms) |
|---|---|---|
| SecondaryNames | 4,351 | 29.0 |
| Lookup | 763 | 44.0 |
| AddEntry | 3,948 | 21.6 |

**Table 11.8.** Elapsed times in milliseconds of key function cache server operations for a scratch build of the complete Vesta release followed by two incremental builds.

Comparing Tables 11.7 and 11.8, we see that cache performance does degrade as the number of cache entries is increased. One cannot, with any confidence, extrapolate quantitatively how the function cache will perform for even larger builds. However, the results presented in Section 11.2.2 indicate that the function cache performs well for medium-size scratch and incremental builds, and it seems reasonable to infer that, while the cost of cache accesses increases significantly with cache size, that cost is nevertheless acceptable overall. To put this in perspective, recall that the cost of a cache access is a few disk operations. In the case of a hit, a large number of disk operations is typically avoided; in the case of a miss, the extra accesses are a small increment to the total.

### 11.4.2 Measurements of the Stable Cache

Recall from Section 8.6.1 that cache entries are partitioned first into PKFiles, and then into CFP groups; only the entries in a single CFP group need be consulted on each Lookup operation. How effective does this organization turn out to be?

| Attribute | Mean Value |
|---|---|
| Number of CFP groups per PKFile | 1.33 |
| Number of entries per CFP group | 1.02 |
| Cache entry size (Kbytes) | 8.24 |
| Function result value size (Kbytes) | 5.82 |
| Number of secondary names per PKFile | 52.4 |
| Percentage of common names per PKFile | 99.1% |
| Percentage of uncommon names per cache entry | 2.5% |

**Table 11.9.** Mean values of various function cache attributes.

The mean values of various function cache properties are shown in Table 11.9. These statistics were measured from a stable cache containing 13,900 cache entries distributed over 10,183 PKFiles. The total disk space required to store these entries was 112 MB, or 8.2KB per cache entry.

The statistics indicate that the separation of entries into CFP groups works well, for the average number of entries per CFP group is only slightly more than 1. Moreover, of the average 52.4 secondary names per PKFile, more than 99% are common. Thus, only a very small number of fingerprints need be compared during a typical Lookup operation.

### 11.4.3 Disk and Memory Usage

The cache server's memory requirements are dominated by the storage used for in-memory cache entries. Much like a virtual memory system, the function cache flushes unused cache entries to disk over time. Its policy can be adjusted to flush entries more aggressively if too many entries are being retained in memory.

Table 11.9 shows that the average function result value occupies 5.82KB, and that the average cache entry in the stable cache occupies 8.24KB. Most of the difference between these numbers is metadata (such as the PKFile and CFP group data structures) and bookkeeping information that allows the stable cache entries to be efficiently shuffled into new CFP groups when a PKFile's set of common names changes. That extra data is not required for cache entries in main memory, so such cache entries average 6KB in size.

These numbers enable us to estimate the main memory requirements as the cache server capacity scales up. 100MB of main memory will accommodate about 16,000 cache entries. To put this in perspective, the entire Vesta system, including the standard environment it requires, generates about 3,500 cache entries. Thus, a system roughly three times larger could fit its entire cache in 100MB of main memory space without inducing any cache flushing. For organizations developing systems beyond this size, an investment in 100MB or more of server memory is negligible. We therefore can tentatively conclude that the function cache's memory usage will scale adequately for large code bases.[12]

Turning to disk space requirements, a stable cache of 12 million entries (the Vesta design target) of 8.24KB each would require about 100GB of disk space. Disks of this size are commonplace today and inexpensive. Thus, disk space needs of the function cache do not impose an impediment to scaling.

### 11.4.4 Function Cache Scalability

The preceding sections touched on the implications of the measurements of medium-sized systems for scalability of the function cache. Here we briefly consider a few other potential scalability bottlenecks and the measures taken to prevent them.

- **Lock Contention.** As the number of clients increases, overall function cache performance might degrade due to lock contention on the cache's in-memory data structures. To avoid this problem, the function cache uses relatively fine-grained locking: there is a separate lock on each in-memory PKFile and its cache entries. Moreover, the lock on the cache's central structures is held as briefly as possible in the places where it is required.
- **Bad Cache Entry Distribution.** The function cache's performance will suffer if the number of cache entries per CFP group grows too large. However, due to

[12] The function cache uses the same garbage collector as the evaluator, so as described in Section 11.2.4, its actual memory usage may be somewhat more than strictly needed. The comments in that section about tuning the collector's heuristics apply equally well to the function cache.

the function cache's scheme of dividing PKFiles into CFP groups (described in Section 8.6.1), this problem is unlikely to be serious. Indeed, this problem occasionally arose during Vesta's development and it was easily corrected by altering bridge models so that the evaluator computed better (that is, less clustered) primary keys for their functions. The **VCacheStats** program that was used to gather the statistics for Table 11.9 can also be used to uncover skewed cache entry distributions, making such problems easy to detect.

- **Disk Latency.** As the number of cache entries per PKFile increases, the files grow larger and more time may be spent waiting on disk reads during cache lookups. Two factors mitigate this effect. First, an increased number of entries per PKFile should account for at most one of the two orders of magnitude in cache entry growth cited above. (The other order of magnitude will appear in the form of an increased number of PKFiles.) Second, the PKFile disk format is designed to minimize the number of disk reads required per lookup. In particular, the index of CFP groups is stored separately from the cache entries in the hope that the entire index can be read in a single disk operation. Similarly, extra cache entry information not required for lookup is stored separately from the entries, again to decrease the number of read and seek operations in a typical lookup.
- **Memory Usage.** There is an obvious time-space tradeoff between the number of cache entries kept in memory and the speed of a typical lookup. As the number of cache entries and clients increases, a smaller fraction of the "working set" entries can be kept in a fixed amount of memory. One solution to this problem is simply to install more memory on the server machine. But even if no entries were kept in memory, the detailed results described in Section 11.4.1 above imply that the overall function cache performance would not degrade badly.

Of course, one can't know if these considerations are sufficient to ensure scalability until Vesta is actually used for large systems. Some anecdotal evidence (presented in Section 12.1) indicates that the cache server's scalability is, indeed, adequate.

## 11.5 Weeder Performance

We turn now from the performance of the cache server proper to the performance of its adjunct, the weeder. We consider two measures: the frequency with which weeding is required, and the time needed to perform a weeding operation when it is needed. These concerns are of lesser weight than the performance of the system components discussed above, since weeding is a background process and nearly invisible to users. However, some administrative effort is needed to run the weeder or to set it up to run automatically, and builds are likely to run a bit more slowly while the weeder is active and competing for resources, so these performance issues are worth some attention.

How often is weeding necessary? The answer depends on how quickly the disk used by the repository and function cache fills up, which in turn is a function of the disk's size, the rate at which new cache entries and deriveds are created, and the sizes of those cache entries and derived files on disk. During the initial use of Vesta, in which three developers were actively doing builds against a 4GB disk, weeding was required about once every two weeks.

When the Vesta system was used by a significantly larger engineering team (more on this in the next chapter), the parameters were rather different. More than 100 developers were using the system, which used a disk cluster comprising 100 GB, and their builds produced roughly 10 GB of derived files per day. They created a script to run the weeder every night, with a weeding operation actually occurring if the disk usage exceeded a predetermined threshold. The same script also ran automatically during the day with a higher threshold to ensure that a spike in the rate of disk consumption would not fill the disk before the next nightly run. In this environment, weeding operations occurred once or twice a week.

How long does it take the weeder to run? Recall from Chapter 9 that the weeder runs in two phases: a mark phase in which the cache entries and derived files to be kept are determined, followed by a deletion phase in which the function cache and repository carry out cache entry deletion and derived file deletion in parallel. Generally, the deletion phase took significantly longer than the mark phase. In particular, the deletion phase took 10–15 minutes when weeding a 4GB disk. By comparison, the engineering group with the 100 GB disk cluster experienced weeding operations that generally took about an hour. One would expect the deletion time to scale linearly with the number of cache entries being deleted, which in turn is bounded linearly by the size of the backing disk.

The performance of the weeder's mark phase is a function of the number of graph log entries buffered in memory (see Section 9.2.1): the smaller the buffer, the more passes over the graph log are required. As one point on the time-space curve, weeding a graph log containing over 30,000 entries using a buffer of 10,000 entries required four scans of the disk file and 10 seconds of elapsed time. There is no trend data, since no experiments have been conducted with different buffer sizes. However, even though more scans of the graph log are required for a given buffer size as the log grows in length, it still seems reasonable to estimate that the mark phase will require no more than 10 minutes on a cache of 1,000,000 entries. If so, the deletion phase will continue to be the dominant factor in the duration of the weeder's execution. Recent anecdotal evidence suggests this projection is accurate.

## 11.6 Interprocess Communication

Before concluding our examination of the Vesta system's performance, we should note the overall characteristics of the communication substrate. For interprocess communication, Vesta uses SRPC, a simple home-grown remote procedure call protocol and library for C++ implemented on top of TCP sockets. SRPC does not include an automatic stub generator, so all of the argument marshaling and unmarshaling stubs were written by hand. To simplify stub coding, SRPC provides methods for sending and receiving common data types like integers, null-terminated strings, arrays of bytes, and sequences. The SRPC implementation uses TCP keep-alives to detect network partitions and other connection failures.

Except where noted in the more recent cross-repository experiments, all of the measurements described in this chapter were carried out on AN2 (see Section 11.1). On this network, the average round-trip elapsed time for a null SRPC (i.e., no arguments or results) is 1.2 milliseconds. Simple bandwidth tests using a range of argument and result sizes indicate a peak transfer rate of 132 Mbit/sec and an average rate of around 100 Mbit/sec. Operationally, these rates have proved adequate; there has been no need to devise optimizations to improve them.

## In Summary

This chapter has presented evidence for the contentions (1) that Vesta delivers superior functionality to the most popular alternative (Make) with equivalent or better performance and (2) that it does so with equipment resources per developer that make it practical to deploy in a large development organization. We have specifically examined resource usage on client and server machines and quantified their use for systems of moderate size. Extrapolation from this data, in the absence of direct measurement, leads one to believe that Vesta's architecture and construction will handle systems of considerably greater size, up to the design targets of Section 3.2. Some possible barriers to scaling were identified, along with potential solutions.

Despite the measurement and analysis covered in this chapter, as well as the design and implementation care presented throughout this book, one cannot know for certain how well Vesta will scale until it is actually used to build large systems. The prospects for that happening are the subject of the next, and concluding, chapter.

# 12

# Conclusions

Section 1.3 set out the Vesta system's objective: to be a software configuration management system that *scales to accommodate large software*, is *easy to use*, and produces *repeatable, incremental, and consistent builds*. Chapters 2-9 explained how Vesta achieves that objective, and Chapters 10-11 evaluated Vesta's functionality and performance against its most widely used competition. To summarize briefly, Vesta:

- preserves source code immutably and immortally,
- supports both simple linear versioning and arbitrarily complex branching for parallel development,
- makes all versions directly accessible through the file system,
- provides very fast check-out and check-in using copy-on-write,
- supports distributed development with source replication, cross-repository check-out and check-in, and cross-realm access control,
- manages storage for source and derived files largely automatically,
- provides a flexible, general description language for the precise description and modular organization of software system construction,
- enables integration of new build tools within the description language without modification of either the tools or the Vesta system,
- builds software configurations repeatably, incrementally, and consistently, and
- runs as fast as Make for scratch builds and outperforms it for incremental ones.

The authors believe that these characteristics make Vesta an attractive and even compelling replacement for conventional configuration management tools. But of course we are hardly unbiased. The real test of any practical system is whether others find it useful. We therefore conclude our assessment of the Vesta system with an examination of its actual use to date and our thoughts on its potential for future adoption.

## 12.1 Vesta in the Real World

Vesta was born as a research project, one with a rather extended history. Once we believed that Vesta brought substantial practical benefits to the software development process, we embarked on a series of technology transfer explorations. This history is described elsewhere [39]. We omit most of it here to focus on the most recent developments.

Vesta has been in daily use by a major engineering group since 1999. This group has evolved over the years, but it started out as DEC/Compaq's Araña group, which at the time it began using Vesta was a team of about 130 developers working on a large microprocessor design. The team was organized as two subgroups, one in New England and the other in California, each with its own Vesta repository. Both the chip design itself and the team's custom design software were stored in the repositories and developed using Vesta's suite of tools. The final code base consisted of about 700,000 lines.

The Araña group didn't move to Vesta overnight, of course. Rather, they introduced its use gradually, beginning with a smaller group (about 20 developers) and expanding as they gained experience and confidence with the system. This initial group served as our first real users, shaking out bugs in the implementation and exposing the need for various small features that we did not initially anticipate.

Overall, the Araña group found Vesta a substantial improvement over their previous build tools. Vesta's strong support for parallel source development and repeatable builds saved them considerable time (3 to 6 months in the architectural design phase alone), and the distributed development features provided answers to some extremely difficult problems they faced in bicoastal software and design database management. They also found Vesta's repeatability and consistency guarantees to be extremely useful for tracking down difficult bugs, a characteristic that gained in importance as they approached completion of the chip design.

After the DEC/Compaq Alpha division was transferred to Intel, the former Araña group continued to use Vesta on new projects. As of February, 2005, the number of developers using Vesta had grown to over 350, and the system being built had exceeded three million source lines.[1] This build is substantially larger than the Araña design, and the complexity of the tools and the input they process is higher, stressing the Vesta implementation and highlighting the scaling bottlenecks. To date, most of the work to eliminate those bottlenecks has been on the repository server implementation, and generally in areas in which the simplifying assumptions made to build the research prototype are no longer valid. This is as we expected.

It is worth noting that the Vesta approach to scaling builds through parallel execution and distributed runtool servers has worked nicely. Collectively, the group at Intel routinely runs 20 simultaneous builds, each performing up to 10 tool invocations in parallel. Thus, 200 separate tools (mostly on distinct machines) are simultaneously competing for the repository's services. Even when running on fast hardware, a single repository server begins to be a performance bottleneck when serving so many

[1] Source lines are not a particularly meaningful metric for some of the components of this build, like schematic diagrams.

clients, so the group uses Vesta's replication machinery to manage multiple repositories (presently three), providing ample capacity for further growth in their build activity.[2]

To our knowledge, Intel has the largest Vesta-based development underway at present. However, Vesta has been ported to Linux (both 32-bit Intel and Alpha versions) and is available as open source under the LGPL [20]. The complete sources have been available through the Vesta web site [62] since late 2001, and there is a continuing modest stream of downloads. We don't really know, therefore, how many Vesta users there are, although it is unlikely that we would be unaware of a large-scale use of the system.

## 12.2 Vesta in the Future

While we believe Vesta usage to date demonstrates its utility, our original goal was more ambitious, since we targeted the system at code bases much larger (tens of millions of source lines). We have claimed in this book that Vesta's algorithms and implementation structure will scale up well, but the jury is still out. We remain hopeful that the system's easy availability and attractive functionality will eventually win it additional users with large code bases.

It is, however, appropriate to consider some potential impediments to Vesta's adoption.

**Generality.** The Vesta builder always creates derived objects from source, using caching of build steps as an essential performance optimization to save work. This paradigm somewhat limits the builder's generality, because some software tool sets or development environments would prefer to be more directly in control of the build process in a more specialized way. For example, an incremental linker increases the speed of linking by modifying a previously linked program, replacing only the parts that have changed, rather than relinking the entire program. Some compilers such as the Modula-3 compiler work most efficiently when given all the source files that go into a program at once, which allows them to parse interface files only once and cache the results for reuse rather than reparsing them for each implementation file that uses them. Java's `javac` compiler [31] includes its own Make-like logic to avoid regenerating a derived file if it deems the existing one to be up-to-date (although it sometimes fails to recompile some sources that it should, producing inconsistent builds.) Finally, some build tools may require human intervention during their execution.

Generally, one can find a way to use tools like these with Vesta by bypassing the incremental features and scripting any human interaction that would otherwise be required, but there can be a performance penalty in doing so. For example, the Unix **ar** tool, which is used in the standard environment (Section 6.2.1) to build libraries, was originally designed to be used incrementally to replace an object file in a library with a newer one, but under Vesta it always rebuilds the entire library file from its

[2] The authors are indebted to Matt Reilly and Ken Schalk for the foregoing assessments of the use of Vesta at DEC/Compaq and Intel.

constituent object files. We decided the performance penalty was tolerable. Similarly, the Araña group made use of a tool that operated in an incremental mode. At the time they adopted Vesta, they were enhancing it with additional incremental features, but they chose instead to discontinue using the incremental features entirely, deeming the performance cost worthwhile in exchange for Vesta's other benefits. Ultimately they were able to modify the tool to work better with Vesta and get back a good deal of the lost performance.

**Maturity.** While Vesta offers robust, attractive functionality, it is not a mature development environment. Vesta hasn't yet acquired the rich collection of tools, utilities, and other supporting facilities that inevitably grow around a system with a broad user base. Thus, Vesta may appear "lean" to a prospective user or user community, lacking as it does a graphical user interface, tools to synthesize simple models automatically, and tutorial user documentation. We note, however, that these deficiencies didn't stop the Araña group, who developed their own specialized versions of each of these items adapted specifically for their development process. Perhaps other "early adopters" of Vesta would do the same, or might generalize the Araña group's work. In this regard, we hope the open-source license under which Vesta is presently available will encourage maturation of its facilities.

**Conversion and Learning Cost.** Because Vesta represents a new and integrated approach to configuration management, software development groups will incur some costs in switching to it. Groups with large code bases already under development using existing configuration management systems will need conversion tools. (The Araña group chose to adopt Vesta at the beginning of their project when very little of the chip design code base had been written, thereby minimizing what would otherwise have been a substantial conversion task.) We have explored designs for tools to help users migrate their files from RCS, CVS, and similar systems to the Vesta repository. We believe such tools would be fairly straightforward to create because of the similarity of the versioning paradigms between Vesta and the other systems. We also have explored designs for tools that could ease the conversion from Makefiles to models. However, neither class of tools exists at present, which presents a barrier to an organization with a substantial code base contemplating Vesta adoption.

Organizations also face a training cost in learning to use Vesta. We have tried to design the repository tools to be simple and intuitive to use, but Vesta's distinctive concepts inevitably cause them to differ somewhat from those of existing (Unix) systems. SDL presents a more substantial training concern. We have worked to make the language as familiar as possible to programmers from the C tradition, and we have shown how to craft a collection of system models (our standard environment) that causes the models users normally see and write to be little more than lists of source files with a few lines of boilerplate. Nevertheless, experience strongly suggests that any organization that adopts Vesta for a large project will need a local SDL expert, and that it takes considerable time for a sophisticated user to understand the standard environment models in sufficient depth to modify them. We note that several Araña users did acquire this knowledge, and a few became quite expert at writing models.

Despite these reservations and uncertainties, we believe that Vesta represents a significant advance in the methodology and technology of software system construction and configuration management. We remain optimistic that its demonstrated strengths will appeal to development organizations with substantial code bases and that it will win increasing acceptance in the years ahead.

# A

# SDL Reference Manual

## A.1 Introduction

This appendix describes the formal syntax and semantics of the Vesta-2 System Description Language (SDL). Because this description is meant to be complete and unambiguous, its treatment is rather formal. A less formal language reference is available [55].

In Vesta, the instructions for building a software artifact are written as an SDL program. Evaluating the program causes the software system to be constructed; the program's result value typically contains the derived files produced by the evaluation.

SDL is a functional language with lexical scoping. Its value space includes Booleans, integers, texts, lists (similar to LISP lists), sequences of name-value pairs called *bindings*, closures, and a unique error value.

The language is dynamically typed; that is, types are associated with runtime values instead of with static names and expressions. Even without static type checking, the language is strongly typed; an executing Vesta program cannot breach the language's type system. The expected types of parameters to language primitives are defined, and those types are checked when the primitives are evaluated. The language includes provisions for specifying the types of user-defined function arguments and local variables, but these type declarations are currently unchecked.

The language contains roughly 60 primitive functions. There is a `_run_tool` primitive for invoking external tools like compilers and linkers as function calls. External tools can be invoked from Vesta without modification.

Conceptually, every software artifact built with Vesta is built from scratch, thereby guaranteeing that the resulting artifact is composed of consistent pieces. Vesta uses extensive caching to avoid unnecessary rebuilding. Vesta records software dependencies automatically. The techniques by which the implementation caches function calls and determines dependencies are described in Chapter 8.

## A.2 Lexical Conventions

This section defines the meta-notation and terminals used in subsequent sections. Section A.3 introduces each language construct by giving its syntax and semantics. The syntax of the complete language is given in Section A.4.

### A.2.1 Meta-notation

Nonterminals of the grammar begin with an uppercase letter, are at least two characters in length, and include at least one lowercase letter. Except for the four terminals listed in Section A.2.2 below, each of which denotes a class of tokens, the terminals of the grammar are character strings not of this form.

The grammar is written in a variant of BNF (Backus-Naur Form). The metacharacters of this notation are:

```
::=   |   [   ]   {   }   *   +   '   '
```

The meaning of the metacharacters is as follows:

| | |
|---|---|
| *NT* ::= *Ex* | Non-terminal *NT* rewrites to expression *Ex* |
| *Ex1* \| *Ex2* | *Ex1* or *Ex2* |
| [ *Ex* ] | optional *Ex* |
| { *Ex* } | meta-parentheses for grouping |
| *Ex** | zero or more *Ex*'s |
| *Ex**, | zero or more *Ex*'s separated by commas, trailing comma optional |
| *Ex**; | zero or more *Ex*'s separated by semicolons, trailing semi optional |
| *Ex*+ | one or more *Ex*'s |
| *Ex*+, | one or more *Ex*'s separated by commas, trailing comma optional |
| *Ex*+; | one or more *Ex*'s separated by semicolons, trailing semi optional |
| '*s*' | the literal character or character sequence *s* |

When used as terminals, square brackets, curly brackets, and vertical bar appear in single quotes to avoid ambiguity with the corresponding metacharacters (i.e., '[', ']', '{', '}', '|').

### A.2.2 Terminals

The following names are used as terminals in the grammar. They denote classes of tokens, and are defined precisely in Section A.4.3.

`Delim` A pathname delimiter. Either forward or backward slashes are allowed within pathnames, but not both.

`Integer` An integer, expressed in either decimal, octal, or hexadecimal.

`Id` An identifier. An identifier is any sequence of letters, digits, periods, and underscores that does not represent an integer. For example, foo and 36.foo are identifiers, but 36 and 0x36 are not.

`Text` A text string. Texts are enclosed in double-quotes. They may contain escape sequences and spaces.

Comments and white space follow C++ conventions. A comment either begins with `//` and ends with the first subsequent newline, or begins with `/*` and ends with `*/` (the latter form does not nest). Of course, these delimiters are only recognized outside text literals. White space delimits tokens but is otherwise ignored (except that the Space character, the ASCII character represented by the decimal number 32, is significant within text literals). The grammar prohibits white space other than the Space character within text literals.

The names of the built-in functions begin with an underscore character, and the identifier consisting of a single period (i.e., "`.`") plays a special role in SDL. It is therefore recommended that SDL programs avoid defining identifiers of these forms.

## A.3 Semantics

The semantics of programs written in SDL are described by a function *Eval* that maps a syntactic *expression* and a *context* to a *value*. That is, Eval(E, C) returns the value of the syntactic expression E in the context C. In addition to syntactic expressions (denoted by the non-terminal Expr in the grammar), the domain of Eval includes additional syntactic constructs. Some of these additional constructs are defined by the concrete grammar, while others are introduced as "intermediate results" during the evaluation process. The latter are noted where they are introduced. Each value returned by Eval is in the Vesta value space, described in the next section. The context parameter C to Eval is a value of type t_binding in the Vesta value space.

### A.3.1 Value Space

Values are typed. The types and values of the language are shown in Table A.1.

The values *true*, *false*, *emptylist* (the list of length zero), *emptybinding* (the binding of length zero), and *err* are not to be confused with the language literals `TRUE`, `FALSE`, `<>`, `[]`, and `ERR` that denote those values.

| Type name | Values of the type |
|---|---|
| t_bool | *true*, *false* |
| t_int | integers |
| t_text | arbitrary byte sequences |
| t_list | sequences of zero or more arbitrary values |
| t_binding | sequences of zero or more (*name*, *value*) pairs |
| t_closure | closures, each of which is a triple $\langle e, f, b\rangle$ |
| t_err | *err* |
| t_value | union of all of the above types |

**Table A.1.** The types and values of the Vesta language.

The type t_bool contains the Boolean values *true* and *false*, denoted in the language by the literals `TRUE` and `FALSE`.

The type t_int contains integers over at least the range $-2^{31}$ to $2^{31}-1$; the exact range is implementation dependent.

The type t_text contains arbitrary sequences of 8-bit bytes. This type is used to represent text literals (quoted strings) in SDL programs as well as the contents of files introduced through the Files nonterminal of the grammar. Consequently, an implementation must reasonably support the representation of large values of this type (millions of bytes), but need not support efficient operations on large text values.

The type t_list contains sequences of values. The elements of a list need not be of the same type.

The type t_binding contains sequences of pairs $(t_i, v_i)$, in which each $t_i$ is a non-empty value of type t_text, each $v_i$ is an arbitrary Vesta value (i.e., of type t_value), and the $t_i$ are all distinct. Note that bindings are sequences; they are ordered. The *domain* of a binding is the sequence of names $t_i$ at its top level. Bindings nest.

The type t_closure contains closure values for the primitive operators and functions (defined in Section A.3.4) as well as for user-defined functions. In a closure $\langle e, f, b\rangle$:

- $e$ is a function body (i.e., a Block as per the grammar below);
- $f$ is a list of pairs $(t_i, e_i)$, where $t_i$ is a t_text value (a formal parameter name) and $e_i$ is either the distinguished expression ⟨emptyExpr⟩ or an Expr (a default parameter value); and
- $b$ is a value of type t_binding (the closure context).

The type t_err consists of the single distinguished value *err*, denoted in the language by the literal `ERR`. Programmers can use this value as they choose; it has no predefined semantics.

### A.3.2 Type Declarations

The language includes a rudimentary mechanism for declaring the expected types of values computed during evaluation. The grammar defines a small sub-language of type expressions, which includes the ability to give names to types and to describe aggregate types (lists, bindings, functions) with varying degrees of detail. Type expressions may be attached to function arguments and results and to local variables, indicating the type of the expected value for these identifiers and expressions during evaluation.

The Vesta evaluator currently treats type names and type expressions as syntactically checked comments; it performs no other checking. Future implementations may type-check expressions at run time and report an error if the value does not match the specified type according to some as yet unspecified definition of what it means for a value to "match" a type specification.

The syntax fragments and semantic descriptions in subsequent sections omit any further reference to type expressions entirely.

### A.3.3 Evaluation Rules

The evaluation of a Vesta program corresponds to the abstract evaluation:

```
Eval( M([]) , C-initial)
```

where *M* is the closure corresponding to the contents of an immutable file (a system model) in the Vesta repository and *C-initial* is an initial context. *M*'s model should have the syntactic form defined by the nonterminal Model described in Section A.3.3.13 below. *C-initial* defines the names and associated values of the built-in primitive operators and functions described in Section A.3.4 below.

The definition of Eval is by cases over the different syntactic forms that E can take. Some cases (generally short forms provided solely to make SDL programs more convenient to write) are defined indirectly, using syntactic rewrite rules that expand them to match a directly defined case. Unless E is handled by either a rewrite rule or an explicit evaluation rule, Eval(E, C) yields a runtime error. As mentioned above, the domain of Eval includes the language generated by the concrete grammar as a proper subset. Thus, in some of the cases below, the expression E can arise only as an intermediate result of another case of Eval. These cases are explicitly noted.

The pseudo-code that defines the various cases of Eval and the primitive functions should be read like C++. That code assumes the declaration for the representation of Vesta values shown in Table A.2. Note that the `operator==` is the one invoked by uses of "==" in the C++ pseudo-code. It is not to be confused with the primitive equality operator defined on various Vesta types in Section A.3.4. The pseudo-code also refers to the constants shown in Table A.3.

```
class val {
  public:
    operator int();
    // converts Vesta t_int or t_bool to C++ int

    val(int);
    // converts a C++ integer to a Vesta t_int

    int operator== (val);
    // compares two Vesta values, returning true (1)
    // if they have the same type and are equal, and
    // false (0) otherwise
}
```

**Table A.2.** A C++ class declaration for Vesta values.

For convenience, the pseudo-code adopts the following notational conventions:

- Eval is defined by cases rather than by one C++ function with an enormous embedded case selection.

```
static val true;         // value of literal TRUE
static val false;        // value of literal FALSE
static val emptylist;    // value of literal < >
static val emptybinding; // value of literal [ ]
static val err;          // value of literal ERR
```

**Table A.3.** Definitions of constants used by the pseudo-code.

- Recursive references to Eval appear inline in the same form that is used to identify the individual cases.
- Primitive functions of the Vesta language, whose names begin with an underscore, are invoked inline from the pseudo-code as if they were ordinary C++ functions. The primitive operators of the Vesta language are invoked in this way too; for example, when the pseudo-code refers to operator+, it means the Vesta primitive function, not the C++ operator. Note that some of the Vesta operators are overloaded by type, but not by arity. For example, operator+ is defined on integers, texts, lists, and bindings, but it always takes two arguments.
- In the pseudo-code for rules that contain the terminal Id, the variable `id` denotes the value of the Id represented as a ttext.
- If the pseudo-statement `error` is reached, evaluation halts with a runtime error and appropriate error message. No value is produced.

Each of the following sections presents a portion of the language syntax with its associated evaluation rules. The complete language syntax is given in Section A.4.

### A.3.3.1 Expr

**Syntax:**

```
Expr      ::= if Expr then Expr else Expr | Expr1
Expr1     ::= Expr2 {  =>  Expr2 }*
Expr2     ::= Expr3 {  ||  Expr3 }*
Expr3     ::= Expr4 {  &&  Expr4 }*
Expr4     ::= Expr5 [ CompareOp Expr5 ]
CompareOp ::= == | != | < | > | <= | >=
Expr5     ::= Expr6 { AddOp Expr6 }*
AddOp     ::= +   |  ++   |  -
Expr6     ::= Expr7 { MulOp Expr7 }*
MulOp     ::= *
Expr7     ::= [ UnaryOp ] Expr8
UnaryOp   ::= -   |   !
Expr8     ::= Primary [ TypeQual ]
Primary   ::= ( Expr ) | Literal | Id | List
            | Binding | Select | Block | FuncCall
```

The grammar lists the operators in increasing order of precedence. The binary operators at each precedence level are left-associative.

**Evaluation Rules:**

The evaluation rules for conditional, implication, disjunction, conjunction, comparison, AddOp, MulOp, UnaryOp, and parenthesized expressions are shown in Tables A.4 and A.5. There are seven remaining possibilities for a Primary: Literal, Id, List, Binding, Select, Block, and FuncCall. These are treated separately in subsequent sections.

### A.3.3.2 Literal

**Syntax:**

```
Literal    ::= ERR | TRUE | FALSE | Text | Integer
```

**Evaluation Rules:**

```
Eval( ERR    , C) = err
Eval( TRUE   , C) = true
Eval( FALSE  , C) = false
Eval( Text   , C) = the corresponding t_text value
Eval( Integer, C) = the corresponding t_int value
```

In the Text evaluation rule, the C++ interpretation of escape characters is used. In the Integer evaluation rule, evaluation halts with a runtime error if the integer is too large or small to be represented by the implementation.

### A.3.3.3 Id

**Evaluation Rules:**

```
Eval( Id , C) = _lookup(C, id)
```

As defined in Section A.3.4.5, `_lookup`(*b*, *nm*) is the value associated with the nonempty name *nm* in the binding *b*. The evaluation halts with a runtime error if *nm* is empty or is not in *b*'s domain.

### A.3.3.4 List

**Syntax:**

```
List        ::= < Expr*, >
```

The use of <, > as both binary operators and list delimiters makes the grammar ambiguous. Section A.4.2 explains how the ambiguity is resolved.

```
// conditional expression
Eval( if Expr1 then Expr2 else Expr3 , C) =
{
  val b = Eval( Expr1 , C);
  if (_is_bool(b) == false) error;
  if (b == true) return Eval( Expr2 , C);
  else return Eval( Expr3 , C);
}

// conditional implication
Eval( Expr1 => Expr2 , C) =
{
  val b = Eval( Expr1 , C);
  if (_is_bool(b) == false) error;
  if (b == false) return true;
  b = Eval( Expr2 , C);
  if (_is_bool(b) == false) error;
  return b;
}

// conditional OR (disjunction)
Eval( Expr1 || Expr2 , C) =
{
  val b = Eval( Expr1 , C);
  if (_is_bool(b) == false) error;
  if (b == true) return true;
  b = Eval( Expr2 , C);
  if (_is_bool(b) == false) error;
  return b;
}

// conditional AND (conjunction)
Eval( Expr1 && Expr2 , C) =
{
  val b = Eval( Expr1 , C);
  if (_is_bool(b) == false) error;
  if (b == false) return false;
  b = Eval( Expr2 , C);
  if (_is_bool(b) == false) error;
  return b;
}
```

**Table A.4.** Evaluation rules for conditionals, implications, disjunctions, and conjunctions.

```
// comparison
Eval( Expr1 == Expr2 , C) =
  operator==(Eval( Expr1 , C), Eval( Expr2 , C))
Eval( Expr1 != Expr2 , C) =
  operator!=(Eval( Expr1 , C), Eval( Expr2 , C))
Eval( Expr1 <  Expr2 , C) =
  operator< (Eval( Expr1 , C), Eval( Expr2 , C))
Eval( Expr1 >  Expr2 , C) =
  operator> (Eval( Expr1 , C), Eval( Expr2 , C))
Eval( Expr1 <= Expr2 , C) =
  operator<=(Eval( Expr1 , C), Eval( Expr2 , C))
Eval( Expr1 >= Expr2 , C) =
  operator>=(Eval( Expr1 , C), Eval( Expr2 , C))

// AddOp
Eval( Expr1 +  Expr2 , C) =
  operator+ (Eval( Expr1 , C), Eval( Expr2 , C))
Eval( Expr1 ++ Expr2 , C) =
  operator++(Eval( Expr1 , C), Eval( Expr2 , C))

// MulOp
Eval( Expr1 -  Expr2 , C) =
  operator- (Eval( Expr1 , C), Eval( Expr2 , C))
Eval( Expr1 *  Expr2 , C) =
  operator* (Eval( Expr1 , C), Eval( Expr2 , C))

// UnaryOp
Eval( ! Expr , C) = operator!(Eval( Expr , C))
Eval( - Expr , C) = operator-(Eval( Expr , C))

// parenthesization
Eval( ( Expr ) , C) = Eval( Expr , C)
```

**Table A.5.** Evaluation rules for comparison, AddOp, MulOp, UnaryOp, and parenthesized expressions.

### Syntactic Rewrite Rules:

```
<Expr1, ..., Exprn>  ⟶  <Expr1> + <Expr2, ..., Exprn>
```

Here, '+' is the concatenation operator on lists.

### Evaluation Rules:

```
Eval( <>       , C) = emptylist
Eval( < Expr > , C) = _list1(Eval( Expr , C))
```

As defined in Section A.3.4.4, `_list1`(*val*) evaluates to a list containing the single value *val*.

### A.3.3.5 Binding

**Syntax:**

```
Binding     ::= '[' BindElem*, ']'
BindElem    ::= SelfNameB | NameBind
SelfNameB   ::= Id
NameBind    ::= GenPath = Expr
GenPath     ::= GenArc { Delim GenArc }* [ Delim ]
GenArc      ::= Arc | $ Id | $ ( Expr ) | % Expr %
Arc         ::= Id | Integer | Text
```

**Syntactic Rewrite Rules:**

```
Id                             ⟶  Id = Id
$ Id                           ⟶  $ ( Id )
% Expr %                       ⟶  $ ( Expr )
GenArc Delim = Expr            ⟶  GenArc = Expr
GenArc Delim GenPath = Expr    ⟶  GenArc = [ GenPath = Expr ]
```

The first rule enables names from the current scope to be copied into bindings more succinctly. For example, the binding value:

```
[ progs = progs, tests = tests, lib = lib ]
```

can instead be written:

```
[ progs, tests, lib ]
```

The final rewrite rule enables nested single-element bindings to be written more succintly. For example, the binding value:

```
[ env_ovs = [ Cxx = [ switches = [ compile =
  [ debug = "-g3", optimize = "-O" ]]]]]
```

can instead be written:

```
[ env_ovs/Cxx/switches/compile =
  [ debug = "-g3", optimize = "-O" ]]
```

**Evaluation Rules:**

First, the rules for constructing empty and singleton bindings:

```
Eval( [ ]              , C) = emptybinding
Eval( [ Arc = Expr ] , C) = _bind1(id, Eval( Expr , C))
```

Here *id* is the t_text representation of Arc. The conversion from an Arc to a t_text is straightforward. If the Arc is an Id, the literal characters of the identifier become the text value. If the Arc is an Integer, the literal characters used to represent the integer in the source of the model become the text value. If the Arc is a Text, the result of Eval(Arc, C) is used. As defined in Section A.3.4.5, `_bind1`(*id*, *v*) evaluates to a singleton binding that associates the non-empty t_text *id* with the value *v*.

The `$(Expr)` syntax allows the name introduced into a binding to be computed:

```
Eval( [ $ ( Expr1 ) = Expr2 ] , C) =
  _bind1(Eval(Expr1, C), Eval( Expr2 , C))
```

When the field name is computed using the `$` syntax, the expression must evaluate to a non-empty t_text (see the `_bind1` primitive in Section A.3.4.5 below).

The following rule handles the case where multiple BindElem's are given.

```
Eval( [ BindElem1, ..., BindElemn ] , C) =
{
  val b1 = Eval( [ BindElem1 ] , C);
  val b2 = Eval( [ BindElem2, ..., BindElemn ] , C);
  return _append(b1, b2);
}
```

As defined in Section A.3.4.5, _append(*b1*, *b2*) evaluates to the concatenation of the bindings *b1* and *b2*; it requires that their domains are disjoint.

#### A.3.3.6 Select

**Syntax:**

```
Select      ::= Primary Selector GenArc
Selector    ::= Delim | !
GenArc      ::= Arc | $ Id | $ ( Expr ) | % Expr %
Arc         ::= Id | Integer | Text
```

A Select expression denotes a selection from a binding, so the Primary must evaluate to a binding value.

**Syntactic Rewrite Rules:**

```
Primary Selector $ Id        ⟶  Primary Selector $ ( Id )
Primary Selector % Expr %    ⟶  Primary Selector $ ( Expr )
```

**Evaluation Rules:**

The Delim syntax selects a value out of a binding by name.

```
Eval( Primary Delim Arc , C) =
  _lookup(Eval( Primary , C), id)
```

Here *id* is the t_text value of Arc, as defined in Section A.3.3.5 above.

The `$(Expr)` syntax allows the selected name to be computed:

```
Eval( Primary Delim $ ( Expr ) , C) =
  _lookup(Eval( Primary , C), Eval( Expr , C))
```

The `!` syntax tests whether a name is in a binding's domain:

```
Eval( Primary ! Arc , C) =
  _defined(Eval( Primary , C), id)
```

Again, *id* is the t_text value of Arc. As defined in Section A.3.4.5, `_defined`(*b*, *nm*) evaluates to *true* if *nm* is non-empty and in *b*'s domain, and to *false* otherwise. As above, the `$(`*`Expr`*`)` syntax can be used to compute the name:

```
Eval( Primary ! $ ( Expr ) , C) =
  _defined(Eval( Primary , C), Eval( Expr , C))
```

In both cases where the GenArc is a computed expression, the Expr must evaluate to a t_text.

#### A.3.3.7 Block

**Syntax:**

```
Block      ::= '{' { Stmt ; }* Result ; '}'
Stmt       ::= Assign | Iterate | FuncDef | TypeDef
Result     ::= { value | return } Expr
```

**Syntactic Rewrite Rules:**

```
return Expr   ⟶   value Expr
```

That is, the keywords `return` and `value` are synonyms, provided for stylistic reasons. The `return`/`value` construct must appear at the end of a Block; there is no analog of the C/C++ return statement that terminates execution of the function in which it appears.

**Evaluation Rules:**

Since SDL is functional, evaluation of a statement does not produce side-effects, but rather produces a binding. Evaluation of a block occurs by augmenting the context with the bindings produced by evaluating the Stmts, then evaluating the final Expr in the augmented context.

```
Eval( { value Expr } , C) = Eval( Expr , C)

Eval( { Stmt1; ...; Stmtn; value Expr } , C) =
{
  val b = Eval( { Stmt1; ...; Stmtn } , C);
  return Eval( Expr , operator+(C, b));
}
```

Notice that this second rule introduces an argument to Eval in the "extended" language that is not generated by any non-terminal of the grammar.

#### A.3.3.8 Stmt

**Evaluation Rules:**

Evaluating a Stmt or sequence of Stmts produces a binding. Note that the binding resulting from the evaluation of a sequence of Stmts is simply the overlay (operator '+') of the bindings resulting from evaluating each Stmt in the sequence, and does not include the context *C*.

```
Eval( { } , C) = emptybinding

Eval( { Stmt1; Stmt2; ...; Stmtn } , C) =
{
  val b0 = Eval( Stmt1 , C);
  val b1 = Eval( { Stmt2; ...; Stmtn }, operator+(C, b0));
  return operator+(b0, b1);
}
```

These rules apply to constructs in the "extended" language. There are three possibilities for a Stmt: Assign, Iterate, and FuncDef. They are covered in the next three sections.

#### A.3.3.9 Assign

Since SDL is functional, assignments do not produce side-effects. Instead, they introduce a new name into the evaluation context whose value is that of the given expression.

**Syntax:**

```
Assign    ::= Id [ TypeQual ] [ Op ] = Expr
Op        ::= AddOp | MulOp
AddOp     ::= +  |  ++  |  -
MulOp     ::= *
```

**Syntactic Rewrite Rules:**

```
Id Op = Expr   ⟶   Id = Id Op Expr
```

**Evaluation Rules:**

```
Eval( Id = Expr , C) = _bind1(id, Eval( Expr , C))
```

where *id* is the t_text representation of `Id`.

### A.3.3.10 Iterate

The language includes expressions for iterating over both lists and bindings. There is also a `_map` primitive defined on lists (Section A.3.4.4) and bindings (Section A.3.4.5). `_map` is more efficient but less general than the Iterate construct.

**Syntax:**

```
Iterate    ::= foreach Control in Expr do IterBody
Control    ::= Id | '[' Id = Id ']'
IterBody   ::= Stmt | '{' Stmt+; '}'
```

The two Control forms are used to iterate over lists and bindings, respectively.

**Evaluation Rules:**

Conceptually, the loop is unrolled *n* times, where *n* is the length of the list or binding resulting from the evaluation of Expr. The evaluation rules for iterating over lists and bindings are shown in Table A.6. Note that the iteration variables (that is, `Id`, `Id1`, and `Id2` in the Table) are not bound in the binding that results from evaluating the `foreach` statement. However, any assignments made in the loop body *are* included in the result binding.

Iteration statements are typically used to walk over or collect parts of a list or binding. For example, Table A.7 presents functions for reversing a list and for counting the number of leaves in a binding.

### A.3.3.11 FuncDef

**Syntax:**

The function definition syntax allows a suffix of the formal parameters to have associated default values.

```
FuncDef     ::= Id Formals+ [ TypeQual ] Block
Formals     ::= ( FormalArgs )
FormalArgs ::= TypedId*,
              | { TypedId = Expr }*,
              | TypedId { , TypedId }* { , TypedId = Expr }+
```

```
// iteration with single-statement body
Eval( foreach Control in Expr do Stmt , C) =
  Eval( foreach Control in Expr do { Stmt } , C)

// iteration over a list
Eval( foreach Id in Expr do { Stmt1; ...; Stmtn } , C) =
{
  val l = Eval( Expr, C);
  if (_is_list(l) == false) error;
  t_text id = Id; // identifier Id as a t_text
  val r = emptybinding;
  for (; !(l == emptylist); l = _tail(l)) {
    val r1 = operator+(C, r);
    r1 = operator+(r1, _bind1(id, _head(l)));
    r = operator+(r, Eval( { Stmt1; ...; Stmtn } , r1));
  }
  return r;
}

// iteration over a binding
Eval(foreach [Id1=Id2] in Expr do {Stmt1; ...;Stmtn}, C) =
{
  val b = Eval( Expr, C);
  if (_is_binding(b) == false) error;
  t_text id1 = Id1; // identifier Id1 as a t_text
  t_text id2 = Id2; // identifier Id2 as a t_text
  val r = emptybinding;
  for (; !(b == emptybinding); b = _tail(b)) {
    val r1 = operator+(C, r);
    r1 = operator+(r1, _bind1(id1, _n(_head(b))));
    r1 = operator+(r1, _bind1(id2, _v(_head(b))));
    r = operator+(r, Eval( { Stmt1; ...; Stmtn } , r1));
  }
  return r;
}
```

**Table A.6.** Evaluation rules for iterating over lists and bindings.

The three alternatives for FormalArgs correspond to the cases in which no arguments are defaulted, all arguments are defaulted, and some arguments are defaulted.

Note that the syntax allows multiple `Formals` to follow the function name. As the rules below describe, the use of multiple Formals produces a sequence of curried functions, all but the first of which is anonymous.

```
/**nocache**/
reverse_list(l: list): list
{
  res: list = <>;
  foreach elt in l do
    res = <elt> + res;
  return res;
}

/**nocache**/
count_leaves(b: binding): int
{
  res: int = 0;
  foreach [ nm = val ] in b do
    res += if _is_binding(val)
      then count_leaves(val) else 1;
  return res;
}
```

**Table A.7.** Two example functions that use `foreach` to iterate over a list and a binding.

**Evaluation Rules:**

```
Eval( Id Formals1 ... Formalsn Block , C) =
  _bind1(id, Eval( e , C1))
```

where:

- `e = LAMBDA Formals1 ... LAMBDA Formalsn Block`
- `C1 = operator+(C, _bind1(id, Eval( e , C1)))`
- *id* is the t_text representation of `Id`.

Notice the recursive definition of C1. This allows functions to be self-recursive, but not mutually recursive. Although this recursive definition looks a little odd, it can be implemented by the evaluator by introducing a cycle into the context C1. This is the only case where any Vesta value can contain a cycle (the language syntax and operators do not allow cyclic lists or bindings to be constructed), and the cycle is invisible to clients. There is no practical difficulty in constructing the cycle because, as will be clear shortly, the "evaluation" of a `LAMBDA` is purely syntactic.

Also note that this rule produces a `LAMBDA` construct in the "extended" language that is not generated by any non-terminal of the grammar. The evaluation of `LAMBDA` produces a t_closure value $\langle e, f, b \rangle$ as described in Section A.3.1.

The following is the simple case of `LAMBDA`, where all actual parameters must be given in any application of the closure. The reason for the restriction on the use of "`.`" as a formal parameter is treated in the next section.

```
Eval( LAMBDA (Id1, ..., Idm)
      LAMBDA Formals2 ... LAMBDA Formalsn Block , C) =
  <LAMBDA Formals2 ... LAMBDA Formalsn Block, f, C>
```

where $f$ is a list of pairs $(id_i, \langle\text{emptyExpr}\rangle)$ such that $id_i$ is the t_text representation of $\texttt{Id}_i$, for $i$ in the closed interval $[1,m]$. If any of the identifiers $\texttt{Id}_i$ is "`.`", the evaluation halts with a runtime error.

In the typical case where only one set of Formals is specified (that is, $n = 1$), the first element of the resulting closure value is simply a Block.

Next is the general case of `LAMBDA`, in which "default expressions" are given for a suffix of the formal parameter list. Functions may be called with fewer actuals than formals if each formal corresponding to an omitted actual includes an expression specifying the default value to be computed. When the closure is applied, if an actual parameter is missing, its formal's expression is evaluated (in the context of the `LAMBDA`) and passed instead. The next section (FuncCall) defines this precisely.

```
Eval(
    LAMBDA (Id_1, ... Id_k, Id_{k+1}=Expr_{k+1}, ... Id_m=Expr_m)
    LAMBDA Formals_2 ... LAMBDA Formals_n Block , C) =
  <LAMBDA Formals_2 ... LAMBDA Formals_n Block, f, C>
```

where $f$ is a list of pairs $(id_i, expr_i)$ such that:

- $id_i$ is the t_text representation of $\texttt{Id}_i$, for $i$ in $[1,m]$,
- $expr_i$ is $\langle\text{emptyExpr}\rangle$, for $i$ in $[1,k]$, and
- $expr_i$ is $\texttt{Expr}_i$, for $i$ in $[k+1,m]$.

As before, if any of the identifiers $\texttt{Id}_i$ is "`.`", the evaluation halts with a runtime error.

#### A.3.3.12 FuncCall

**Syntax:**

```
FuncCall    ::= Primary Actuals
Actuals     ::= ( Expr*, )
```

**Evaluation Rules:**

The function call mechanism provides special treatment for the identifier consisting of a single period, called the *current environment* and pronounced "dot". Dot is typically assigned a binding that contains the tools, switches, and file system required for the rest of the build. The initial environment, *C-initial* (see Section A.3.3 above), does not bind dot (that is, `_defined(`*`C-initial`*`, ".")` is *false*).

When a function is called, the context in which its body executes may bind "`.`" to a value established as follows:

- if the function is defined with $n$ formals and called with $n$ or fewer actuals, then the value bound to the implicit formal parameter "`.`" is the value of "`.`" at the point of call;
- if the function is defined with $n$ formals and called with $n+1$ actuals, then the value bound to the implicit formal parameter "`.`" is the value of the last actual.

Thus, the binding for "`.`", if any, is passed through the dynamic call chain until it is altered either explicitly by an Assign statement (Section A.3.3.9) or implicitly by calling a function with an extra actual parameter. The pseudo-code shown in Table A.8 makes this precise. In this code, the comparison with ⟨emptyExpr⟩ has not been formalized, but it should be intuitively clear.

#### A.3.3.13 Model

**Syntax:**

```
Model        ::= Files Imports Block
```

**Evaluation Rules:**

The nonterminal Model is treated like the body of a function definition (i.e., like a FuncDef (Section A.3.3.11), but without the identifier naming the function and with an empty list of formal parameters). More precisely:

```
Eval( Files Imports Block , C) =
{
  val C0 = Eval( Files Imports , emptybinding);
  return Eval( LAMBDA () Block , _append(C0, C));
}
```

As this rule indicates, the Files and Imports constructs are evaluated in an empty context, and they add to the closure context in which the model's `LAMBDA` is evaluated. In practice, the context C will always be the initial context *C-initial* when this rule is applied (cf. Sections A.3.3 and A.3.3.15).

The Files nonterminal introduces values corresponding to the contents of ordinary files and directories. The Imports nonterminal introduces closure values corresponding to other SDL models.

The evaluation rules handle Files and Imports clauses by augmenting the context using the `_append` primitive, thereby ensuring that the names introduced by these clauses are all distinct, just as if the Files and Imports clauses of the Model were a single binding constructor. The Files and Imports clauses are evaluated independently:

```
Eval( Files Imports , C) =
  _append(Eval( Files , C), Eval( Imports , C))
```

The following two sections give the rules for evaluating Files and Imports clauses individually. It should be noted that the evaluation context C is ignored in those rules.

#### A.3.3.14 Files

A Files clause introduces names corresponding to files or directories in the Vesta repository. Generally, these files or directories are named by relative paths, which are interpreted relative to the location of the model containing the Files clause. Absolute paths are permitted, though they are expected to be rarely used.

```
Eval( Primary ( Expr_1, ..., Expr_n ) , C) =
{
  val cl = Eval( Primary , C);
  if (_is_closure(cl) == false) error;

  /* cl.e is the function body, cl.f are the formals, and
     cl.b is the context */
  int m = _length(cl.f);          // number of formals
  if (n > m + 1) error;           // too many actuals
  val C1 = cl.b;                  // t_binding
  val f = cl.f;                   // t_list (of (t, e) pairs)

  /* augment C1 to include formals bound to corresponding
     actuals */
  int i;
  for (i = 1; i <= m; i++) {
    val form = _head(f);          // i-th formal
    val act;                      // corresponding actual
    if (i <= n)
      act = Eval( Expr_i , C); // value for i-th actual
    else {
      if (form.e == <emptyExpr>) {
        // a required actual is missing
        error;
      }
      act = Eval( form.e , cl.b); // defaulted formal value
    }
    C1 = operator+(C1, _bind1(form.t, act));
    f = _tail(f);
  }

  // bind "." in C1
  val dot;
  if (n <= m)
    dot = _lookup(C, ".");       // inherit "." from C
  else
    dot = Eval( Expr_n , C);  // last actual value supplied
  C1 = operator+(C1, _bind1(".", dot));

  /* C1 is now a suitable environment.  If the closure is
     a primitive function, then invoke it by a special
     mechanism internal to the evaluator and return the
     value it computes. Otherwise, perform the following:
  */
  return Eval( cl.e , C1);
}
```

**Table A.8.** Evaluation rule for FuncCall.

**Syntax:**

```
Files        ::= FileClause*
FileClause   ::= files FileItem*;
FileItem     ::= FileSpec | FileBinding
FileSpec     ::= [ Arc = ] DelimPath
FileBinding ::= Arc = '[' FileSpec*, ']'

DelimPath    ::= [ Delim ] Path [ Delim ]
Path         ::= Arc { Delim Arc }*
Arc          ::= Id | Integer | Text
```

Each FileItem in a Files clause takes one of two forms: a FileSpec or a FileBinding. Each form introduces (binds) exactly one name. In the FileSpec case, the name corresponds to the contents of a single file or directory; in the FileBinding case, the name corresponds to a binding consisting of perhaps many files or directories. In both cases, the identifier introduced into the Vesta naming context or the identifiers introduced into the binding can be specified explicitly or derived from an Arc in the Path.

For example, consider the following `files` clause:

```
files
  scripts = bin;
  c_files = [ utils.c, main.c ];
```

Suppose the directory containing this model also contains a directory named `bin` and files named `utils.c` and `main.c`. Then this `files` clause introduces the two names `scripts` and `c_files` into the context. The former is bound to a binding whose structure corresponds to the `bin` directory. The latter is bound to a binding that maps the names `utils.c` and `main.c` to the contents of those files, respectively. The file contents are values of type t_text.

**Syntactic Rewrite Rules:**

When multiple FileItem's are given in a FileClause, the `files` keyword simply distributes over each of the FileItem's. That is:

$\texttt{files FileItem}_1\texttt{; ...; FileItem}_n\texttt{;}$

$\longrightarrow$

$\texttt{files FileItem}_1\texttt{;}$
$\texttt{...;}$
$\texttt{files FileItem}_n\texttt{;}$

When the initial Arc is omitted from a FileSpec, the rightmost Arc of the path is used in its place. That is,

```
files [ Delim ] { Arc Delim }* Arc [ Delim ];
```

$\longrightarrow$

```
files Arc = [ Delim ] { Arc Delim }* Arc [ Delim ];
```

**Evaluation Rules:**

Multiple FileClauses are evaluated independently:

```
Eval( FileClause0 FileClause1 ... FileClausen , C) =
{
  val C2 = Eval( FileClause1 ... FileClausen , C);
  return _append(Eval( FileClause0 , C), C2);
}
```

That leaves only two cases to consider: FileSpec (in which the initial Arc is specified) and FileBinding.

```
// FileSpec
Eval( files Arc = DelimPath , C) = _bind1(id, v)
```

where:

- *id* is the t_text representation of Arc, as defined in Section A.3.3.5 above.
- If DelimPath begins with a Delim, it is interpreted as an absolute path, which must nevertheless resolve to a file or directory in the Vesta repository. If DelimPath does not begin with a Delim, it refers to a file or directory named relative to the directory of the enclosing Model.
- If the entity named by DelimPath is a file, *v* is a t_text value formed by taking the file's contents. If DelimPath names a directory, *v* is a t_binding value constructed from the contents of the directory, treating the files (if any) in the directory as above (i.e., as t_text values) and the directories (if any) recursively (i.e., as bindings). The members of the resulting binding are in an unspecified order. If DelimPath does not correspond to either an extant file or a directory, the evaluation halts with a runtime error.

```
// FileBinding
Eval( files Arc = [ FileSpec1, ..., FileSpecn ] , C) =
  _bind1(id, Eval( files FileSpec1; ...; FileSpecn , C))
```

Again, *id* is the t_text representation of Arc.

The FileBinding form of the Files clause provides a convenient way to create a binding containing multiple FileSpecs. Without this construct, it would be necessary to name each file twice, once in the FileSpec and once in a subsequent binding constructor. Making a binding with FileBinding is semantically similar to constructing a file system directory, with the additional property that there is an enumeration order for the component files.

Notice that the grammar and evaluation rules given above for FileSpec and FileBinding allow a general Arc on the left-hand side of each equal sign, not just an Id. This simplifies the definitions and rewrite rules. However, it would be useless to write constructs like the following, which introduce names that cannot be referenced in the body of the model:

```
files
  33;
  34 = 34;
  "hash-table.c";
  "foo bar" = [ foo, bar ];
```

Therefore, the context created by a Files clause is constrained to bind only names that are legal identifiers; that is, names that match the syntax of the Id token.

If files whose names are not legal identifiers must be introduced, they can either be given legal names using the equal sign syntax or embedded in a binding. For example:

```
// Choose a legal name
files
  f33 = 33;
  f34 = 34;
  hash_table.c = "hash-table.c";
  foo_bar = [ foo, bar ];

// Embed in a binding
files
  f = [ 33, 34 ];
  src = [ "hash-table.c" ];
```

### A.3.3.15 Imports

The Imports clause enables one SDL model to reference and use others; that is, it supports modular decomposition of SDL programs.

**Syntax:**

```
Imports    ::= ImpClause*
ImpClause  ::= ImpIdReq | ImpIdOpt
```

There are two major forms of the Imports clause: one where identifiers are required (ImpIdReq), and one where they are optional (ImpIdOpt). Both forms have two sub-forms in which either a single model or a list of models may be imported.

First, consider the ImpIdReq case. This form is typically used to import models in the same package as the importing model. Each ImpItemR in the ImpIdReq clause takes one of two forms: an ImpSpecR or an ImpListR. Each form binds exactly one name.

```
ImpIdReq   ::= import ImpItemR*;
ImpItemR   ::= ImpSpecR | ImpListR
ImpSpecR   ::= Arc = DelimPath
ImpListR   ::= Arc = '[' ImpSpecR*, ']'

DelimPath  ::= [ Delim ] Path [ Delim ]
Path       ::= Arc { Delim Arc }*
Arc        ::= Id | Integer | Text
```

In the ImpSpecR case, the name is bound to the t_closure value that results from evaluation of the contents of a file according to the Model evaluation rules of Section A.3.3.13. For example, consider the Import clause:

```
import self = progs.ves;
```

This clause binds the name `self` to the closure corresponding to the local *progs.ves* model in the same directory as the model in which it appears.

In the ImpListR case, the name is bound to a binding of such values. For example:

```
import sub =
  [ progs = src/progs.ves, tests = src/tests.ves ];
```

This clause binds the name `sub` to a binding containing the names `progs` and `tests`; these names within the binding are bound to the closures corresponding to the models named `progs.ves` and `tests.ves` in the package's `src` subdirectory.

Because the Imports clause often mentions several files with names that share a common prefix, a syntactic form is provided to allow the prefix to be written once. This is the ImpIdOpt form. It is used to import models from other packages. The semantics are defined so that many identifiers are optional; when omitted, they default to the name of the package from which the model is being imported. As in the ImpIdReq case, ImpIdOpt has forms for importing both single models and lists of multiple models.

```
ImpIdOpt    ::= from DelimPath import ImpItemO*;
ImpItemO    ::= ImpSpecO | ImpListO
ImpSpecO    ::= [ Arc = ] Path [ Delim ]
ImpListO    ::= Arc = '[' ImpSpecO*, ']'
```

Here are some examples of ImpIdOpt imports:

```
from /vesta/west.vestasys.org/vesta import
  cache/12/build.ves;
  libs = [ srpc/2/build.ves, basics/5/build.ves ];
```

This construct binds the name `cache` to the closure corresponding to version 12 of that package's `build.ves` model, and it binds the name `libs` to a binding containing the names `srpc` and `basics`, bound to versions 2 and 5 of those package's `build.ves` models. (As the evaluation rules below describe, the three occurrences of "`/build.ves`" in this example could actually have been omitted.)

**Syntactic Rewrite Rules:**

When multiple ImpItemR's are given in a ImpIdReq, the `import` keyword distributes over each of the ImpItemR's. That is:

```
import ImpSpec1; ...; ImpSpecn;
```

$\longrightarrow$

```
import ImpSpec1;
...;
import ImpSpecn;
```

Similarly, the `from` clause distributes over the individual imports of an ImpId-Opt. In particular:

```
from DelimPath import ImpItemO1; ...; ImpItemOn;

  ⟶

from DelimPath import ImpItemO1;
...;
from DelimPath import ImpItemOn;
```

The use of `from` makes it optional to supply a name for the closure value being introduced; if the name is omitted, it is derived from the Path following the `import` keyword as follows:

```
from DelimPath import
  [ Arc1 = ] [ Delim ] Arc2 { Delim Arc }* [ Delim ]

  ⟶

import Arc =
  DelimPath Delim Arc2 { Delim Arc }* [ Delim ]
```

where the *Arc* to the left of the equal sign is $\texttt{Arc}_1$ if it is present and is $\texttt{Arc}_2$ otherwise. Similarly:

```
from DelimPath import Arc = [
  [ Arc11 = ] [ Delim ] Arc21 { Delim Arc }* [ Delim ],
  ...,
  [ Arc1n = ] [ Delim ] Arc2n { Delim Arc }* [ Delim ] ]

  ⟶

import Arc = [
  Arc1 = DelimPath Delim Arc21 {Delim Arc }* [ Delim ],
  ...,
  Arcn = DelimPath Delim Arc2n {Delim Arc }* [ Delim ] ]
```

where $\text{Arc}_i$ is $\text{Arc1}_i$ if it is present and is $\text{Arc2}_i$ otherwise.

**Evaluation Rules:**

Multiple ImpClause's are evaluated independently:

```
Eval( ImpClause0 ImpClause1 ... ImpClausen , C) =
{
  val C2 = Eval( ImpClause1 ... ImpClausen , C);
  return _append(Eval( ImpClause0 , C), C2);
}
```

This leaves two fundamental forms of the Imports clause, whose semantics are defined as follows:

```
// ImpSpecR
Eval( import Arc = DelimPath , C) =
  _bind1(id, Eval( model , C-initial))
```

where:

- *id* is the t_text representation of *Arc*, as defined in Section A.3.3.5 above.
- Let *f* be the sequence of Delims and Arcs that constitute the DelimPath.
  1. If *f* does not begin with a Delim, prepend "`Delim Path0 Delim`" to *f*, where Path0 names the directory containing the Model in which this Imports clause appears.
  2. Look up the path *f* in the Vesta repository. (See Section A.3.3.16 below.) If *f* names a directory, append a Delim (if *f* doesn't already end in one) and the string "`build.ves`", then look up the augmented path *f* in the repository again. If *f* does not name a directory and its final element does not end in "`.ves`", append the string "`.ves`" to the final element of *f*, and look it up in the repository again.
- *model* is the SDL Model represented by the contents of the file in the Vesta repository named by the sequence *f*. If no such expression can be produced (e.g., the file doesn't exist, or can't be parsed as an expression), evaluation halts with a runtime error.

```
// ImpListR
Eval( import Arc = [ ImpSpecR1, ..., ImpSpecRn ] , C) =
  _bind1(id, Eval( import ImpSpecR1; ...; ImpSpecRn , C))
```

Again, *id* is the t_text representation of Arc.

As with the Files clause, and for the same reason, the context created by an Imports clause is constrained to bind only names that are legal identifiers; that is, names that match the syntax of the Id token.

#### A.3.3.16 File Name Interpretation

The evaluation rules for the Files and Imports clauses do not specify how the sequence of Arcs and Delims making up a DelimPath is converted into a file name in the underlying file system. While this is somewhat system-dependent, it is nevertheless intended to be intuitive. In particular,

- Multiple adjacent Delims are replaced by a single one. (The grammar above doesn't permit adjacent Delims, but they can be produced by the rewrite rules.)
- SDL syntax allows the arbitrary intermingling of "`/`" and "`\`" as arc separators. However, the implementation actually requires that Vesta programs use one or the other uniformly. When creating a file name from a sequence of Arcs and Delims, the implementation inserts the appropriate arc separator required by the underlying file system. The choice is not influenced by the choice of Delim that appears in the SDL program.

- The grammar permits an Arc to be an arbitrary Text. An Arc in a file name, however, is forbidden to contain a Delim character (i.e., forward or backward slash), and the Arcs "`..`" and "`.`" are forbidden in file names as well.

### A.3.3.17 Pragmas

The evaluator recognizes two stylized comments, or *pragmas*, which can be used to control how it caches calls of user-defined functions. The two pragmas are `/**nocache**/` and `/**pk**/`.

By default, evaluations of all user-defined functions are cached. However, if a function definition is immediately preceded by `/**nocache**/`, then calls to that function are not cached. The `/**nocache**/` pragma is useful to avoid cluttering the cache with values that would be faster to recompute than to look up.

By default, the primary key (see Section 8.4.3) used to index the function cache is a combination of the function body being called and the values of all actual arguments that are not composite values (that is, are not lists, bindings, or closures). If the `/**pk**/` pragma appears immediately before the name of a function's formal parameter, the value of the corresponding actual parameter is also included in the function's primary key, even if it is a composite value. The `/**pk**/` pragma is useful when a function's result is known to depend on the entire composite value and leaving this value out of the computation would result in a large number of different cache entries having the same primary key.

## A.3.4 Primitives

The primitive names and associated values described below are provided by the SDL evaluator in *C-initial*, the initial context. Most of these values are closures with empty contexts; that is, they are primitive functions.

In the descriptions that follow, the notation used for the function signatures follows C++, with the result type preceding the function name and each argument type preceding the corresponding argument name. Defaulting conventions also follow C++; if an argument name is followed by "`= value`", then omitting the corresponding actual argument is equivalent to supplying *value*.

Some of the function signatures use the C++ operator definition syntax, which should be understood as defining a function whose name is not an Id in the sense of the grammar above. Such operator names cannot be rebound. These operators are frequently overloaded, as the descriptions below indicate. Uses of these built-in Vesta primitives within C++ code are denoted by the `operator` syntax.

The pseudo-code of this section assumes the definition of the Vesta value class given at the start of Section A.3.3. Invocation of a Vesta operator primitive within the pseudo-code is denoted by the `operator` syntax. All other operators appearing in the pseudo-code denote the C++ operators.

In these descriptions, the argument types represent the natural domain; the result type is the natural range. If a primitive function is passed a value that lies outside its natural domain, evaluation halts with a runtime error. This type-checking occurs when the primitive function is called, not before.

#### A.3.4.1 Functions on Type t_bool

Recall that *true* and *false* are Vesta values, not C++ quantities.

```
t_bool
operator==(t_bool b1, t_bool b2)
```

Returns *true* if *b1* and *b2* are the same, and *false* otherwise.

```
t_bool
operator!=(t_bool b1, t_bool b2)
  operator!(operator==(b1, b2))
```

```
t_bool
operator!(t_bool b)
```

Returns the logical complement of *b*.

#### A.3.4.2 Functions on Type t_int

```
t_bool
operator==(t_int i1, t_int i2)
```

Returns *true* if *i1* and *i2* are equal, and *false* otherwise.

```
t_bool
operator!=(t_int i1, t_int i2) =
  operator!(operator==(i1, i2))
```

```
t_int
operator+(t_int i1, t_int i2)
```

Returns the integer sum *i1* + *i2* unless it lies outside the implementation-defined range, in which case evaluation halts with a runtime error.

```
t_int
operator-(t_int i1, t_int i2)
```

Returns the integer difference *i1* - *i2* unless it lies outside the implementation-defined range, in which case evaluation halts with a runtime error.

```
t_int
operator-(t_int i) =
  operator-(0, i)
```

```
t_int
operator*(t_int i1, t_int i2)
```

Returns the integer product *i1* * *i2* unless it lies outside the implementation-defined range, in which case evaluation halts with a runtime error.

```
t_int
_div(t_int i1, t_int i2)
```

Returns the integer quotient *i1 / i2* (that is, the floor of the real quotient) unless it lies outside the implementation-defined range, in which case evaluation halts with a runtime error. This error is possible only if *i2* is zero or if *i2* is -1 and *i1* is the largest implementation-defined negative number.

```
t_int
_mod(t_int i1, t_int i2) =
  operator-(i1, operator*(_div(i1,i2), i2))
```

```
t_bool
operator<(t_int i1, t_int i2)
```

Returns *true* if and only if *i1* is less than *i2*.

```
t_bool
operator>(t_int i1, t_int i2) =
  operator<(i2, i1)
```

```
t_bool
operator<=(t_int i1, t_int i2)
```

Returns *true* if and only if *i1* is at most *i2*.

```
t_bool
operator>=(t_int i1, t_int i2) =
  operator<=(i2, i1)
```

```
t_int
_min(t_int i1, t_int i2) =
{ if (operator<(i1, i2)) return i1; else return i2; }
```

```
t_int
_max(t_int i1, t_int i2) =
{ if (operator>(i1, i2)) return i1; else return i2; }
```

### A.3.4.3 Functions on Type t_text

The first byte of a t_text value has index 0.

```
t_bool
operator==(t_text t1, t_text t2)
```

Returns *true* if *t1* and *t2* are identical byte sequences, and *false* otherwise.

```
t_bool
operator!=(t_text t1, t_text t2) =
  operator!(operator==(t1, t2))
```

```
t_text
operator+(t_text t1, t_text t2)
```

Returns the byte sequence formed by appending the byte sequence *t2* to the byte sequence *t1* (concatenation).

```
t_int
_length(t_text t)
```

Returns the number of bytes in the byte sequence *t*.

```
t_text
_elem(t_text t, t_int i)
```

If $0 \leq i <$ `_length(t)`, returns a byte sequence of length 1 consisting of byte *i* of the byte sequence *t*. Otherwise, returns the empty byte sequence.

```
t_text
_sub(t_text t, t_int start = 0, t_int len = _length(t)) =
{
  int w = _length(t);
  int i = _min(_max(start, 0)), w);
  int j = _min(i + _max(len, 0), w);
  // 0 <= i <= j <= _length(t); extract [i..j)
  t_text r = "";
  for (; i < j; i++) r = operator+(r, _elem(t, i));
  return r;
}
```

Extracts from *t* and returns a byte sequence of length *len* beginning at byte *start*. Note the boundary cases defined by the pseudo-code; `_sub` produces a runtime error only if it is passed arguments of the wrong type.

```
t_int
_find(t_text t, t_text p, t_int start = 0) =
{
  int j = _length(t) - _length(p);
  if (j < 0) return -1;
  int i = _max(start, 0);
  if (i > j) return -1;
  for (; i <= j; i++) {
    int k = 0;
    while (k < _length(p) &&
           _elem(t, i+k) == _elem(p, k)) k++;
    if (k == _length(p)) return i;
  }
  return -1;
}
```

Finds the leftmost occurrence of *p* in *t* that begins at or after position *start*. Returns the index of the first byte of the occurrence, or -1 if none exists.

```
t_int
_findr(t_text t, t_text p, t_int start = 0) =
{
  int j = _length(t) - _length(p);
  if (j < 0) return -1;
  int i = _max(start, 0);
  if (i > j) return -1;
  for (; i <= j; j--) {
    int k = 0;
    while (k < _length(p) &&
           _elem(t, j+k) == _elem(p, k)) k++;
    if (k == _length(p)) return j;
  }
  return -1;
}
```

Finds the rightmost occurrence of *p* in *t* that begins at or after position *start*. Returns the index of the first byte of the occurrence, or -1 if none exists.

### A.3.4.4 Functions on Type t_list

```
t_bool
operator==(t_list l1, t_list l2)
```

Returns *true* if *l1* and *l2* are lists of the same length containing (recursively) equal values, and *false* otherwise.

```
t_bool
operator!=(t_list l1, t_list l2) =
  operator!(operator==(l1, l2))
```

```
t_list
_list1(t_value v)
```

Returns a list containing a single element whose value is *v*.

```
t_value
_head(t_list l)
```

Returns the first element of *l*. If *l* is empty, evaluation halts with a runtime error.

```
t_list
_tail(t_list l)
```

Returns the list consisting of all elements of *l*, in order, except the first. If *l* is empty, evaluation halts with a runtime error.

```
t_int
_length(t_list l)
```

Returns the number of (top-level) values in the list *l*.

```
t_value
_elem(t_list l, t_int i)
```

Returns the *i*-th value in the list *l*. If no such value exists, evaluation halts with a runtime error. The first value of a list has index 0.

```
t_list
_append(t_list l1, t_list l2)
```

Returns the list formed by appending *l2* to *l1*.

```
t_list
operator+(t_list l1, t_list l2)
```

Equivalent to `_append(l1, l2)`.

```
t_list
_sub(t_list l, t_int start = 0, t_int len = _length(l))
{
  int w = _length(l);
  int i = _min(_max(start, 0)), w);
  int j = _min(i + _max(len, 0), w);
  // 0 <= i <= j <= _length(l); extract [i..j)
  t_list r = emptylist;
  for (; i < j; i++) r = operator+(r, _elem(l, i));
  return r;
}
```

Returns the sub-list of *l* of length *len* starting at element *start*. Note the boundary cases defined by the pseudo-code; `_sub` produces a runtime error only if it is passed arguments of the wrong type.

```
t_list
_map(t_closure f, t_list l) =
{
  t_list res = emptylist;
  for (; !(l == emptylist); l = _tail(l)) {
    t_value v = f(_head(l)); // apply the closure "f"
    res = operator+(res, v);
  }
  return res;
}
```

Returns the list that results from applying the closure *f* to each element of the list *l*, and concatenating the results in order. The closure *f* should take one value (of type t_value) as argument and return a value of any type. If *f* has the wrong signature, the evaluation halts with a runtime error.

```
t_list
_par_map(t_closure f, t_list l)
```

Formally equivalent to `_map`, but the implementation may perform each application of *f* in a separate parallel thread. External tools invoked by `_run_tool` in different threads may be run simultaneously on different machines. If a runtime error occurs in one thread, the other threads may still run to completion before the evaluation terminates.

### A.3.4.5 Functions on Type t_binding

```
t_bool
operator==(t_binding b1, t_binding b2)
```

Returns *true* if *b1* and *b2* are bindings of the same length containing the same names (in order) bound to (recursively) equal values, and *false* otherwise.

```
t_bool
operator!=(t_binding b1, t_binding b2) =
  operator!(operator==(b1, b2))
```

```
t_binding
_bind1(t_text n, t_value v)
```

If *n* is not empty, returns a binding with the single (name, value) pair (*n*, *v*). If *n* is empty, the evaluation halts with a runtime error.

```
t_binding
_head(t_binding b)
```

Returns a binding with one (name, value) pair equal to the first element of *b*. If *b* is empty, the evaluation halts with a runtime error.

```
t_binding
_tail(t_binding b)
```

Returns the binding consisting of all elements of *b*, in order, except the first. If *b* is empty, the evaluation halts with a runtime error.

```
t_int
_length(t_binding b)
```

Returns the number of (name, value) pairs in *b*.

```
t_binding
_elem(t_binding b, t_int i)
```

Returns a binding consisting solely of the *i*-th (name, value) pair in the binding *b*. If no such pair exists, the evaluation halts with a runtime error. The first pair of a binding has index 0.

```
t_text
_n(t_binding b)
```

If `_length(b) = 1`, returns the name part of the (name, value) pair that constitutes *b*. Otherwise, the evaluation halts with a runtime error.

```
t_value
_v(t_binding b)
```

If `_length(b) = 1`, returns the value part of the (name, value) pair that constitutes *b*. Otherwise, the evaluation halts with a runtime error.

```
t_bool
_defined(t_binding b, t_text name)
```

If *name* is empty, the evaluation halts with a runtime error. Otherwise, the function returns *true* if the binding *b* contains a pair (*n*, *v*) with *n* identical to *name*, and *false* otherwise.

```
t_value
_lookup(t_binding b, t_text name)
```

If *name* is nonempty and is defined in *b*, returns the value associated with it; otherwise, the evaluation halts with a runtime error.

```
t_binding
_append(t_binding b1, t_binding b2)
```

Returns a binding formed by appending *b2* to *b1*, but only if all the names in *b1* and *b2* are distinct. Otherwise, the evaluation halts with a runtime error.

```
t_binding
operator+(t_binding b1, t_binding b2) =
{
  val r = emptybinding;
  for (; !(b1 == emptybinding); b1 = _tail(b1)) {
    val n = _n(_head(b1));
    val v;
    if (_defined(b2, n) == true)
      v = _lookup(b2, n);
    else v = _v(_head(b1));
    r = _append(r, _bind1(n, v));
  }
  for (; !(b2 == emptybinding); b2 = _tail(b2)) {
    if (_defined(b1, _n(_head(b2)) == false)
      r = _append(r, _head(b2));
  }
  return r;
}
```

Returns a binding formed by appending *b2* to *b1*, giving precedence to *b2* when both *b1* and *b2* contain (name, value) pairs with the same *name*.

```
t_binding
operator++(t_binding b1, t_binding b2) =
{
  val r = emptybinding;
  for (; !(b1 == emptybinding); b1 = _tail(b1)) {
    val n = _n(_head(b1));
    val v;
    if (_defined(b2, n) == true) {
      val v2 = _lookup(b2, n);
      if (_is_binding(v2) == true) {
        v = _v(_head(b1);
        if (_is_binding(v) == true)
```

```
          v = operator++(v, v2);
        else v = v2;
      }
      else v = v2;
    }
    else v = _v(_head(b1));
    r = _append(r, _bind1(n, v));
  }
  for (; !(b2 == emptybinding); b2 = _tail(b2)) {
    if (_defined(r, _n(_head(b2)) == false)
      r = _append(r, _head(b2));
  }
  return r;
}
```

Similar to operator+, but performs the operation recursively for each name *n* that is associated with a binding value in both *b1* and *b2*.

```
t_binding
operator-(t_binding b1, t_binding b2) =
{
  val r = emptybinding;
  for (; !(b1 = emptybinding); b1 = _tail(b1)) {
    val n = _n(_head(b1));
    if (_defined(b2, n) == false)
      r = _append(r, _head(b1));
  }
  return r;
}
```

Returns a binding formed by removing from *b1* any pair (*n*, *v*) such that the name *n* is defined in *b2*. The value *v* associated with *n* in *b2* is irrelevant.

```
t_binding
_sub(t_binding b, t_int start = 0, t_int len = _length(b))
{
  int w = _length(b);
  int i = _min(_max(start, 0)), w);
  int j = _min(i + _max(len, 0), w);
  // 0 <= i <= j <= _length(b); extract [i..j)
  t_binding r = emptybinding;
  for (; i < j; i++) r = _append(r, _elem(b, i));
  return r;
}
```

Returns the sub-binding of *b* of length *len* starting at element *start*. Note the boundary cases defined by the pseudo-code; `_sub` produces a runtime error only if it is passed arguments of the wrong type.

```
t_binding
_map(t_closure f, t_binding b) =
{
  t_binding res = emptybinding;
  for (; !(b == emptybinding); b = _tail(l)) {
    // apply the closure "f"
    t_binding b1 = f(_n(_head(b)), _v(_head(b)));
    res = _append(res, b1);
  }
  return res;
}
```

Returns the binding that results from applying the closure *f* to each (*name*, *value*) pair of the binding *b*, and appending the resulting bindings together. The closure *f* should take the *name* (of type t_text) and *value* (of type t_value) as arguments, and return a value of type t_binding. If *f* has the wrong signature, the evaluation halts with a runtime error.

```
t_binding
_par_map(t_closure f, t_binding b)
```

Formally equivalent to `_map`, but the implementation may perform each application of *f* in a separate parallel thread. External tools invoked by `_run_tool` in different threads may be run simultaneously on different machines. If a runtime error occurs in one thread, the other threads may still run to completion before the evaluation terminates.

#### A.3.4.6 Special Purpose Functions

```
t_closure _self
```

Unless redefined, the name `_self` always refers to the model in which it textually occurs. In effect, every model imports itself under this name, prior to the first `import` clause that appears explicitly in the SDL program text.

```
t_text
_model_name(t_closure m)
```

The value *m* must be a model; that is, a closure defined by importing an immutable file from the Vesta repository. `_model_name` returns a text value that gives one name for *m* within the repository. If a model with identical contents in an identical directory has multiple pathnames in the repository, the name returned by this primitive may be any of these pathnames, not necessarily the one that was actually imported in the current evaluation.

```
t_text
_fingerprint(t_value v)
```

The `_fingerprint` primitive returns a text representation of the given value's *fingerprint*, a 128-bit internal identifier for the value. Fingerprints are chosen so that with very high probability, two different values will always have different fingerprints. A given value may have different fingerprints in different evaluations or when computed at different points in the same evaluation, but the implementation tries to avoid this when practical.

Specifically, a source with a particular absolute name in the Vesta repository always has the same fingerprint, while two sources with different names but with the same value will have the same fingerprint if they were fingerprinted *by content* when inserted into the repository. See the documentation of the **vadvance** program for details on when sources are fingerprinted by name and when by content. A derived value returned by any Vesta primitive other than `_run_tool` has a fingerprint that depends deterministically on the fingerprints of its arguments. Derived values returned by `_run_tool` have either arbitrary unique fingerprints or deterministic content-based fingerprints; see Section A.3.4.8 for details.

These properties make fingerprints useful as version stamps for Vesta evaluations, sometimes more useful than `_model_name`. If *m1*, *m2* are models with identical contents that reside in identical directories, then `_fingerprint(m1) = _fingerprint(m2)` will often be true even when `_model_name(m1) != _model_name(m2)`.

### A.3.4.7 Type Manipulation Functions

```
t_text
_type_of(t_value v)
```

Returns a text value corresponding to the type of the value *v* as shown in Table A.9.

```
t_bool
_same_type(t_value v1, t_value v2) =
   operator==(_type_of(v1), _type_of(v2))
```

```
t_bool
_is_bool(t_value v)
```

Returns *true* if *v* is of type t_bool; returns *false* otherwise.

```
t_bool
_is_int(t_value v)
```

Returns *true* if *v* is of type t_int; returns *false* otherwise.

| Value | Text returned by `_type_of` |
|---|---|
| true, false | "t_bool" |
| integer | "t_int" |
| byte sequence | "t_text" |
| err | "t_err" |
| list | "t_list" |
| binding | "t_binding" |
| closures | "t_closure" |

**Table A.9.** Text values returned by the `_type_of` primitive for each possible input value.

```
t_bool
_is_text(t_value v)
```

Returns *true* if *v* is of type t_text; returns *false* otherwise.

```
t_bool
_is_err(t_value v)
```

Returns *true* if *v* is of type t_err; returns *false* otherwise.

```
t_bool
_is_list(t_value v)
```

Returns *true* if *v* is of type t_list; returns *false* otherwise.

```
t_bool
_is_binding(t_value v)
```

Returns *true* if *v* is of type t_binding; returns *false* otherwise.

```
t_bool
_is_closure(t_value v)
```

Returns *true* if *v* is of type t_closure; returns *false* otherwise.

#### A.3.4.8 Tool Invocation Function

```
t_binding
_run_tool(
  t_text platform,
  t_list command,
  t_text stdin = "",
  t_text stdout_treatment = "report",
  t_text stderr_treatment = "report",
  t_text status_treatment = "report_nocache",
  t_text signal_treatment = "report_nocache",
  t_int  fp_content = -2,
  t_text wd = ".WD",
  t_bool existing_writable = FALSE)
```

The `_run_tool` primitive is the mechanism by which external programs like compilers and linkers are executed from an SDL program. It provides functionality that is fairly platform-independent. The following description, however, is somewhat Unix-specific (for example, in its description of exit codes and signals).

The *platform* argument specifies the platform on which the tool is to be executed. `_run_tool` selects a specific machine for the given platform. The legal values for *platform* and the mechanism by which a machine of the appropriate platform is chosen are implementation dependent.

The tool to be executed is specified by the *command* argument. This argument is a t_list of t_text values. The first member of the list is the name of the tool (interpretation of the name is discussed below); the remaining members of the list are the arguments passed to the tool as its command line. The tool is executed on the specified *platform* in an environment with the following characteristics:

- The file system is encapsulated so that absolute paths (i.e., those beginning with a Delim) are interpreted relative to `./root`, where '.' is the implicit final parameter to `_run_tool`. Non-absolute paths are interpreted relative to `./root/$`*wd*, where *wd* is a parameter to `_run_tool`. The interpretation of file names is discussed in more detail below.
- The environment variables are taken from `./envVars`, where '.' is the implicit final parameter to `_run_tool`.
- The content of standard input is the value of the *stdin* `_run_tool` parameter.
- Treatment of standard output and standard error is specified by the *stdout_treatment* and *stderr_treatment* parameters. These parameters may be one of the t_text values `"ignore"`, `"report"`, `"report_nocache"`, `"value"`, or `"report_value"`. If the treatment is `"ignore"`, any bytes written to the corresponding output stream (stdout or stderr) are discarded. If the treatment is `"report"`, the corresponding output is made visible to the user. If the treatment is `"report_nocache"`, the corresponding output is made visible to the user and, if it is not empty, the evaluator does not cache the result of the `_run_tool` call. If the treatment is `"value"`, the output stream is converted to a Vesta value of type t_text and returned as part of the `_run_tool` result, as described below. If the treatment is `"report_value"`, the output stream is both made visible to the user and returned as part of the result.
- The *status_treatment* and *signal_treatment* arguments may take on the t_text value `"report"` or `"report_nocache"`. Regardless of their values, the `code` and `signal` fields of the result value will be set as described below. If the value of *status_treatment* is `"report_nocache"`, this `_run_tool` call will not be cached if the result `code` is nonzero; similarly, if *signal_treatment* is `"report_nocache"`, the `_run_tool` call will not be cached if the result `signal` is nonzero. Additionally, in the present implementation, a runtool call that is not cached because of its return code or signal is considered a runtime error and halts the evaluation with an error message, unless the -k ("keep going") flag is given on the evaluator command line.
- The *fp_content* argument controls how fingerprints are assigned to any derived files created by the tool execution, including derived files created for stdout or stderr when the value of the *stdout_treatment* or *stderr_treatment* parameter is "value". A value of -1 causes the fingerprints of all such derived files to be computed deterministically from their contents. A non-negative *fp_content* value of *x* causes only those files less than *x* bytes in length to have their fingerprints computed from the file contents; an arbitrary unique fingerprint is chosen for files at least *x* bytes in length. Hence, a value of 0 causes all derived files to be assigned arbitrary fingerprints. Setting *fp_content* to -2 selects a site-dependent default value (set by the [Evaluator]/FpContent configuration variable, in our implementation). The SDL values *true* and *false* are accepted as synonyms for -1 and 0, respectively.

  The cost of fingerprinting a file's contents is non-trivial (approximately 1 second per megabyte on the prototype implementation), but doing so allows for cache hits in cases where two evaluations depend on a value that is identical, but was computed in two different ways.

- The *existing_writable* argument controls whether the tool is permitted to write to files that already exist in its encapsulated file system when it is started. If the argument is *true*, such files may be opened for writing and written to; if it is *false*, they may not. The value *false* gives better file system performance on some implementations and should be used unless the tool being invoked requires the ability to write files named in the encapsulated file system.

The `_run_tool` primitive returns a binding that contains the results of the command execution. This binding has type:

```
type run_tool_result = binding [
  code   : int,
  signal : int,
  stdout_written : bool,
  stderr_written : bool,
  stdout : text,
  stderr : text,
  root   : binding
]
```

If *r* is of type `run_tool_result`, then:

- `r/code` is an integer value that characterizes how the command terminated (i.e., the exit status of the Unix process).
- `r/signal` is an integer value identifying the Unix signal that terminated the process, or 0 if the process exited voluntarily.
- `r/stdout_written` and `r/stderr_written` indicate whether data was written to the stdout and stderr streams, respectively.
- `r/stdout` is defined if and only if the *stdout_treatment* `_run_tool` parameter is `"value"` or `"report_value"`, in which case it contains the bytes written to stdout.
- `r/stderr` is defined if and only if the *stderr_treatment* `_run_tool` parameter is `"value"` or `"report_value"`, in which case it contains the bytes written to stderr.
- `r/root` is a binding containing all files created by the command that are extant upon exit. See the description under "File System Encapsulation" below for details.

Fine points relating to the results of `_run_tool`:

- If the tool cannot be invoked — for example, because of errors in the parameters to `_run_tool` — the evaluator always prints a diagnostic and halts with a runtime error. However, errors that occur during the execution of the tool are reported in a tool-specific fashion, as discussed under *status_treatment* and *signal_treatment* above.

- If `report_nocache` is specified as the treatment for an output stream (stdout or stderr) or the exit or signal status, the evaluator will not make a cache entry for the `_run_tool` call if any output is produced on the corresponding output stream or if the exit or signal status is nonzero, respectively. In addition, none of the ancestor functions of the failing `_run_tool` call in the call graph are cached. Since no cache entries are made, a subsequent re-evaluation of the model will produce the same output (on stdout or stderr). This can be useful for reproducing error messages from a compiler or other external tool that are displayed through the Vesta user interface.

**File System Encapsulation:**

- When the command process (or any subprocess it creates) executes a Unix system call that includes a file path as a parameter, the file path is translated into a reference into the '.' binding that is the last parameter to `_run_tool`.
- The path is interpreted relative to `./root` if it is absolute (i.e., if it begins with "`/`"), and relative to `./root/$wd` otherwise, where `$wd` is the value of the *wd* parameter to `_run_tool`. Each component of the path — except possibly the final one — must name a Vesta binding. The interpretation of the final component of the path depends on the semantics of the system call. If the system call expects an extant file, the final component must name a Vesta value of type t_text. If the system call expects an extant directory, the Vesta value must be of type t_binding. If the system call expects an unbound name, the name must not be bound by the binding corresponding to the penultimate path component.
- The command name itself is first looked up according to the rule just given — that is, relative to `./root` if it begins with "`/`" or relative to `./root/$wd` otherwise. If this lookup fails, a `PATH` environment variable exists in `./envVars`, and the command name does not contain a "`/`", then the value of `PATH` is interpreted as a colon-separated list of directory names and the command name is looked for in each of them until it is found or the list is exhausted.
- A file created or modified by the command process (or a subprocess) remains visible in the name space throughout the remainder of the process's execution (or until deleted), just as in a regular file system. This is achieved by modeling file creation, modification, and deletion as a suitable overlaying of `./root`. For example, if the process creates "foo.o" in its working directory, this has the effect of:

```
./root/$wd += [ foo.o = <bytes of file> ];
<subsequent execution of the command process>
```

- File modification is handled in exactly the same way. For example, if the process opens the existing file "foo.db" in its working directory and writes to it, this has the effect of:

```
./root/$wd += [ foo.db = <new contents of file> ];
<subsequent execution of the command process>
```

  Note that modification of preexisting files is forbidden if the *existing_writable* argument to `_run_tool` is set to *false* (the default).

- File deletions are modeled similarly, but the files are removed from the context using the binding difference (-) operator, instead of added using the binding overlay (+) operator.
- When the command process exits, the accumulated effects of the file creations and deletions it has performed are returned as part of the `_run_tool` result (in `r/root`). In this binding, the names of files that existed in `./root` before the tool was invoked but were deleted by the tool are bound to *false*.

  Thus, if `./root` represents the state of the file system visible to the command process at the time it is launched, then the state of the file system when it exits can be described as:

```
./root ++ r/root
```

  So, if the invoker of `_run_tool` wanted to update `./root` to reflect the changes made by calling `_run_tool`, the code might look like this:

```
r = _run_tool( <suitable parameters> );
new_fs = ./root ++ r/root;
. += [ root = new_fs ];
```

  After the last assignment, names in `./root` bound to *false* are files that were deleted by the tool. Here is a recursive function for removing such files:

```
/**nocache**/
remove_deleted(b: binding): binding
{
  res: binding = [];
  foreach [ n = v ] in b do
    res += if v = false then [] else
      if _is_binding(v)
        then [ $n = remove_deleted(v) ]
        else [ $n = v ];
  return res;
};
```

#### A.3.4.9 Diagnostic Functions

```
t_value
_print(t_value v, t_int deps = 0, t_bool verbose = FALSE)
```

Print the value $v$ to standard output followed by a newline, and return $v$. What gets printed depends on $v$'s type. If $v$ is of type t_err, `ERR` is printed. If $v$ is of type t_bool, `TRUE` or `FALSE` is printed. If $v$ is of type t_int, its decimal value is printed.

The printed representation of a t_text value is `<file 0x`*XXXXXXXX*`>` if *verbose* is false and the text is represented by a backing file, in which case *XXXXXXXX* is the file's hexadecimal identifier. Otherwise, it is the text value's contents enclosed in double quotes.

The printed representation of a t_list value containing the values $v_1, v_2, \ldots, v_k$ is $< p_1, p_2, \ldots, p_k >$, where $p_i$ denotes the printed representation of the value $v_i$.

The printed representation of a t_binding value containing the (name, value) pairs $(n_1, v_1), (n_2, v_2), \ldots, (n_k, v_k)$ is `[` $n_1 = p_1, \ldots, n_k = p_k$ `]`, where again $p_i$ denotes the printed representation of the value $v_i$.

The printed representation of a t_closure value is `<Model` *name*`>` if the closure is represented by a model, in which case *name* is a name for the model file in the repository. Otherwise, if *verbose* is true, it is the complete list of formals, body, and context; if not it is simply `<Closure>`.

If *deps* is greater than zero, the value's dependencies are also printed. In the current implementation, values of 1 and 2 provide different levels of detail. This feature is meant for debugging the evaluator itself.

Typically, `_print` is used for debugging purposes, and its result is ignored. A call of the `_print` function is never cached, but it does not prevent caching of a call to the function that calls it.

```
t_bool
_assert(t_bool cond, t_value msg)
```

If the value *cond* is *true*, return *true*. Otherwise, print the value *msg* as with the `_print` primitive, then terminate the evaluation with a runtime error. Command-line options to the evaluator permit the context of a false assertion and/or a stack trace to be printed as well.

## A.4 Concrete Syntax

### A.4.1 Grammar

**Models:**

```
Model       ::= Files Imports Block
```

**Files Clauses:**

```
Files       ::= FileClause*
FileClause  ::= files FileItem*;
FileItem    ::= FileSpec | FileBinding
FileSpec    ::= [ Arc = ] DelimPath
FileBinding ::= Arc = '[' FileSpec*, ']'
```

**Import Clauses:**

```
Imports     ::= ImpClause*
ImpClause   ::= ImpIdReq | ImpIdOpt
ImpIdReq    ::= import ImpItemR*;
ImpItemR    ::= ImpSpecR | ImpListR
ImpSpecR    ::= Arc = DelimPath
ImpListR    ::= Arc = '[' ImpSpecR*, ']'
```

```
ImpIdOpt     ::= from DelimPath import ImpItemO*;
ImpItemO     ::= ImpSpecO | ImpListO
ImpSpecO     ::= [ Arc = ] Path [ Delim ]
ImpListO     ::= Arc = '[' ImpSpecO*, ']'
```

**Paths and Arcs:**

```
DelimPath    ::= [ Delim ] Path [ Delim ]
Path         ::= Arc { Delim Arc }*
Arc          ::= Id | Integer | Text
```

**Blocks and Statements:**

```
Block        ::= '{' { Stmt ; }* Result ; '}'
Stmt         ::= Assign | Iterate | FuncDef | TypeDef
Result       ::= { value | return } Expr
```

**Assignment Statements:**

```
Assign       ::= TypedId [ Op ] = Expr
Op           ::= AddOp | MulOp
AddOp        ::= +  |  ++  |  -
MulOp        ::= *
```

**Iteration Statements:**

```
Iterate      ::= foreach Control in Expr do IterBody
Control      ::= TypedId | '[' TypedId = TypedId ']'
IterBody     ::= Stmt | '{' Stmt+; '}'
```

**Function Definitions:**

```
FuncDef      ::= Id Formals+ [ TypeQual ] Block
Formals      ::= ( FormalArgs )
FormalArgs   ::= TypedId*,
               | { TypedId = Expr }*,
               | TypedId { , TypedId }* { , TypedId = Expr }+
```

**Expressions:**

```
Expr         ::= if Expr then Expr else Expr | Expr1
Expr1        ::= Expr2 {  =>  Expr2 }*
Expr2        ::= Expr3 {  ||  Expr3 }*
Expr3        ::= Expr4 {  &&  Expr4 }*
Expr4        ::= Expr5 [ CompareOp Expr5 ]
CompareOp    ::= == | != | < | > | <= | >=
```

```
Expr5        ::= Expr6 { AddOp Expr6 }*
Expr6        ::= Expr7 { MulOp Expr7 }*
Expr7        ::= [ UnaryOp ] Expr8
UnaryOp      ::= -  |  !
Expr8        ::= Primary [ TypeQual ]
Primary      ::= ( Expr ) | Literal | Id | List
               | Binding | Select | Block | FuncCall
```

Binary operators with equal precedence are left-associative.

**Literals:**

```
Literal      ::= ERR | TRUE | FALSE | Text | Integer
```

**Lists:**

```
List         ::= < Expr*, >
```

**Bindings:**

```
Binding      ::= '[' BindElem*, ']'
BindElem     ::= SelfNameB | NameBind
SelfNameB    ::= Id
NameBind     ::= GenPath = Expr
GenPath      ::= GenArc { Delim GenArc }* [ Delim ]
GenArc       ::= Arc | $ Id | $ ( Expr ) | % Expr %
```

**Binding Selections:**

```
Select       ::= Primary Selector GenArc
Selector     ::= Delim | !
```

**Function Calls:**

```
FuncCall     ::= Primary Actuals
Actuals      ::= ( Expr*, )
```

**Type Definitions:**

```
TypeDef      ::= type Id = Type
TypedId      ::= Id [ TypeQual ]
TypeQual     ::= : Type
Type         ::= any | bool | int | text
               | list [ ( Type ) ]
               | binding ( TypeQual )
               | binding [ ( TypedId*, ) ]
               | function { ( TypedForm*, ) }* [ TypeQual ]
               | Id
TypedForm    ::= [ Id : ] Type
```

### A.4.2 Ambiguity Resolution

The grammar as given above is ambiguous. The ambiguity is resolved as follows.

The Vesta parser accepts a modified grammar in which the > token is replaced by two distinct tokens: GREATER in the production for Expr4 and RANGLE in the production for List. The modified grammar is unambiguous and can easily be parsed by an LL(1) or LALR(1) automaton.

The Vesta tokenizer is responsible for disambiguating between GREATER and RANGLE wherever > appears in the input. It does so by looking ahead to the next token after the >. If the next token is one of

```
- ! ( ERR TRUE FALSE Text Integer Id < [ {
```

then the > is taken as GREATER; otherwise, it is taken as RANGLE.

Why is this solution reasonable? Inspection of the grammar shows that in a syntactically valid program, the next token after GREATER must be one of those in the list above. The next token after RANGLE must be one of the following:

```
: * + ++ - == != < GREATER <= >= && || =>
; do , ) then else RANGLE ] % / \ ! (
```

These sets overlap in the tokens `-`, `!`, `(`, and `<`. Given the choice to resolve these cases as GREATER, it is impossible to write certain syntactically valid programs containing RANGLE. However, any such program can be rewritten by replacing every List nonterminal by `(` List `)`, yielding a semantically equivalent program in which the closing > of the List is correctly resolved as RANGLE. Moreover, any program in which RANGLE is followed by `-`, `!`, `(`, or < must have a runtime type error, due to the paucity of operators defined on the list type, so in practice such programs are never written.

### A.4.3 Tokens

Table A.10 gives a BNF description of the tokens of the language. The token classes Delim, Integer, Id, and Text, and the individual tokens in the classes Punc, TwoPunc, and Keyword, serve as terminals in the BNF of earlier sections.

Newline is defined as an ASCII new line sequence, either CR, LF, or CRLF. NonNewlineChar is any ASCII character other than CR and LF. CommentBody is any sequence of ASCII characters that does not contain '*/'. Tab is the ASCII TAB character.

The ambiguities in the token grammar are resolved as follows. The tokenizer interprets the program as a TokenSeq. It scans from left to right, repeatedly matching the longest possible Token beginning with the next unmatched character. The tokens Whitespace and Comment are discarded after matching; other tokens are passed on for parsing by the main grammar. When a string of characters matches both Integer and Id, it is tokenized as Integer. When a string matches both Keyword and Id, it is tokenized as Keyword.

```
TokenSeq    ::= Token*
Token       ::= Integer | Id | Text | Punc | TwoPunc
              | Keyword | Whitespace | Comment

Delim       ::= /  |  \

Integer     ::= DecimalNZ Decimal*
              | 0 Octal* | 0 { x | X } Hex+
Decimal     ::= 0 | 1 | 2 | 3 | 4 | 5 | 6 | 7 | 8 | 9
DecimalNZ   ::= 1 | 2 | 3 | 4 | 5 | 6 | 7 | 8 | 9
Octal       ::= 0 | 1 | 2 | 3 | 4 | 5 | 6 | 7
Hex         ::= Decimal
              | A | B | C | D | E | F
              | a | b | c | d | e | f

Id          ::= { Letter | Decimal | IdPunc }+
Letter      ::= A | B | C | D | E | F | G | H | I | J | K
              | L | M | N | O | P | Q | R | S | T | U | V
              | W | X | Y | Z
              | a | b | c | d | e | f | g | h | i | j | k
              | l | m | n | o | p | q | r | s | t | u | v
              | w | x | y | z
IdPunc      ::= .  |  _

Text        ::= " TextChar* "
TextChar    ::= Decimal | Letter | Punc | Escape
Punc        ::= ~ | ‘ | ! | @ | # | $ | % | ^ | & | *
              | ( | ) | _ | - | + | = | ‘{’ | ‘[’ | ‘}’
              | ‘]’ | : | ; | ‘|’ | ’ | , | < | . | >
              | ? | / | Space
Escape      ::= \ EscapeChar
EscapeChar  ::= n | t | v | b | r | f | a | \  | "
              | Octals |  Hexes
Octals      ::= Octal [ Octal [ Octal ] ]
Hexes       ::= { x | X } Hex [ Hex ]

TwoPunc     ::= ++ | == | != | <= | >= | => | || | &&

Keyword     ::= any | binding | bool | do | else | ERR
              | FALSE | files | foreach | from | function
              | if | import | in | int | list | return
              | text | then | TRUE | type | value

Whitespace ::= ‘ ’ | Tab | Newline

Comment     ::= // NonNewlineChar* Newline
              |  ‘/*’ CommentBody ‘*/’
```

**Table A.10.** BNF for the tokens of SDL.

### A.4.4 Reserved Identifiers

Here are SDL's reserved identifiers; they should not be redefined:

```
_append _assert _bind1 _defined _div _elem _find _findr
_fingerprint _head _is_binding _is_bool _is_closure
_is_err _is_int _is_list _is_text _length _list1 _lookup
_map _max _min _mod _model_name _n _par_map _print
_run_tool _same_type _self _sub _tail _type_of _v
```

# B

# The Vesta Web Site

The Vesta system has a website, `http://www.vestasys.org`, that contains a number of additional resources for readers who seek more information about Vesta. The home page has links to publications, reference documents, and user documentation (in Unix jargon, "man" pages).

The code of the Vesta system is licensed under the LPGL and is available via the download link on the home page. The committed reader who wants to install and run Vesta should first follow the link "Getting Started with Vesta" on the home page, as the installation is not automatic (as with any server-based system) and this link provides quite a bit of helpful documentation. But for the more casual reader who simply wants to browse the code, there is a link on the home page entitled "A web interface to the Vesta repository". This link provides easy access to the code of Vesta (in C/C++) and to the SDL code for Vesta's bridges and standard environment models. These latter packages are particularly recommended to those who want to understand the full power and flexibility afforded by SDL to designers of complex, large-scale development environments.

# References

1. Martín Abadi, Butler Lampson, and Jean-Jacques Lévy. Analysis and caching of dependencies. In *Proceedings of the 1996 ACM SIGPLAN International Conference on Functional Programming (ICFP '96)*, pages 83–91, May 1996.
2. AccuRev, Inc. Accurev. http://www.accurev.com/.
3. Larry Allen, Gary Fernandez, Kenneth Kane, David Leblang, Debra Minard, and John Posner. ClearCase MultiSite: Supporting geographically-distributed software development. In *Software Configuration Management: ICSE SCM-4 and SCM-5 Workshops Selected Papers*, pages 194–214, 1995. Available as volume 1005 in *Lecture Notes in Computer Science*, Springer-Verlag.
4. Atria Software, Inc., 24 Prime Park Way, Natick, MA 01760. *ClearCase Concepts Manual*, 1992.
5. Dave Belanger, David Korn, and Herman Rao. Infrastructure for wide-area software development. In *Proceedings of the 6th International Workshop on Software Configuration Management*, pages 154–165, 1996. Available as volume 1167 in *Lecture Notes in Computer Science*, Springer-Verlag.
6. A. D. Birrell, R. Levin, R. M. Needham, and M. D. Schroeder. Grapevine: An exercise in distributed computing. *Communications of the ACM*, 25(4):260–274, April 1982.
7. Andrew D. Birrell, Michael B. Jones, and Edward P. Wobber. A simple and efficient implementation for small databases. In *Proceedings of the 11th ACM Symposium on Operating Systems Principles*, pages 149–154. The Association for Computing Machinery, November 1987.
8. BitMover, Inc. Bitkeeper. http://www.bitkeeper.com/.
9. Robert S. Boyer and J Strother Moore. *A Computational Logic Handbook*. Academic Press, 1988.
10. Andrei Broder. Some applications of Rabin's fingerprinting method. In R. Capocelli, A. De Santis, and U. Vaccaro, editors, *Sequences II: Methods in Communications, Security, and Computer Science*, pages 143–152. Springer-Verlag, 1993.
11. Mark R. Brown and John R. Ellis. Bridges: Tools to extend the Vesta configuration management system. SRC Research Report 108, Digital Equipment Corporation, Systems Research Center, June 1993. http://www.hpl.hp.com/techreports/Compaq-DEC/SRC-RR-108.html.
12. B. Callaghan, B. Pawlowski, and P. Staubach. NFS version 3 protocol specification. Network Working Group Request for Comments 1813, Sun Microsystems, Inc., June 1995. http://www.ietf.org/rfc/rfc1813.html.

13. Sheng-Yang Chiu and Roy Levin. The Vesta repository: A file system extension for software development. SRC Research Report 106, Digital Equipment Corporation, Systems Research Center, June 1993. http://www.hpl.hp.com/techreports/Compaq-DEC/SRC-RR-106.html.
14. Computer Associates. AllFusion Harvest Change Manager (formerly CCC/Harvest). http://www.ca.com/.
15. Connectathon test suites. http://www.connectathon.org/nfstests.html.
16. M. E. Conway. How do committees invent? *Datamation*, 14(4):28–31, April 1968.
17. Jacky Estublier and Rubby Casallas. The Adele configuration manager. In Walter Tichy, editor, *Configuration Management*, volume 2 of *Trends in Software*, pages 99–134. John Wiley and Sons Ltd., 1994. Available from http://www-adele.imag.fr/.
18. S. I. Feldman. Make—A program for maintaining computer programs. *Software—Practice and Experience*, 9(4):255–265, April 1979.
19. Glenn Fowler. A case for Make. *Software—Practice and Experience*, 20(S1):S1/35–S1/46, June 1990.
20. Free Software Foundation. GNU Lesser General Public License. http://www.fsf.org/licenses/lgpl.html.
21. Cary G. Gray and David R. Cheriton. Leases: An efficient fault-tolerant mechanism for distributed file cache consistency. In *Proceedings of the 12th ACM Symposium on Operating Systems Principles*, pages 202–210. The Association for Computing Machinery, December 1989.
22. Jim Gray and Andreas Reuter. *Transaction Processing: Concepts and Techniques*. Morgan Kaufmann Publishers, San Mateo, CA, 1993.
23. Dick Grune, Brian Berliner, and Jeff Polk. *cvs(1) manual page*. Free Software Foundation.
24. Carl A. Gunter. Abstracting dependencies between software configuration items. *ACM Transactions on Software Engineering and Methodology*, 9(1):94–131, January 2000.
25. Christine B. Hanna and Roy Levin. The Vesta language for configuration management. SRC Research Report 107, Digital Equipment Corporation, Systems Research Center, June 1993. http://www.hpl.hp.com/techreports/Compaq-DEC/SRC-RR-107.html.
26. Allan Heydon, Roy Levin, Timothy Mann, and Yuan Yu. The Vesta approach to software configuration management. SRC Research Report 168, Compaq Computer Corporation, Systems Research Center, March 2001. http://www.hpl.hp.com/techreports/Compaq-DEC/SRC-RR-168.html.
27. Allan Heydon, Roy Levin, Timothy Mann, and Yuan Yu. The Vesta software configuration management system. SRC Research Report 177, Compaq Computer Corporation, Systems Research Center, January 2002. http://www.hpl.hp.com/techreports/Compaq-DEC/SRC-RR-177.html.
28. Allan Heydon, Roy Levin, and Yuan Yu. Caching function calls using precise dependencies. In *Proceedings of the ACM SIGPLAN 2000 Conference on Programming Language Design and Implementation*, pages 311–320, June 2000.
29. Allan Heydon and Greg Nelson. The Juno-2 constraint-based drawing editor. SRC Research Report 131a, Digital Equipment Corporation, Systems Research Center, December 1994. http://www.hpl.hp.com/techreports/Compaq-DEC/SRC-RR-131A.html.
30. John H. Howard, Michael L. Kazar, Sherri G. Menees, David A. Nichols, M. Satyanarayanan, Robert N. Sidebotham, and Michael J. West. Scale and performance in a distributed file system. *ACM Transactions on Computer Systems*, 6(1):51–81, February 1988.
31. *javac(1) manual page*. http://java.sun.com/j2se/1.4.2/docs/tooldocs/solaris/javac.html.
32. Juno-2 home page. http://www.research.compaq.com/SRC/juno-2/.

33. Brian Kernighan and Rob Pike. *The UNIX$^{TM}$ Programming Environment*. Prentice-Hall Software Series. Prentice-Hall, Englewood Cliffs, New Jersey, 1984.
34. Brian W. Kernighan and Dennis M. Ritchie. *The C Programming Language*. Prentice Hall, 1988.
35. Butler W. Lampson and Eric E. Schmidt. Organizing software in a distributed environment. In *Proceedings of the 1983 ACM SIGPLAN Symposium on Programming Language Issues in Software Systems*, June 1983.
36. Butler W. Lampson and Eric E. Schmidt. Practical use of a polymorphic applicative language. In *Proceedings of the Tenth Annual ACM Symposium on Principles of Programming Languages (POPL)*, pages 237–255, January 1983.
37. David B. Leblang and Robert P. Chase, Jr. Computer-aided software engineering in a distributed workstation environment. *SIGPLAN Notices*, 19(5):104–112, May 1984.
38. David B. Leblang, Robert P. Chase, Jr., and Gordon D. McLean, Jr. The DOMAIN software engineering environment for large-scale software development efforts. In *Proceedings of the 1st International Conference on Computer Workstations*, pages 266–280, San Jose, CA, November 1985. IEEE Computer Society, IEEE Computer Society Press.
39. Roy Levin. A technology transfer retrospective. In Andrew Herbert and Karen Spärck-Jones, editors, *Computer Systems: Theory, Technology, and Applications*, Monographs in Computer Science, pages 185–194. Springer, New York, 2004.
40. Roy Levin and Paul R. McJones. The Vesta approach to precise configuration of large software systems. SRC Research Report 105, Digital Equipment Corporation, Systems Research Center, June 1993. http://www.hpl.hp.com/techreports/Compaq-DEC/SRC-RR-105.html.
41. J. MacDonald, P. N. Hilfinger, and L. Semenzato. PRCS: The project revision control system. In *Proceedings of the 8th International Workshop on System Configuration Management*, pages 33–45, 1998. Available as volume 1439 in *Lecture Notes in Computer Science*, Springer-Verlag.
42. Boris Magnusson and Ulf Asklund. Fine grained version control of configurations in COOP/orm. In *Proceedings of the 6th International Workshop on System Configuration Management*, pages 31–48, 1996.
43. Timothy Mann. Partial replication in the Vesta software repository. SRC Research Report 172, Compaq Computer Corporation, Systems Research Center, August 2001. http://www.hpl.hp.com/techreports/Compaq-DEC/SRC-RR-172.html.
44. Timothy Mann, Andrew Birrell, Andy Hisgen, Charles Jerian, and Garret Swart. A coherent distributed file cache with directory write-behind. *ACM Transactions on Computer Systems*, 12(2):123–164, May 1994.
45. McCabe & Associates. TRUEchange (formerly known as Aide-De-Camp or ADC). http://www.mccabe.com/.
46. Peter Miller. Aegis. http://aegis.sourceforge.net/.
47. Modula-3 resource page. http://www.m3.org/.
48. Greg Nelson, editor. *Systems Programming with Modula-3*. Series in Innovative Technology. Prentice Hall, Englewood Cliffs, New Jersey, 1991.
49. Bill Nowicki. NFS: Network file system protocol specification. Network Working Group Request for Comments 1094, Sun Microsystems, Inc., March 1989. http://www.ietf.org/rfc/rfc1094.html.
50. John Ousterhout. Why aren't operating systems getting faster as fast as hardware? In *Proceedings of the Summer USENIX Conference*, pages 247–256, Anaheim, CA, Summer 1990.
51. Perforce Software. Perforce. http://www.perforce.com/.

52. M. O. Rabin. Fingerprinting by random polynomials. Report TR–15–81, Department of Computer Science, Harvard University, 1981.
53. Marc J. Rochkind. The Source Code Control System. *IEEE Transactions on Software Engineering*, SE–1(4):364–370, December 1975.
54. Russel Sandberg, David Goldberg, Steve Kleiman, Dan Walsh, and Bob Lyon. Design and implemention of the Sun network filesystem. In *Proceedings of the Summer USENIX Conference*, pages 119–130, June 1985.
55. Kenneth C. Schalk. Vesta SDL programmer's reference. http://www.vestasys.org/doc/sdl-ref/.
56. R. Srinivasan. Remote procedure call protocol specification version 2. Network Working Group Request for Comments 1831, Sun Microsystems, Inc., August 1995. http://www.ietf.org/rfc/rfc1831.html.
57. R. Srinivasan. XDR: External data representation standard. Network Working Group Request for Comments 1832, Sun Microsystems, Inc., August 1995. http://www.ietf.org/rfc/rfc1832.html.
58. Telelogic AB. Telelogic SYNERGY/CM (formerly Continuus/CM). http://www.telelogic.com/products/synergy/.
59. W. Tichy. Design, implementation, and evaluation of a revision control system. In *Proceedings of the 6th International Conference on Software Engineering*, pages 58–67. IEEE Computer Society Press, 1982.
60. W. Tichy. RCS—A system for version control. *Software—Practice and Experience*, 15(7):637–654, July 1985.
61. André van der Hoek, Antonio Carzaniga, Dennis Heimbigner, and Alexander L. Wolf. A testbed for configuration management policy programming. *IEEE Transactions on Software Engineering*, 28(1):79–99, January 2002.
62. Vesta home page. http://www.vestasys.org/.

# Index

The letter "n" following a page number denotes a reference to a footnote.

MIX
Papier aus verantwortungsvollen Quellen
Paper from responsible sources
FSC® C105338

If you have any concerns about our products,
you can contact us on
**ProductSafety@springernature.com**

In case Publisher is established outside the EU,
the EU authorized representative is:
**Springer Nature Customer Service Center GmbH**
**Europaplatz 3, 69115 Heidelberg, Germany**

Printed by Libri Plureos GmbH
in Hamburg, Germany